London's Lost Rivers

A Walker's Guide

Volume Two

D1164353

Tom Bolton

with photography by SF Said

London's Lost Rivers: A Walker's Guide – Volume Two
Published by Strange Attractor Press 2019

Maps: Lorna Ritchie
Design: Maia Gaffney-Hyde / Mark Pilkington

ISBN: 9781907222856

Strange Attractor Press
BM SAP,
London, WC1N 3XX, UK
www.strangeattractor.co.uk

Distributed by The MIT Press, Cambridge, Massachusetts.
And London, England.

Printed and bound in Estonia by Tallinna Raamatutrukikoda.

Contents

Foreword

by Tom Holland

It is hard to live in London and not occasionally feel haunted by the ghosts of its vanished rivers. For years, whether it was reading about Tyburn Hill, or crossing Fleet Street, or stocking up on Effra Ale, I would sense their shadows flit across my imaginings. Vaguely, I began to feel a yearning to track them: to start at the source of a vanished river, and then to follow every turn, every meandering, all the way to the Thames. It was only when I saw Tom Bolton's guide in a bookshop, however, that I realised quite how strong the yearning had become. Picking it up, skimming through its pages, looking at how rivers snaked under the beautifully-drawn street plans, I felt with an absolute sense of certainty that this was the guide-book for me. And so it proved.

For the past year my wife and I, sometimes accompanied by friends, sometimes just doing it by ourselves, have been following the routes outlined in the first volume of *London's Lost Rivers: A Walker's Guide*. I have tramped along many trails – from the Camino de Santiago to Offa's Dyke – but never have any given me as much pleasure as the ones detailed in Tom's book. It may seem odd to rate Croydon or Bermondsey above the Pyrenees or the Black Mountains, but such is the magic of following a river as it flows beneath concrete and tarmac. Beauty is discovered in ugliness; mystery in the seemingly forgettable; wonder in the mundane. Take Tom Bolton's guide with you, and trace-elements of London's lost rivers can be found everywhere. In street names; in the curving of valleys; in the rushing of waters dimly heard through metal grates. To follow their line is to journey back in time, and explore the contours of the vanished history of the most inexhaustible city on the face of the planet. The thrill is that of a treasure hunt: discovering in the curve of a railway concourse or in the jutting of a stink-pipe hints of vanished geological ages or of urban legends.

To walk across Piccadilly and recognise it as a river valley is to contemplate what, before it was swallowed up by cityscape, it would once have looked like: a boggy expanse of fields. To see a pub named 'The Boathouse' stranded next to a railway viaduct, miles from the sea, is to imagine what the environment around it would have been like a hundred, two hundred, three hundred years ago. Urban topography and history, seen through such a prism, come vividly alive. There is no better way of exploring a city.

And there is no better guide to it than Tom Bolton. My only complaint about his first book on London's lost rivers was that it only covered eight of them. Every one was so enjoyable and so full of fascinating detail that it did not take long for my wife and I to start rationing them, to ensure that we did not binge on them all at once. Now, with the publication of a second volume, our prayers are answered. Just to read the names of the rivers covered – the Black Ditch, the Cock and Pye Ditch, Falcon Brook – is to feel the call of the urban. London, as you will never have seen it before, awaits. Happy walking!

Introduction

by Tom Bolton

London's Lost Rivers Volume 1, published in 2010, followed nine partly or wholly buried rivers. It covered the best known – rivers such as the Fleet, the Tyburn, the Walbrook and the Effra – but many more had to be left out. *Volume 2* aims to make up for that a little by tracking another nine, more obscure rivers, often unknown even to those living on their banks, and therefore all the more intriguing to explore. It includes rivers that seem culturally, as well as physically, lost such as Counter's Creek, which has left no place names behind to remember it by, or the Falcon Brook, which never recovered its profile when Falcon Bridge Station was renamed Clapham Junction. Also included are rivers, such as the network of channels that make up Stamford Brook and the Bollo Brook, that follow complex and disputed courses and remain, to some extent, a mystery. And there are rivers only known from their function as 'sewers' – originally drainage channels removing water, not sewage, from surrounding land, that became polluted, and were covered and denied as the city closed in around them. These include the least promising, in name, of all the rivers – the Black Ditch – which has received little attention despite, or because, of its forbidding designation. Also included are the Cock and Pye Ditch and its companion the Bloomsbury Ditch, surprisingly rarely discussed or traced despite running through central London, passed daily by millions. And two of the rivers in *Volume 2* empty into the River Lea, not the Thames. The Hackney Brook and the Moselle, both with a strong local presence, are behind the easterly alignment of both Hackney and Haringey that help to give this part of North East London a sense of separation from the wider city.

Volume 2 includes a selection of lost rivers, but many more remain untraced. There are more rivers in Greater London than can ever be mapped – including an uncountable number of local tributaries with names that, if they ever had them, were never recorded. I have chosen the rivers that are the hardest to detect above ground, and in most need of a guide, leaving out many others. In particular, the Ravensbourne and its substantial tributaries the Quaggy and the Pool River, are not included. This long river system provides essential London walking routes but is mostly above ground, ducking briefly below part of Lewisham, and therefore easier to follow without directions.

London's Lost Rivers has also, inevitably, become a project tracking the history of the recent past. Monitoring long strips of London, like a tissue sample, discloses the myriad changes that, localised in themselves, combine to alter the condition of an entire metropolis. The rivers have, despite the constant flow of water under the pavements, provided still points that allow the constant shifting of the city all around them to be observed. The walking routes along the buried rivers remain the same, but cumulative change means that a new edition of *London's Lost Rivers Volume 1* has recently been published. A decade's worth of redevelopment – estate demolition, transport rethinks, safety deposit boxes in the sky, and the Thames Tideway sewer remaking even the Thames itself – have rendered the London of 2010 only semi-recognisable. The lost rivers attract change because, although they are no longer visible, they still mark borders and transition points within the city. The interzones between London boroughs have traditionally been neglected in favour of the local centres, leaving places such as Wormwood Scrubs, Gunnersbury or Tottenham Hale as indeterminate locations, waiting for the time when they become noticed again. The damper conditions along the valley floors tended to attract industry, making strips of London ripe for replacement with flats – lots of flats.

There is a word for the lowest point along the length of a valley: thalweg, from the German for valley way. The thalweg is what these walks

Black Ditch

' The under-appreciated Black Ditch follows a distinctive, looping course and folds Poplar in a tight embrace.. '

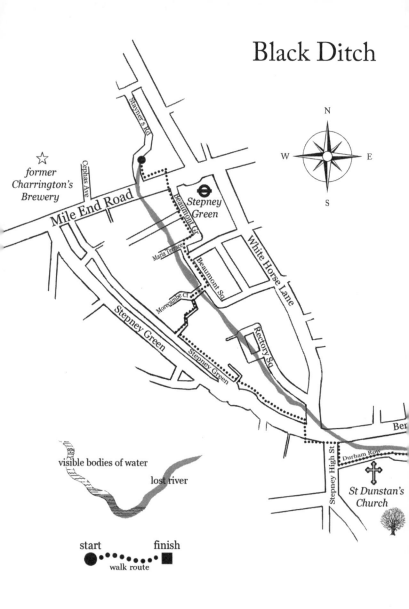

Black Ditch

N
W   E
S

Stayner's Rd

former
Charrington's
Brewery

Cephas Ave

Mile End Road

Beaumont Gr

Stepney
Green

Maria Terrace

Beaumont Sq

White Horse Lane

Morecambe Cl

Stepney Green

Stepney Green

Rectory Sq

Ber

Durham Row

Stepney High St

St Dunstan's
Church

visible bodies of water

lost river

start   finish

walk route

Practicalities

Distance – 3 miles
Start – Stayner's Road, Stepney
Getting there – Stepney Green Station

End – Limekiln Dock, Limehouse
Getting back – Limehouse Station *or* Canary Wharf Station

Introduction

In its very name the Black Ditch reveals its status as an unappreciated river. Despite its route, which runs through the heart of the East End, the Ditch is generally dismissed as no more than a sewer. It is contained in the Limekiln Dock Diversion Sewer, which connects to the main system in Stepney and follows the Ditch's curving course to the Thames. For a hidden river so close to the centre of London it has been little studied and, although it is marked on maps, misconceptions persist about its course. Few have successfully tracked the full length of the stream. A rare acknowledgment comes from Ben Aaronovitch, who personifies the lost rivers as mystical entities in *Rivers of London*. One is a plump, smiley, young woman, a daughter of Mama Thames, "whose formal name was the Black Ditch. Not that anyone called her that."[1]

The Black Ditch is essentially a default name that refers, as with other similarly polluted London watercourses, to its function as a sewer. Black Ditches are also to be found at the Holywell Priory in Shoreditch, possibly part of the lost Walbrook, on the buried Earl's Sluice in Rotherhithe and at Enfield Lock. On Horwood's 1799 map its lower course is labelled 'Common Sewer', and its upper reaches disappear into a muddle of thin lines representing field boundaries and street edges, appearing in its own right only here and there. The Ditch is thought to have two sources to the east of Brick Lane, both running east down from "the Brick Lane ridge"[2], and a third at Stepney Green. The first two are spectral streams, a double-header originating on Weavers' Fields in

1 Aaronovitch, Ben, *Rivers of London*. Gollancz, 2012, p387
2 Barton, Nicholas and Myers, Stephen, *The Lost Rivers of London*. Historical Publications, 2016, p118

Bethnal Green and on the south side of Buxton Street, meeting near the Brady Street Jewish Cemetery, and another that flows from behind the East London Mosque to Stepney Green. The Whitechapel ducking pond, where the tube station now stands, may have been fed by one of these. Here it is thought that they meet the branch followed on this walk, which can be traced on the 1799 Horwood Map of London.

The Black Ditch has a role in local origin myth, a frequently repeated story. Stepney, through which much of the river flows, was first recorded was as Stybbanhythe in around 1000, meaning a landing place belonging to a Saxon individual called Stybba. This is likely to have been the first settlement in this place but the story – that Stybba rowed up the Black Ditch to found it – cannot be confirmed. However, the mouth of the watercourse at Limekiln Dock, the only section of river now above ground, is short but definitely wide enough for a brief row at high tide.

The Ditch follows a distinctive, looping course through modern Stepney, Poplar and Limehouse that mirrors the Neckinger on the south side of the Thames, a river which also flowed through marshland and was able to meander. From Stepney Green the Ditch runs due east to Mile End Park, where it begins a curve that brings it through 180 degrees, folding Poplar in a tight embrace, before entering the Thames not much more than half a mile from where it began its arc. By the late 18th century the stream was culverted and built over west of Rhodeswell Common, and parts of its lower course appeared to have been straightened, presumably as a local drainage channel and, inevitably, sewer. The rest of the river disappeared under the unstoppable Victorian East End.

Route

• *Starting point: Stayner's Road.*

The Horwood Map of 1799 includes a dead-end street called Spring Garden Court that has now become Stayner's Road. Its name is highly suggestive of a spring on this site. There is, however, no trace on the ground of what was here and only a hint, on late 18th century maps, of what may be a stream flowing along the side street towards Mile End Road.

Just behind Stayner's Road, off Globe Road, the Charrington's brewing firm built a street of houses for their workers at the nearby Blue Anchor Brewery. The road became a local curiosity because of its name, XX Place. Apparently named after Charrington's XX Mild, it featured in books about quaint London, although not in the Post Office Directory which refused to recognise the name. It was closed off in 1903, and demolished in the 1950s during slum clearance.

• *Turn left along Mile End Road, cross and turn first right along Beaumont Grove.*

The buildings and perimeter wall on the right, around the Anchor Retail Park, are the remains of Charrington's Blue Anchor Brewery which at one time was the second largest in London. It closed in 1975 when Charrington's merged with Bass. It is likely that the brewery tapped into the underground springs that fed the Black Ditch which, at least at its source, would have provided clean water.

Stepney was a village, a mile outside Aldgate, the nearest entrance to the City of London, until the Industrial Revolution linked it to surrounding places, filling in the fields with workers' housing. The old centre of Stepney was a small cluster around Stepney Green and Mile End Road, or Mile End Old Town. At the end of the 18th century London stopped at this point but, although it was surrounded by pasture, the course of the Ditch itself had been built over for some time.

The stream seems to have crossed Mile End Road and run under the buildings between Beaumont Square and Stepney Green, where it was covered over in the 1790s.

• At the T-junction turn right and follow the right-hand side of Beaumont Square.

Beaumont Square was badly bombed during the Blitz, and its 19th century buildings entirely demolished. In Nigel Balchin's novel *Darkness Falls from the Air*, bomb damage in Stepney was "worse than anything I'd seen so far. In some of the really slum streets the places hadn't waited to be hit. They'd just fallen down at the thought of it."[3] Central Stepney was hit particularly hard, and the destruction around the miraculously preserved St Dunstan's Church was almost complete.

The London Jewish Hospital was in the north-eastern corner of the square, on the site of an earlier building, the Beaumont Philosophical Institution "for the mental and moral improvement" of the people, which was a smaller hall attached to the People's Palace in Mile End, formerly a famous concert hall, now occupied by Queen Mary University of London.

• Turn second right into Morecambe Close. Bear left around a small square, and follow a path between the houses to Stepney Green. Turn left along Stepney Green.

Stepney Green has large houses built mainly for merchants from the late 1600s. The green space is the last remaining strip of the much larger Mile End Green, preserved as something too large to be described as a verge, but too small to be a park. In the late 19th century Stepney Green became a centre of the Jewish East End. An 1899 map of the Jewish population, produced by cab driver and statistician George Arkell, shows its expansion from the heartland of Spitalfields and Whitechapel, where many streets are estimated as one hundred per cent Jewish, to Stepney

---

3 Balchin, Nigel, *Darkness Falls from the Air*. Collins, 1942, p212

where most are less than five per cent Jewish except around Stepney Green, where the proportions are around twenty-five per cent.

The red brick blocks immediately to the left are Stepney Green Court, a large development from 1895 for Jewish artisans. Further along a building in sandy London brick, set back from the road and now housing, was the first large synagogue built in the East End, in the 1870s, which closed in 1987.

Stepney, however, is a lost borough, abolished in 1965 when London government was reorganised and incorporated into Tower Hamlets. Its alternative, earlier name was Stebunheath, a version of Stybbanhythe, which was still in use when a barony was created in 1906.

• *Continue straight ahead along Stepney Green until it reaches a mini-roundabout. Cross the road and turn right along Stepney High Street.*

Stepney Way, further along on the right, was previously called Spring Garden Place. This street was probably the reason for the name change to Stayner's Road at our starting point, reducing local confusion. In the 18th century there was a Spring Gardens Coffee House on this street, "a wooden edifice"[4] which is shown in an engraving from 1764, 'The Treat of Stepney'. Sailors dressed up for shore leave drink and carouse in the gardens, enjoying the company of several young ladies. An explanatory verse begins "At Stepney now, with Cakes and Ale, our Tars their Mistresses regale." This was originally the site of Great Place, a Tudor mansion built, characteristically for Stepney, as a retreat for city noblemen. It belonged to the Colet family, including Henry Colet, Dean of St Paul's Cathedral, drawn by Holbein. Later, it is thought to be where Thomas Cromwell spent much of his time while at the height of his power as Henry VIII's right-hand man. It was later replaced by the Stepney Meeting House, an independent Congregational chapel, one of several radical non-conformist meeting houses in Stepney during the second half of the 1600s. The chapel demolished the surviving Tudor gatehouse from the original house

---

4 Hughson, David and Reid, William Hamilton, *Walks Through London*. Shirley, Neely and Jones et al., 1817, p322

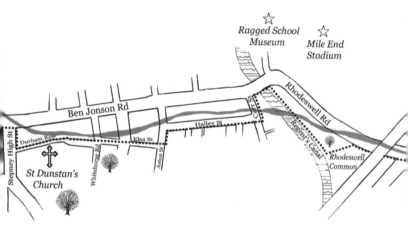

N
W E
S

Ragged School
Museum

Mile End
Stadium

Rhodeswell Rd

Ben Jonson Rd

Cliff St

Regent's Canal

Rhodeswell
Common

Stepney High St

Durham Row

Whitehorse Rd

Elsa St

Aston St

Halley St

St Dunstan's
Church

but was destroyed by bombing leaving, in turn, the ruined gateway that survives today.

• *At the gates to St Dunstan's Church turn left along a path that runs outside the churchyard, beside the railings. Where the path ends, continue straight ahead along Durham Row.*

The stream runs along the edge of the churchyard, forming its northern boundary. St Dunstan's and All Saints, Stepney High Street is, according to the Buildings of England "the principal medieval church of East London."[5] It was rebuilt in 952 by St Dunstan and contains rare, pre-Norman Conquest carvings.

Bishops of Stepney have a history of becoming influential figures in the Church of England. Previous incumbents include Cosmo Lang, later Archbishop of Canterbury, John Sentamu, later Archbishop of York, social campaigner Jim Thompson and anti-Apartheid activists Trevor Huddleston and Joost de Blank. They also included Evered Lunt who, being a lower impact figure than some of his predecessors, was unkindly nicknamed 'Evered the Unready'.

As well as the Black Ditch, the Elizabeth Line also passes underground at the church. It splits at St Dunstan's, dividing into separate branches to Shenfield and Abbey Wood which pass either side of the churchyard.

• *Cross Whitehorse Road and continue straight ahead along Elsa Street.*

The area to the left was known in the 19th century as Pedlar's Orchard, a neighbourhood of very poor housing. The notebooks of the Booth Survey, delivering a judgement in typically direct fashion, describe the area as "costers – thieves – good for nothing unfortunates. hatless girls & women, doors open, bread about, rough.'[6] Along with much of Stepney, Pedlar's Orchard vanished in the Blitz and the clearance that followed.

---

5 Cherry, Bridget, O'Brien, Charles & Pevsner, Nikolaus, *London 4: North. Buildings of England.* Yale University Press, 2005, p445
6 Booth/B/350 p63

• *At a T-junction turn left along Aston Street, then first right on to Halley Street.*

The Ditch runs between Halley Street and Ben Jonson Road, further to the left, before cutting right towards the canal where it is channelled underneath.

Before the construction of the estate, Elea Street ran straight ahead all the way to the canal. In the 1890s this was North Street and, along with the two parallel streets – Eastfield and Catherine – was a noted concentration of poverty known as 'Donkey Row' and described by local police as "as bad as Notting Dale" (a notorious West London slum – see Chapter 4: Counter's Creek). They claimed that people here "think nothing of assaulting the policeman."[7] The eastern part of the neighbourhood beside the canal was a fish curing district with "cartloads of fresh haddock standing at doors."[8] A living based on haddock was precarious, because it only sold when prices were low.

• *At a T-junction turn left along Carr Street, then right on to Ben Jonson Road.*

Housing on the opposite side of the road was built in the 2000s on the Commercial Gas Works site, which occupied an entire block beside the canal and boasted four smaller gasholders and one enormous double-sized structure. In 1843, balloonist Charles Green attempted to make the first Channel crossing, ascending from the grounds of the gas works but coming down in Sussex.

• *Cross the bridge over the Regent's Canal and turn right immediately after the bridge, taking the path through Rhodeswell Common beside the canal.*

The Ragged School Museum, on the left on the far side of the canal bridge, recreates the classroom set up by Dr Barnardo in 1876 in a warehouse. Before public education Ragged Schools fed, clothed and taught destitute children, and Barnardo's institution ran for 50 years before the building became a warehouse again.

---

7 Booth/B/350 p149
8 Booth/B/350 p149

The Horwood map of the 1790s shows Rhodes Well Common, the south-east section of the park, occupied by a teardrop-shaped pond labelled 'Rhodes Well' (once perhaps 'Rogues' Well'). The well evidently combined with the Black Ditch stream to generate a substantial flow of water, enough to fill the pond and create a wider, more distinctive watercourse from this point onwards. The canal had not yet been built, and Rhodes Well sat out in the middle of nowhere, beyond the edge of Stepney. However, the map shows signs of coming change. Immediately to the north is a rope walk – the premises of a rope manufacturer – a third of a mile long, laid out across Bow Common. Ropes were made at full length and ropewalks therefore needed a long space to operate in. This is the first sign of the impending arrival of the docks and the industrial East End that would create and define this place.

A drain cover sits beside an area of the park that has been deliberately left wild, on the site of the lost pond. However, the history of the site is more complicated than it appears. Rhodeswell Common is now a detached southern section of Mile End Park but, before the Second World War, the entirety of the park, including the common, was Victorian streets. Bombing caused destruction to the north beyond Mile End Stadium, but the houses on the common were only lightly damaged. Nevertheless, the area was cleared to create the open space previously lacking in the East End. The stadium is built on the site of several lost streets, three churches, three schools, and the Sun Iron Works. The standalone chimney is the only remnant of the houses on the common, which faced both on to the canal towpath and Rhodeswell Road, and a small street called Georgiana Place.

• *Cross the green space to return to Rhodeswell Road. Turn right and follow to the junction (it is now St Paul's Way).*

From Rhodeswell Common until it reaches the Thames, the Black Ditch is a boundary even today, and despite its sharply curved course. It marks the parish boundaries, and now local council wards. This shows that it had some significance as a local watercourse, being above ground and identifiable when housing arrived, bringing a need for smaller parishes.

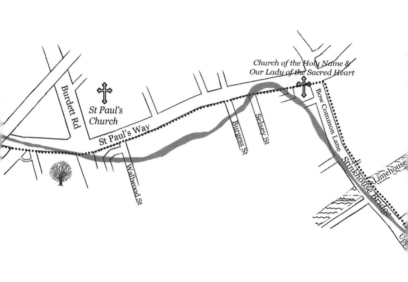

Burdett Rd

St Paul's
Church

St Paul's Way

Wallwood St

Burgess St

Selsey St

Church of the Holy Name &
Our Lady of the Sacred Heart

Bow Common Lane

Shirkhouse Bridge

Limehouse

Up

N

W   E

S

The boundary line that separates the Tower Hamlets wards of Mile End East and Limehouse to the west, and Bromley-by-Bow, East India and Lansbury to the east clearly reflects the exact course of the Ditch, starting at the canal halfway across Rhodeswell Common, where the Rhodes Well pond sat.

The water of the Black Ditch passed through an increasingly, notoriously overcrowded part of London as the 19th century progressed and drainage was poor, managed parish-by-parish and by the Commissioners of Sewers. Arrangements for waste disposal were limited, to say the least. The Poplar Board of Health kept a brush, bucket and supply of lime at the town hall, which residents could borrow. When cholera reached London in 1832, preceded by an extensive panic but little action, up to 7,000 people died, mostly in East London. However, there would be a further three major outbreaks before sanitation brought the disease under control, including by placing the Black Ditch and others like it underground.

• *Cross Burdett Road at the lights and continue straight ahead along St Paul's Way.*

At the junction with Burdett Road there are twin drains in the middle of the street. There is too much traffic to allow a closer examination, but these mark the course of the storm sewer that carries the Black Ditch. To the right the road dips down towards Wallwood Street, revealing the course of the Ditch as it crosses Burdett Road to run beside St Paul's Way.

To the left, where the viaduct crosses, is the site of the lost Burdett Road Station on the Great Eastern mainline. It closed in 1941 after bomb damage, never reopening.

To the right, a Patent Cable Manufactory ran alongside Burdett Road, a next generation ropewalk stretching all the way to the Limehouse Cut canal.

The inscription over the porch at St Paul's, Bow Common announces it, boldly, to be 'The Gate of Heaven'. It opened in 1960, replacing a bombed 19th century church. Designed by architects Robert Maguire and Keith Murray its modernity, including a central altar and deliberate use of cheap materials such as concrete, shocked contemporaries and remains very striking.

• Follow St Paul's Way for ¼ mile until it reaches a crossroads with Bow Common Lane, at the red brick Holy Name Church.

There are prominent drain covers in middle of the road at the junction, again marking the course of the Ditch. Although it sounds as though water can be heard underneath, this is in fact the tinkling of the grotto in the grounds of Holy Name and Our Lady of the Sacred Heart Vietnamese Church.

• Turn right along Bow Common Lane.

To the left after the junction is the former Bow Common Gas Works, run by the Gas, Coke and Light Company. Although derelict at the time of writing and surrounded by a brick wall, it will not remain so for long. The site, although smaller than the Commercial Gas Works, had its own railway tracks connecting to the mainline, and four gasholders that have only recently been dismantled.

Further along the road opposite the Acqua Vista development a square drain cover in the road emits a low roar which is, at last, the Black Ditch itself still flowing out of sight.

The new blocks occupy part of a district known in the 1890s as 'The Fenian Barracks'. The police claimed that "All are Irish Cockneys" and that "This block sends more police to hospital than any other block in London" adding, for good measure "They are not human. They are wild beasts".[9] The Booth Survey also reported that in summer, after rain, it was possible to see "thousands and tens of thousands" of rats on the streets here, "not small rats but big & fat, the size of cats." This story, which sounds exaggerated, nevertheless carries enough detail to suggest it has a basis in reality: "You knock with your book and away they go with a rush and hissing sound from their feet upon the pavements that will make your blood run cold."[10]

---

9 Booth/B/346 p31
10 Booth/B/346 p33-35

• Follow Bow Common Lane to the bridge over the Limehouse Cut canal.

Poplar, "so called from the trees with which it once abounded"[11] as an early 19th century account neatly puts it, begins after the canal. According to Anthony Trollope, it was where old London ended before the coming of the railways: "London will soon assume the shape of a great starfish. The old town, extending from Poplar to Hammersmith, will be the nucleus, and the various railway lines will be the projecting rays."[12]

A fat pipe runs beside the canal bridge, but it appears to carry the gas main rather than the Ditch, which is probably routed under the canal. The Limehouse Cut is London's oldest canal, built in the 1760s as a short-cut from the River Lea to Limehouse Basin, speeding up transport by avoiding the need for ships to wait for the tide on the long journey along the loops of the Lower Lea and around the Isle of Dogs. It is mostly dead straight. The bridge has been known as 'Stinkhouse Bridge' since the late 18th century, because of industry that was already clustering. Bob Gilbert describes the "bouquets of my boyhood; the cloying, hot sweetness of a biscuit factory and the sharp vinegary smells of a pickle cannery… the sourness of the tanneries, the pepper and spice of the warehouses, the dark brown maltiness of the Anchor Brewery… The winner, by a margin, was ammonia from the chemical works."[13]

In J.B. Priestley's 1930 novel *Angel Pavement* the fraudster Golspie, leaving London by ship, looks back on the "haze of smoke above the multitudinous chimney pots of Poplar and Bow."[14] At the area's industrial peak, a remarkable quantity of industry was concentrated along the canal at this bridge. Around the turn of the century the Phoenix Cement Works were located to the left, with a Tar and Resin Distillery located behind. To the right were the Royal National Life Boat [sic] Association Stores, the Thames Fish Guano and Oil Works, a felt works, the Eagle Chemical Works, and a dry grain works. On the north side of the Cut, lined with

11 Hughson, David & Reid, William Hamilton, *Walks Through London*. Shirley, Neely and Jones et al., 1817, p334
12 Trollope, Anthony, *The Three Clerks*. Alan Sutton, 1858 [1984], p21
13 Gilbert, Bob, *Ghost Trees: nature and people in a London parish*. Saraband, 2018, Chapter 4
14 Priestley, J.B., *Angel Pavement*. Penguin Books, 1930, p496

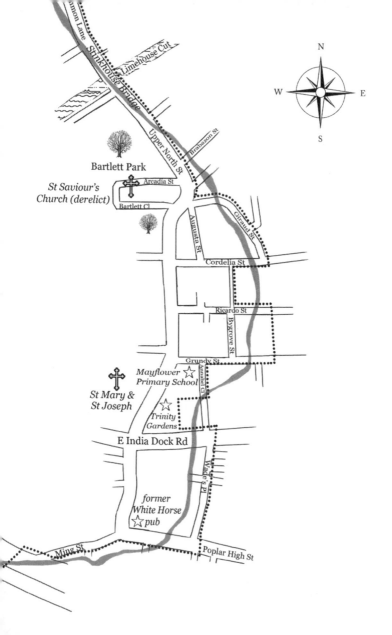

wharves and factories, were a sack and bag works, a gold and silver refinery, a varnish works and a chemical manure works. Most were the kind of factories you would only live near if you needed to work in them.

• *Continue straight ahead (the road now Upper North Street).*

Although part of Poplar, the whole area between the Limehouse Cut and East India Dock Road to the south is known as Lansbury, after local MP and Labour leader George Lansbury. Its two-storey Victorian houses were heavily bombed during the Second World War, and designated for reconstruction as 'Neighbourhood 9'. It then became part of the Festival of Britain, a satellite to the South Bank site that hosted the Exhibition of Live Architecture. Buses took Festival visitors out to East London to see the model housing of the future, part of the Lansbury Estate which was under construction, and pavilions illustrating the bad ways of the past and the enlightened buildings of the future.

Further along, Bartlett Park was created by clearing badly bombed streets after the Second World War. It is named after a long-standing vicar but his church, St Saviour's, is now a shell. It was burned out in 2007 in a disastrous fire and Bartlett Close is now a very strange place to live, an island of houses grouped around an alarmingly ruined church.

• *After the Essex House tower block, turn first left along Giraud Street. Follow the road round to the right.*

The river's route is under the angled terrace to the right. This is the Lansbury Estate, built during and after the Festival of Britain with the explicit intention of creating self-sufficient communities equipped with all the facilities they needed. George Lansbury, who resigned as Labour leader in 1935 over his refusal to support rearmament, left a significant legacy in the area. He had led a revolt in Poplar against the unequal burden on poorer boroughs, refusing to set a rate and being imprisoned as a result, along with more than 20 councillors. Despite this, he won a reduction in local rates and the political doctrine of local authority support for the poor became known as Poplarism.

• *At a T-junction, turn right along Cordelia Street, then first left past a vehicle barrier alongside Elgin House.*

To the left along Cordelia Street, Balfron Tower can be seen in the distance. It was architect Erno Goldfinger's first public housing project, a sister building to the taller, more famous Trellick Tower in West London. It was controversially refurbished in 2019, with the replacement windows coming in for particular criticism.

The ornamental 1950s tower belongs to Chrisp Street Market, which opened in 1951 as part of the Exhibition of Live Architecture. It was designed by Frederick Gibberd as the first post-war pedestrian market square in Britain, a typology that was to fall in popularity as rapidly as it rose in the decades to come.

• *Turn left along Ricardo Street. After No.73 turn right through an archway along an unmarked path with two round bollards. The path leads to Elizabeth Close.*

On the left at the junction with Ricardo Street, a tall, pale green stink pipe tells us this is the course of the Ditch.

The Black Ditch formed the eastern boundary of Randall's Estate, an area of speculative development owned by local pub landlord Onesiphorus Randall, whose first name meant 'to bring profit'. The two storey, grey brick houses, which have now disappeared, were of notoriously poor quality. The central street, Randall's Market, struggled to compete with nearby Chrisp Street. In the 1890s it contained mostly furniture shops owned by the same man, with "odd statues running along the roofs of the houses".[15] After bomb damage, it lay derelict for several years into the 1950s before being pulled down. The street has now vanished, covered by Bygrove Primary School and the housing behind.

---

15 Booth/B/346 p97

• At the T-junction, turn right along Grundy Street, then second left along Annabel Close.

On the corner of Duff Street, the former African Queen pub is virtually the only surviving pre-war building in the neighbourhood.

At the end of the road, St Mary and St Joseph Church was, remarkably, completed in 1954. It was designed by Adrian Gilbert Scott, grandson of George. Its brooding, Gothic appearance, reminiscent of his brother Giles's Liverpool Cathedral, is a strange contrast with the surrounding Festival of Britain era housing.

• After the Mayflower School playground, turn right along an unnamed alley alongside the school wall.

Beside the school a drain cover can be found, sitting on low ground, and the sound of the Ditch can be heard beneath.

The Black Ditch, as an open sewer running through Poplar and Limehouse, was the cause of much local concern, especially after cholera reached East London in 1832. Residents petitioned Parliament to complain that the sewers "are for the most part shallow, narrow, inconvenient, filthy, and out of repair" and, being above ground, were "liable to be choked up and the waters thereof rendered stagnant from dead animals, offal, broken vessels and other materials of an offensive kind."[16] Some improvements were made as a result, but these involved covering open sewers on Ropemakers' Fields. The Black Ditch was left open until the Bazalgette sewer improvements of the 1860s eventually placed it underground.

• Turn left through the small park (Trinity Gardens).

Trinity Gardens, not to be confused with Trinity Green further up the same road, is the site of the original Mayflower School destroyed in one of the worst events of the German bombing raids on London during the First World War. A Zeppelin dropped a bomb through the school's roof,

---

16 Marriott, John, *Beyond the Tower: A History of East London*. Yale University Press, 2011, p128

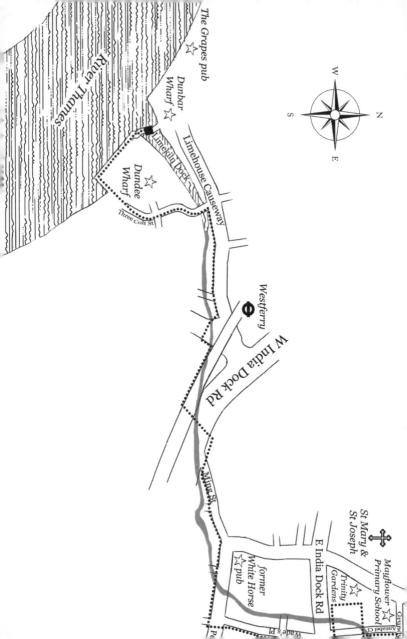

killing 18 young children. Afterwards, the school was demolished, and the site left open as a memorial.

The rest of the immediate surroundings were destroyed in the Second World War, including St Stephen's Church on a site to the right, and Trinity Congregational Chapel to the left. The elegant copper and concrete 1950s former Trinity Methodist Church stands on its site, and was part of the Exhibition of Live Architecture.

• *Turn left along East India Dock Road, and cross both carriageways at the lights opposite Queen Victoria Seamen's Rest. Turn right along the opposite side of the road, and then left along Wades Place.*

A now-demolished terrace at Nos.105-115 East India Dock Road, where Trinity Gardens is now located, was built over the line of the Ditch in the 1840s.

Turn right along unmarked a dead end (Shirbutt Street) before the school to venture into the valley of the Ditch, where another drain cover, loud with the sound of water.

• *At the T-junction, turn right along Poplar High Street.*

At the end of Poplar High Street, a white horse atop a pole is a reminder of the White Horse inn which stood on this corner site until demolition in 2003, after more than 300 years. A watering place for livestock, Stonebridge Pond, is recorded in front of the pub, fed by the Black Ditch. A stone bridge, first mentioned in 1452, took the road across the Ditch at this point.

• *Where the road swings right by the white horse sign, carry on straight ahead, bearing left along a wide pedestrian and cycle path (Ming Street).*

The long block to the right is the Will Crooks Estate, named after a radical Mayor of Poplar and early 20th century Labour MP, who also had one of the Woolwich ferries named after him. The entire area from here to the East India Dock Road was demolished during 1930s slum clearance.

Ming Street was called King Street until its name was changed in a neat nod to the Limehouse Chinatown district. The next street to the north is Pennyfields, one of the two central streets of Limehouse Chinatown. At the end of the 19th century, the legend of Chinatown grew rapidly and between the 1890s and the 1920s these streets became a destination for visitors from more respectable parts of London, seeking the supposed exoticism of the East End. What they found was a small semi-permanent population of Chinese, Japanese and Lascar sailors, some of whom had settled and married English women, there being virtually no Chinese women in London. The foggy streets and opium dens gained popularity in fiction and films, driven by racist tropes about the mysterious, devious men of the Orient, but the reality was a much more prosaic set of shops, clubs and laundrettes serving sailors on shore leave. There was opium, legal until the First World War, but the responsibility lay at the door of the British and the East India Company, who manufactured it in India and forced its sale on reluctant Chinese ports.

None of the buildings that existed at the height of the street's notoriety survive. The area, where slum clearance had already begun before the Second World War, was entirely destroyed by bombing and its aftermath, and London's Chinese population moved on to reestablish itself in the streets of southern Soho, where it remains today.

• *Turn right along West India Dock Road to cross at the pedestrian crossing. On the other side of the road walk straight ahead along Garford Street, then turn immediately right along Premiere Place, beside the viaduct.*

The gates to the West India Dock stood to the left, all traces eliminated by the widening of the road into a dual carriageway as part of the redevelopment of the Docks in the 1980s. The vanished West India Dock Station, on the London and Blackwall Railway, was on the site of the round corner building that signals the start of Canary Wharf.

The area beyond the railway viaduct, now unrecognisable, was described as "one of the blackest spots in London"[17] in the late 19th

---

17 Booth/B/346 p89

century, a warren of streets around Chusan Place where pickpockets would climb over walls and disappear, after helping themselves to your belongings in the West India Dock Road.

• *After Westferry Station, cross Westferry Road, continue straight ahead for a short distance along Salter Street, then turn left along Limehouse Causeway.*

Limehouse Causeway, which led into Pennyfields until the widening of West India Dock Road, was also part of Limehouse Chinatown. It was the less respectable part of the neighbourhood, although the Chinese were not to blame. To the right, streets such as Rich Street, Gill Street and the lost Chusan Street housed the roughest areas of the docks dominated by brothels for sailors, the kind that also robbed their customers. Chusan Street was described memorably by the Booth Survey as "a favourite thieves' resort. You are robbed in the West India Dock Road: off goes the thief down Chusan Street; you follow and if you are close enough behind him you manage to land yourself in Chusan Street. There he suddenly disappears. You are glad enough to get out of the place without further mishap."[18]

• *Turn second left along Three Colt Street.*

The unnecessarily striped pub on the left was originally the Five Bells and Bladebone. Its name, one of the most atmospheric in London, referred to the breastbone of a whale.

Potter Dwellings, which sits over the line of the Ditch, is Stepney Borough housing from the start of the 20th century. The buildings next door are the street frontage of Limekiln Dock, which can be glimpsed through railings further along. This is the outlet of the Black Ditch, the only stretch of water that remains above ground. There is no way through, so the walking route detours around to the left to reach the dock from the Thames.

---

18 Booth/B/346 p91

• Follow Three Colt Street as it crosses Milligan Street and reaches the Thames. Turn right along the river path.

This riverside area was known as Limehouse Hole, and was a ship building centre with "shipbuilders, barge-builders, boat-builders, ropemakers, sailmakers, mastmakers, blockmakers and ship-chandlers, as well as general wharfingers."[19] The name has disappeared, along with the neighbourhood and most of its buildings. Westferry Circus, a large roundabout to the south, now dominates, occupying the former entrance to West India Dock which was filled in during the 1980s reconstruction of the Isle of Dogs as a financial district.

• Follow the Thames Path on to the suspension bridge over Limekiln Dock.

It is possible to walk along the near side of dock beside Dunbar Wharf, where the inlet is clearly visible. This is filled by the tide, but the very last few feet of the Black Ditch also still flow through the mud, evidence at last that the river really does exist in hidden form.

Ship building began at Limekiln Dock in 1633, when John Graves established a shipyard. Until the 18th century warships were built here for the Royal Navy, based on the other side of the Thames at Deptford. The warehouses grouped around the inlet were built in the 19th century and were owned by Duncan Dunbar & Sons who ran sailing ships from the confusingly similar Dundee Wharf next door. Ships began their voyages here to North America, India and Australia, including the first voluntary transport to the latter.

Although the wharf was destroyed by bombing it was rebuilt, but was out of use by the end of the 1960s. The flats here were designed by CZWG in the mid-1990s and feature what the Buildings of England accurately describes as "sinister crane-like attachments".[20]

The best pub for a post-river drink is celebrated local landmark The Grapes, a little way along Narrow Street.

---

19 Hobhouse, Hermione, (ed.), *Survey of London Volumes 43 and 44, Poplar, Blackwall and Isle of Dogs*. London County Council, 1994, p388

20 Cherry, Bridget, O'Brien, Charles & Pevsner, Nikolaus, *London 4: North. Buildings of England*. Yale University Press, 2005, p674

Bollo Brook

*' An apparently low key river, the Bollo Brook
delivers a spectacular appearance in one of
Britain's most famous landscaped gardens. '*

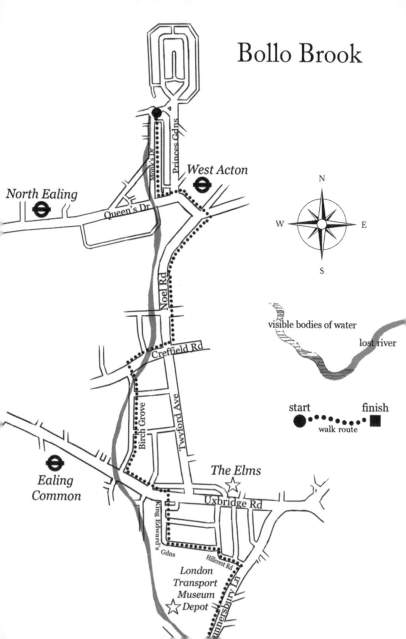

Bollo Brook

North Ealing

West Acton

Queen's Dr

Mott's Dr

Princes Gdns

Noel Rd

Creffield Rd

Birch Grove

Twyford Ave

Ealing Common

The Elms

Uxbridge Rd

King Edward's Gdns

Hillcrest Rd

Summersbury Ln

London Transport Museum Depot

N
W   E
S

visible bodies of water

lost river

start ● ● ● ● ● ● ● ● ● ● ■ finish
walk route

Practicalities

Distance – 4½ miles
Start – junction of Vale Lane and Monks Drive, West Acton
Getting there – West Acton Station, then a 5-minute walk to Vale Lane
End – Duke's Meadows, Chiswick

Getting back – Chiswick Station or Barnes Bridge Station
Note – this walk should be followed between 7am and dusk to allow access to Chiswick House Gardens, which is open between these hours every day of the year.

Introduction

The Bollo Brook has a particularly memorable name, but it is a low-key river until its final, spectacular appearance in the grounds of Chiswick House, as the central attraction in one of the most famous landscaped gardens in Britain. For much of its relatively short course it runs through a combination of early 20th century suburbs on the edge of Acton, and the industrial fringe of South Acton. It is a boundary stream, and marks the place where West London towns meet, a zone which is neither Ealing nor Acton, and neither Acton nor Chiswick. It is a typical lost London river, shaping the places around it before disappearing almost without trace. Following its course almost guarantees encounters with places the walker, unless they happen to live nearby, has never before visited.

The river's name seems to come from Bollo Bridge, the bridge that crossed Bollo Lane, which in turn gave its name to the rest of the river, although not very effectively. It is debatable how much of the course of the Brook traced here was known by this name, apart from the middle section through South Acton and Acton Green. The bridge and the Lane were recorded in medieval times under several variations – Bolebregge, Bolholbregge, Bolhollane – which suggest that the underlying meaning could be Bull Hollow. The river is also referred to in the 1820s as Bollar Brook, and Bollo Lane was also called Bellow Lane, a different sort of bull reference. Whatever its origins, the name lives on along the central section of the route in Bollo Lane and Bollo Bridge Road, and places named after them including the Bollo Brook Youth and Community Centre in South Acton.

The course of the Brook becomes hard to trace around Turnham Green, where a short section south is missing and cannot be traced. Some conjecture is needed to piece together the full route followed by this walk. The route below follows the likely route of this mysterious linking section, connecting to an easily identified stream that passes through the grounds of Chiswick House. Others suggest the river turned east along Chiswick High Road, either instead or as well as heading south towards Chiswick House, and could have met the western Stamford Brook at Goldhawk Road. It seems likely that the Brook crossed Acton Common in this direction when it was in flood. Leigh's map from 1819, at tantalisingly large scale, suggests the stream swung west at Turnham Green, heading towards Kew Bridge. Meanwhile, Barton and Myers trace a separate stream flowing from Kew Bridge to Chiswick House, now part of the Chiswick Sewer. The only definite conclusion is that we cannot be sure.

Because of the surprising level of uncertainty around its lower reaches, confusion has developed between the Bollo Brook and the nearby Mill Hill Brook. The two run close to each other, separated only by the length of Mill Hill Road, in Acton. However, they are clearly separate streams, and the Mill Hill Brook is in fact part of the Stamford Brook, itself a complicated river with several branches (see Chapter 9: Stamford Brook West).

The local significance of the Brook can be seen in the way modern boundaries follow its buried course. From Uxbridge Road to Acton Town Station, the Brook is also the local ward boundary. Before it was merged with Ealing, this was the western boundary of the Borough of Acton. The Brook is also the boundary between the Boroughs of Ealing and Hounslow from Acton Town to the Gunnersbury Triangle.

Route

• *Starting point: roundabout at the junction of Vale Lane and Monks Drive.*

Not only is the course and identity of the Bollo Brook slightly unclear: so is its source. Barton and Myers locate it on Ashbourne Road in Hanger Hill, but this walk starts from a little further south where a stream begins on mid-19th century maps. It appears to the north of West Acton Underground Station, as an unmistakable watercourse flowing towards the Uxbridge Road.

The stream can be seen on maps of the countryside north of Ealing and Acton, which remained still-undeveloped until after the First World War. A stream emerges at the junction of Vale Lane with Monks Drive, marked by a roundabout. There is no visible trace now of the spring that feeds the Brook, which is buried under the inter-war suburban houses that crowd the slopes of Hanger Hill which slopes away to the south, the course followed by the Brook.

The houses in this street are part of the Hanger Hill Garden Estate, "the beau ideal of romantic, rural Metroland",[1] built between 1929 and 1936. It was designed by the architect's firm Douglas Smith & Barley, and has the kind of high mock Tudor houses that set the standard for suburbia which, a generation later, had become easy to mock. These houses seem to take themselves and their links to a fairy-tale past very seriously indeed.

To the north is more inter-war suburbia, the Haymills Estate. Its half-moon shape occupies the space between the District Line and the Western Avenue which, when built in the 1920s as an ultra-modern expressway carrying the A40, signalled the age of the car. Haymills looks to the future, with smart modern movement houses that have aged well in contrast to the backward-gazing Hanger Hill.

---

1 Cherry Bridget & Pevsner, Nikolaus, *London 2: South. Buildings of England.* Yale University Press, 2001, p179

• *Turn left along Monks Lane. At a T-junction turn left along Queen's Drive.*

The Hanger Gardens Estate was built on land that had been a very early airfield. Acton Aerodrome, as it became, started in 1909 when a man called Harold Piffard rented a field next to Masons Green Lane where an aircraft he had built travelled a foot or two off the ground over a hundred yards. Building on this achievement, he set up an aerodrome on the site which was used by the London Aviation Company and then the Ruffy-Baumann School of Flying, training First World War pilots. In 1918 the Alliance Airplane Company took over the aerodrome to produce De Havilland and Handley Page biplanes during the final year of the war. The company closed in 1920 after the experimental Alliance P2 Seabird crashed in Surbiton attempting a flight to Australia, killing its crew of two, and the airfield was sold for housing.

• *Follow Queen's Drive as it turns right and passes West Acton Underground Station. At the roundabout afterwards turn right along Noel Road.*

The route of the Brook continues straight ahead, passing under the West Coast mainline, but the walk route detours to the left to find a route through.

Before development in the 1920s, maps labelled the spot occupied by West Acton Station as Masons Green. This is the final appearance of a lost village called Masons Green, probably a row of houses along the lane that disappeared following the Black Death of 1348. Masons Green Lane leads north from the starting point of the walk, a back alley that predates all the roads around it.

• *Cross the railway and, at a mini-roundabout, continue straight ahead along Twyford Avenue. Turn first right along Creffield Road.*

West Acton has a relatively long-standing Japanese population, with associated facilities. The Japanese School is on Creffield Road, in a building built for Haberdashers' Aske's School for Girls, and the parade of shops at Ealing Common Station, unlike most tube stations, includes a Japanese supermarket. In the early 1990s *The Economist* reported that lower-ranked Japanese workers in London lived in Croydon, middle managers in Ealing, Finchley or Golders Green and their bosses in Hampstead or St John's Wood. The mock-Tudor Englishness of the Hanger Gardens Estate has proved particularly popular.

The Creffield area is another suburban estate, less flamboyant than those to the north, built in the late 19th century in the grounds of The Elms, a large house on the Uxbridge Road that is, remarkably, still there.

• *Turn first left along Birch Grove.*

The walk rejoins the route of the Brook where it crosses Creffield Road, a little way past the junction with Birch Grove. It flows behind the houses on the right-hand side of the street, forming the boundaries separating their gardens from those of Fordhook Avenue, behind. Walking down Birch Grove, a gradient becomes apparent.

Fordhook Avenue was built on the site of a large house called Fordhook, demolished at the start of the 20th century. It had been the home of, among others, author and jurist Henry Fielding who lived there towards the end of his life. As well as the novels for which he is particularly remembered Fielding, as chief magistrate of London, helped found the first police force with his brother John. He left Fordhook in 1754 for Lisbon seeking a cure for his numerous ailments, and died there not long after arrival.

• *At the T-junction turn left to walk along Uxbridge Road.*

After rain, water gathers rapidly along both sides of the main road at this point, making crossing surprisingly difficult. This reflects the presence of water flowing under Uxbridge Road, the main road from London to Oxford. The stream crosses Uxbridge Road between the two large mansion blocks at No.400 and No.409. It crossed the Brook on Fordhook Bridge, which was last recorded here in 1826.

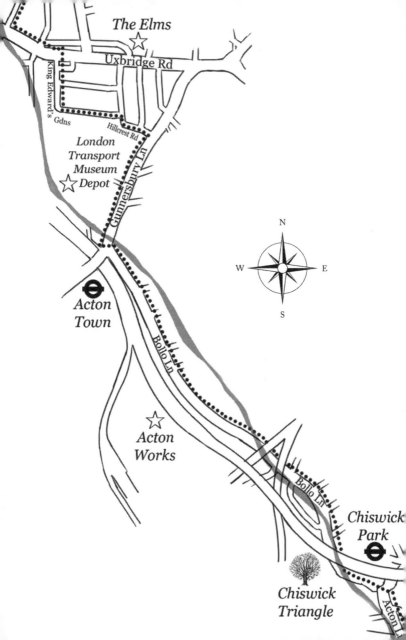

• With green space on your left, cross Uxbridge Road, and turn right into King Edward's Gardens.

Twyford Gardens, on the left, occupies the site of a large fishpond, which was big enough to have its own boathouse. It belonged to The Elms which is the oldest surviving building in Acton, built in 1735 and now used as a school. The house was a factory for many years, at one time the J.K. Farnell soft toy factory. At first the firm made toys from rabbit skin, but had moved on to mohair by the time they produced the bear that A.A. Milne gave to his son, Christopher Robin, in 1926 which soon became known as Winnie the Pooh.

The pond was filled in to create a park when the land around the house was bought by Acton Urban District Council in 1903, to build the Creffield estate. This development also filled in the remaining space between Ealing and Acton, separate villages that met each other in the late 19th century as ribbon development along the Uxbridge Road. However, the buried Bollo still marks the separation between the two, and was the boundary between the boroughs of Ealing and Acton until they were merged in 1965.

• Follow King Edward's Gardens as the street turns ninety degrees to the left.

The first indication of the Bollo, beyond the general slope along its route, is Brook Close, a small street just out of sight off West Lodge Avenue, a block away to the right, where it flows behind the houses. However, there is no way through so the route sweeps to the east to rejoin the route of the river near Acton Town Station.

• At the T-junction turn right on to Hillcrest Road, and follow the street as it turns to the left.

Perched up above the Bollo on a gravel subsoil, which it proudly advertised, Ealing became the prosperous 'Queen of Suburbs' in the late 19th century. It claimed to be healthy, with a good sewer system and a low death rate compared to other London boroughs, lacking 'nuisances' such as large cemeteries, asylums and cheap trains, and even kept the trams at bay. Down in the valley of the Brook, however, Acton also had its share of respectable suburbia. The streets around Hillcrest Road are handsome and overlooked.

They are tucked between Uxbridge Road and the railway – the District Line – which follows the line of the Brook to Acton Town. Between the houses and the tracks is the enormous Ealing Common Depot for the tube and the TfL Transport Museum Depot, a treasure house of retired trains, buses and ephemera that is very difficult to visit, being opened to the public only three times every year. Before railways took over the site in the early 1900s it was occupied by a large fish pond fed by the Brook.

• *At the T-junction turn right along Gunnersbury Lane.*

Gunnersbury Lane leads to Gunnersbury Park, a mansion now owned by Ealing that once belonged to the Rothschilds, its landscaped grounds complete with fake ruins.

On the right, is the hidden Mill Hill Park Estate, walled off from the street to the north and the south (although Mill Hill Road, where the author first lived in London, is outside its boundaries). The name comes from a windmill which stood on a mound in what is now Avenue Road. At the other end of Mill Hill Road the Mill Hill Brook crosses, part of the Stamford Brook (see Chapter 9: Stamford Brook West), making it one of the very few streets in London with two lost rivers.

The estate was built in the 1870s by a family called the Willetts. However, William Willett the Younger, who lived in Avenue Road, is remembered today as the promoter of Daylight Saving Time. He published a pamphlet in 1907 called 'The Waste of Daylight', which began the campaign that led, eventually, to the introduction of British Summer Time in 1916, mostly to save fuel during the First World War. Willett also lived in Pett's Wood, where he is remembered at the Daylight Inn.

The former Acton War Memorial Hospital on the right is a typical cottage hospital which, also typically, closed in 2001. The Ark Acton Academy on the right is the latest version of Acton High School, former pupils including Ian Gillan, lead singer of Deep Purple and three quarters of The Who (Keith Moon went to Alperton Secondary Modern). After the school a deep dip crosses Gunnersbury Lane, revealing the course of the stream as it passes beneath the road, and a block of flats called Brook House. This is the site of Bollo Bridge, first recorded in 1239. The Bishop of London paid for it to be repaired in 1554 and again in 1663, and it was marked on maps until the end of the 19th century. The Brook remained visible above ground until then, with a fishpond on either side of the road.

• *At the mini-roundabout by Acton Town underground station, turn left along Bollo Lane. Follow Bollo Lane for ¾ mile over two level crossings and under a bridge until you reach Chiswick Park underground station.*

Acton Town Station was called Mill Hill Park when it opened in 1879 on the Hounslow and Metropolitan District Railway, reflecting ambitions for the Willetts' development to rival Bedford Park, nearby in Chiswick. However, the architecture was not up to the standards of Bedford Park where Richard Norman Shaw created what John Betjeman described as "the most significant suburb built in the last century, probably in the western world". Today it bristles with listed buildings while Mill Hill Park, which has none, is generally forgotten. In 1910 the name of the station was changed but the station building dates from the 1930s, a classic modernist Charles Holden Piccadilly Line design.

Bollo's Peri Peri Restaurant and the parade of shops on the corner of Bollo Lane sit over the course of the Brook, which flows along the north side of the street in a more or less straight line for three-quarters of a mile. The three handsome blocks of Gunnersbury Court occupy the site of another long, thin fish pond that formed part of the Brook's course.

The Brook ran along the north side of Bollo Lane for half a mile. Beyond the station on the right side of Gunnersbury Lane is the site of Gunnersbury Lodge. This was an 18th century farm which became a gentleman's house, with residents including General Charles Dumouriez, former interior minister under Louis XVI, in exile after the French Revolution. Maps from the 19th century show a lake with a boat house, and more ponds to the north.

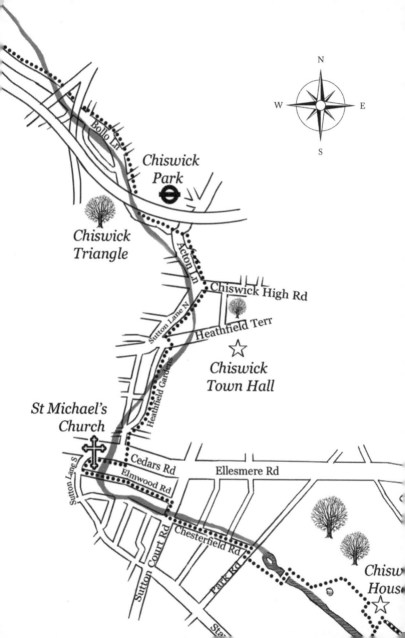

The redevelopment, including new blocks of flats on Bollo Lane, is part of the remodelling of a vast area of the South Acton Estate, built in the 1860s. This was the laundry district for London, as discussed in Chapter 9: Stamford Brook West. When the modernist estate was built in the 1960s land was freed for other industries on Bollo Lane as part of the redevelopment, when new industrial units were built. In the 1950s the area was said to be the largest industrial estate in southern England.

The Acton Works on the right, also known as Frank Pick House after the man responsible amongst other things for the Tube's roundel signs, looks like a cheaper version of the Pompidou Centre in Paris. It was the central engineering works for London Underground, and is now the main depot for Tubelines. During the Second World War tanks were prepared here for the D-Day landings. Several buildings on the site, including the canteen, date from the 1920s.

Bollo Bridge Road marks the location of another Bollo Bridge, a railway crossing that has been demolished, leaving only the abutments. The bridge carried a branch of the District Line that ran to South Acton Station, a little way along the tracks to the left. The train service was an extremely short, one-stop shuttle service to Acton Town, and it was said that drivers could pour a cup of tea, make the trip to Acton Town and return to South Acton in time to drink it before it was cold. The service ended in 1959, and the girder bridge collapsed while being dismantled.

After the level crossings, the Brook passes under Bollo Lane to run along the south side, just before the junction with Rothschild Road. On the corner of Antrobus Road and Bollo Lane is a rare 'anonymous' post box, made between 1879 and 1892 without a Royal cypher to show which monarch's reign it belonged to. Next door, the Bollo House pub was originally the Railway Tavern, built for the workers nearby and also, wackily, the Orange Kipper for several years in the late 20th century.

Just before Chiswick Park Station, a path on the right is the only entrance to the Gunnersbury Triangle Nature Reserve, saved from development by campaigners in the early 1980s. It is surrounded on all sides by railway lines. A pond on the site is filled by groundwater, not directly by the Bollo Brook.

Behind the Triangle is Chiswick Business Park, on the site of the Chiswick Works. This belonged to the London General Omnibus Company and was the bus equivalent of the Acton Works, including a notorious 'skid pan' where drivers were required to test their control of a double-decker.

• *At the mini-roundabout after Chiswick Park Station, turn right to cross the railway and walk along Acton Lane.*

The indeterminate nature of the end of Bollo Lane is reflected in the underground station, originally Acton Green, then Acton Green and Chiswick Park, now Chiswick Park. The brick tower is designed to make it visible from Chiswick High Road. Until 19th century development, Acton Green was a separate hamlet between Acton and Chiswick and is now the name given to the open space just beyond the station, once also called Acton Common.

• *At the junction with Chiswick High Road, cross Acton Lane via the pedestrian lights to the left, then cross Chiswick High Road via lights to Turnham Green.*

At this point the course of the Bollo Brook becomes controversial. It is said that a stream flowed east towards Turnham Green Station, connecting with the Stamford Brook. However, this may have been confused with a separate watercourse, flowing down from Acton Lane along the top of Acton Green. It seems likely that the Bollo Brook turned south, crossing Chiswick High Road and passing along the west side of Turnham Green (confusingly, some distance from Turnham Green Station). In the 19th century there was a pond on the west side of the Green, and this side was also prone to flooding.

• *Walk along Sutton Lane, with Turnham Green on your left.*

Turnham Green has a battle named after it, more of stand-off than an engagement, that took place in 1642 during the Civil War. Following the Battle of Edgehill, the Royalist army advanced through Oxfordshire and Berkshire towards London. After Prince Rupert's cavalry sacked Brentford, the Earl of Essex gathered an army of 24,000 including many Londoners, who were armed civilians from the 'trained bands'. They blocked the Royalists' path into the capital, and Charles I held back from attacking a large group of what were, in fact, untrained soldiers. He retreated to Oxford after some symbolic cannon fire.

In A.P. Herbert's 1930 novel *The Water Gipsies*, a character stops his motorbike at Turnham Green as the drizzle comes down "under the shadow of the great Tank which Chiswick has set up to be a perpetual memorial of the Great War."[2] In 1919, 265 towns in Britain, including Chiswick, received decommissioned tanks as memorials in thanks for their contribution to the war effort. However, they were viewed as grim reminders of something people preferred to forget, and were gradually removed. The Chiswick tank was dismantled in 1937.

On the right, a plaque marks the flat which was E.M. Forster's London home from 1939 until his death in 1970. He moved here from Bloomsbury when war began and to be closer to his lover Bob Buckingham, a policeman who was married and lived in Shepherd's Bush.

• *Follow the zebra crossing over Heathfield Terrace and walk ahead along Heathfield Gardens.*

A gentle gradient slopes away along Heathfield Gardens in the direction of the Thames, supporting the theory that the Brook is likely to have followed this route.

To the left along Heathfield Terrace, Chiswick Town Hall and the surrounding streets are on the site of the Royal Horticultural Society's experimental gardens, opened in 1821. It held flower and vegetable competitions and fêtes there until it was replaced in 1904 by new gardens at Wisley. The red brick building further along, now flats, was originally the 3rd Middlesex and Royal Westminster Light Infantry Militia Barracks, then the Sandersons wallpaper factory and the Army and Navy Stores Furniture Depository, eventually closing in 1980.

---

2 Herbert, A.P. 1930 [1979], *The Water Babies*. Peacock, p222

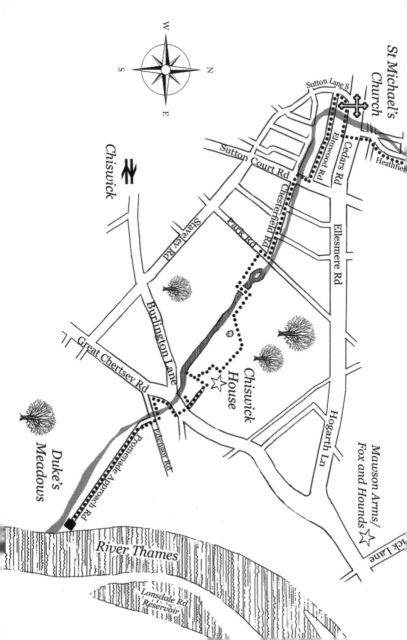

• At the mini-roundabout, walk straight ahead along a short, unsigned road (Sutton Lane North) to the A4. At the A4 (Cedars Road) turn right and walk to the underpass to cross the main road. Emerging from the underpass, turn right at the top of the stairs. Turn first left along Elmwood Road.

The A4 cuts a grim path between Chiswick's High Road and its riverfront, creating an extremely hostile environment for anyone not travelling through at speed. In wet weather the passing lorries send waves of water crashing into the underpass, in accidental tribute to the missing Brook.

On the other side of the A4, the turning into Elmwood Road marks the point where, in the 1890s, there was a fish pond shaped like the bends in a stream and, beside it, a small rivulet flowing above ground to the west. This, as far as we can tell, is the lower section of the Bollo Brook reemerging. From here to the Thames its course is clear. It now flows underground behind the church and along the backs of the houses on the right-hand side of the road.

A stream also rose near Kew Bridge Station, ¾ mile away on the north bank of the river, flowing to this spot. This is now Chiswick Sewer, which can be traced through the curved lines of various streets, gardens and open spaces along its route, including Harvard Hill Recreation Ground, just to the west of the walking route.

St Michael's Church was built in 1908 as a replacement for St Michael's Burleigh Street, off the Strand, "the demolition of which to meet the needs of the time has enabled a house of god to be erected in this district", as the foundation stone explains.

• At the T-junction cross and turn right along Sutton Court Road. Take the first left on to Chesterfield Road.

The Brook crosses to the right-hand side of Chesterfield Road at the junction with Sutton Court Road, and then back to the other side a little further along.

Local names – Chesterfield Road, Chatsworth Road – reflect the influence of the Dukes of Devonshire, who came to own Chiswick House, now close by, and their Derbyshire estates.

• *At the T-junction turn right along Park Road, then left into Chiswick House Gardens.*

The landscaped park dates from the 1720s, when the 3rd Earl of Burlington built Chiswick House and expanded its grounds, buying the neighbouring Sutton Court Estate on the other side of the Bollo Brook. The Brook became the centrepiece rather than the boundary of his park, and it now emerges dramatically from hiding into perhaps the most impressive setting of any lost London river. It was widened into what is described as a 'canal', but bears little resemblance to the Grand Union. It is, in fact, carefully designed to look like a natural river, which is strange because that is what it was before landscape designer William Kent widened it to create an artificially 'natural' version of itself.

A long lake runs the full length of the grounds. It is now fed, like other ornamental lakes formed from rivers, by springs while the Brook is piped underneath. The laundries of South Acton, and the lack of a sewer system, must have undermined the Arcadian atmosphere of the lake.

• *Follow the path straight ahead. Further along, turn left to cross the Classic Bridge.*

The impressive Classic Bridge was built in 1774, replacing a wooden bridge. The gardens of Chiswick House were exceptionally influential during the 18th century, and often painted. William Kent's designs use the water of the Brook and a series of striking, classical elements including a doric column with a replica of the Venus de Medici on top, a pavilion with a mirror pond and obelisk, Coade stone urns and antique statues lining the path to the house, a wilderness garden and an Inigo Jones gate.

• *On the opposite bank of the lake turn right to follow the path to Chiswick House.*

Lord Burlington himself – who also owned a town house, now the Royal Academy – became fascinated with Palladian architecture after visiting

Italy in the early 1700s. He took his interest much further than most, designing what is described by the *Buildings of England* as "The most famous English c18 Palladian villa, a small but splendid recreation of the antique spirit."[3] It is inspired by Palladio's Villa Rotonda near Vicenza, but incorporates ideas from other classical buildings he admired, including the Pantheon and the Baths of Diocletian.

The house was built as an extension to a larger Jacobean manor house. The Fifth Earl of Burlington and his wife, Georgiana, Duchess of Devonshire – famous for her glamour, troubled life and involvement in Whig politics – knocked down the old house and added wings to Jones' building. These were controversially demolished by the Ministry of Works in the 1950s, when the building was in poor repair which explains why the surviving house, a perfect cube, is so small.

In 1966 The Beatles, who no longer played live, made videos to show on *Top of the Pops* for 'Paperback Writer' and its B-side, 'Rain', in the grounds of Chiswick House in the glasshouse, posing among the statues and sitting in the branches of the cedars.

• *Walk round the right-hand side of the house and through a small gate. Turn right to detour to the cascade.*

William Kent's cascade is accessed from a bridge built with the earth dug out to widen the Bollo Brook. It shows the water off with the help of a Cyclopean masonry grotto – a style using massive boulders inspired by the walls of Bronze Age Mycenae, in Greece.

• *Retrace your steps, carry on straight ahead past the small gate, and turn right to leave the park.*

Just before the main gates, a path runs to the right inside the perimeter fence. This leads to a small wooden bridge that crosses the last of the Brook as it leaves the park. It disappears under a brick arch which can be seen between the bridge and the fence, taking the Brook under the road.

---

3 Cherry, Bridget & Pevsner, Nikolaus, *London 2: South. Buildings of England*. Yale University Press, 2001, p395

• *Turn right along Burlington Lane.*

The perimeter wall above the outfall of the Brook is cracked, and appears to be under some strain, as though the landscaped gardens are on the verge of bursting into Burlington Lane. The Brook disappears under the road here and into a culvert for the rest of its journey to the Thames.

• *Cross Burlington Lane and turn left along Edensor Road.*

More names on this side of Burlington Lane – Cavendish Primary School, Edensor Road – refer to the Devonshire family's Derbyshire estates, and show that the family owned all the lands between here and the Thames. This is also the unlikely location for the Embassy of Moldova, perhaps the most obscure piece of foreign territory in the whole of London.

• *After Cavendish Primary School, turn right through gates on to Promenade Approach.*

Promenade Approach is built on top of the Bollo Brook, a canal that was filled in during the 1930s. The often-empty road and the avenue of trees are river ghosts. The Brook flowed beside the orchards that occupied Duke's Meadows until the 1920s, when industrialisation began. For thirteen years between the wars, gravel companies dug the meadows to the south, the Great Chertsey Road was built to a new Thames crossing at Chiswick Bridge and factories such as the Cherry Blossom shoe polish works opened. The area to the left of the avenue became a sewage works, which was replaced by the Edensor Gardens estate after the Second World War.

• *Bear left around a boarded-up brick building to reach the Thames.*

The outfall of the Bollo Brook can be seen over a low fence beside the Thames. A sluice gate is clearly visible, managing the flow of the Brook into the river.

For a post-Brook drink turn right along the river to follow Chiswick Mall, then turn left on to Chiswick Lane South. The Mawson Arms/Fox and Hounds, a pub with a curious double identity, is the brewery tap for the Fuller's Griffin Brewery and an appropriate place to end the walk.

Cock and Pye Ditch

' Remnants of the lost marshes, the ditch systems of Covent Garden still flow somewhere beneath the pavements. '

Cock and Pye Ditch

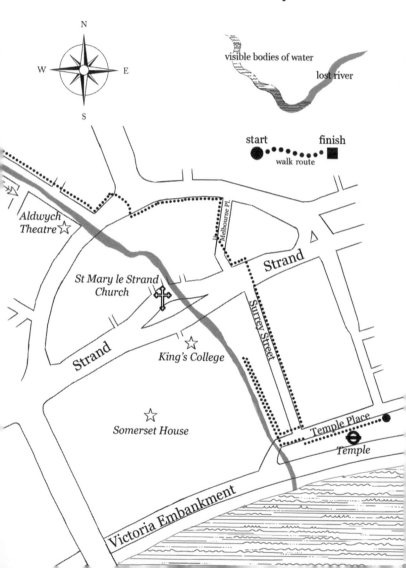

N
W E
S

visible bodies of water

lost river

start   finish

walk route

Aldwych
Theatre ☆

St Mary le Strand
Church

Strand

Melbourne Pl.

Strand

Surrey Street

King's College ☆

☆
Somerset House

Temple Place

Temple

Victoria Embankment

Practicalities

Distance – 1¾ miles
Start – Victoria Embankment Gardens, Temple
Getting there – Temple Station
End – Cleopatra's Needle, Victoria Embankment
Getting back – Embankment Station

Note – this walk should be completed between 7.30am and dusk (or 9pm, whichever is earlier) to allow access to Embankment Gardens, open between these hours every day of the year.

Introduction

The Cock and Pye Ditch, the Bloomsbury Ditch and their associated channels may or may not have, at one time, been rivers, but they certainly carried water. They drained land that is now Covent Garden, carrying water to the Thames at Embankment and Temple. The ditches were the most prominent part of a system that kept roads relatively passable and drained the marshy land around the village of St Giles, surrounded by fields on the road to Oxford, outside the City of London. With no known natural watercourses between the Fleet, to the east, and the Tyburn, to the west, Covent Garden and Soho are gaps in the London river map. It is, however, quite possible that the ditches rechannelled small streams that existed before the earliest maps. Today, the sewer system still sends water along the routes of the two ditches. This walking route follows the two linked ditches, tracking them from outfall to outfall and, unusually for a lost river walk, both starting and ending at the River Thames.

Until the 17th century, when it became absorbed into London and rapidly transmuted into a notorious slum, St Giles-in-the-Fields was a small collection of houses in the grounds of a leper hospital, which had been founded in 1101 by Matilda, Henry I's queen. The Cock and Pye Ditch encircled a marshy field called, appropriately, Marshland. Until its name changed to reflect the nearby pub, it was called the Marshland Ditch. The last open area to be developed in Covent Garden, Marshland was covered by Seven Dials and its radiating streets in the 1690s. The Ditch made a full circuit around the entire field – a rectangular watercourse. The Pituance Croft Ditch, which drained a field outside the hospital gates, seems to have been next to the Marshland and may have been connected to the Cock and Pye Ditch. Several ponds are also said to have been scattered across St Giles, and another field in the hospital grounds, Pool Close, sounds very much as though it contained one, and was possibly the source of some of the water that fed the ditches.

Connections from the Cock and Pye Ditch to the Thames are harder to track. We know that the Ditch connected into a channel that ran along St Martin's Lane in the direction of Whitehall. In the 1670s it was arched over to make St Martin's Lane more passable, and its water diverted east into the Bloomsbury Ditch. The Bloomsbury Ditch, also known as Bloomsbury Great Ditch or the Southampton Sewer, is part of a system of connected drains that separated the parishes of St Giles and Bloomsbury, and continued to act as a boundary as the city developed. In the 19th century the entire route could still be traced as a parish boundary, from the Cock and Pye Ditch at Seven Dials to the Thames at Surrey Lane. Its name was originally, according to 19th century historian John Parton, Blemund's Dyche after William Blemund, medieval owner of a large house in St Giles. While these were the two main ditches that drained St Giles, the local network also included Spencer's Ditch, which ran along the south side of Holborn, and another unnamed ditch that surrounded Lincoln's Inn Fields.

Any walk along lost rivers in this part of town is also haunted by the mythical or semi-mythical watercourses of Soho. The two key players in these stories are the Cranbourn and the Dean, two rivers which may be explained by the Cock and Pye Ditch. The Cranbourn is said to flow under the London Hippodrome, on the corner of Charing Cross Road and Cranbourn Street. The latter, however, is a title belonging to the local landowners, the Earls of Salisbury, not a river. Further north into Soho, authors Nicholas Barton and Stephen Myers report a watercourse that was visible through a grating in the basement of No.4 Meard Street when it was the Mandrake Club, a bohemian post-War Soho venue.

These supposed rivers are debated in the surprising context of a Lord Peter Wimsey mystery *Thrones, Dominations*, in which a taxi driver tells the detective "I don't know as how the marsh under Seven Dials ever did drain into the Fleet". Wimsey suggests the Cranbourn may have connected the two, but the sewerman doubts the existence of the Cranbourn and suggests that if the marsh drains into the Fleet it does so "down lots of little courses that have lost their names long ago along with their daylight."[1] Illegal sewer diversions in the 17th century may have been responsible for redirecting water from St Giles into Soho. The Westminster Commissioners for Sewers concluded that Richard Frith – who built houses on Soho Fields in the 1670s and has left his name at Frith Street – had connected a sewer in Soho to the St Giles and St Martin's parish sewer without permission. The latter was the Cock and Pye Ditch, and its flow may have been diverted under Soho, generating the illusion of a river to occasionally be glimpsed under its theatres and clubs.

This walk traces the probable course of the St Martin's parish sewer from the Thames at Embankment to the Cock and Pye Ditch, and then follows the latter into the Bloomsbury Ditch and back to the Thames, to reveal something of the deeply obscure watercourses of WC2.

1 Sayers, Dorothy & Paton Walsh, Jill, *Thrones, Dominations*. New English Library, 1998, p311

Route

• *Starting point: the separate rooftop section to Victoria Embankment Gardens, above Temple underground station.*

The walk starts at the Thames, following the Bloomsbury Ditch, which drained the Cock and Pye Ditch back to the marshes of Seven Dials. The Bloomsbury Ditch, or Southampton Sewer, no longer has a visible outfall into the Thames. It was channelled into the main low-level interceptor sewer contained within the Victoria Embankment, which was completed in 1870. Temple Place marks the line of the river bank before the Thames was pushed back by Joseph Bazalgette's huge engineering project. The sewer emptied directly into the Thames at the foot of Strand Lane, to the left. The gradient on Temple Place, which falls to the west, reveals the route taken by the sewer.

The raised section of Victoria Embankment Gardens, an intriguingly hidden spot, is a perfect point to survey the Thames. It narrowly survived the proposal to build the Garden Bridge across the Thames, which would have landed on the north bank on this spot. Look carefully to see whether you can spot the £43m of public funds spent on the aborted project.

• *With your back to the Thames, take the steps down from Temple Gardens furthest from the tube station. Turn left along Temple Place, then second left on to Strand Lane.*

The sewer flowed along the line of Strand Lane. This is now a dead-end, cut off by the main King's College building on the Strand, which is partly why it remains such an atmospheric street. The walk follows the Lane as far as possible, before retracing its steps to an adjacent through route.

Surrey Steps, climbing to the right, show how much lower Strand Lane is than Surrey Street and reveal a sense of a valley. A map from 1676 shows Strand Lane, or 'Strand Bridg (sic) Lane' which then ran between the gardens of neighbouring riverside palaces – Somerset House, where

King's College is now, and Arundel House. A stretch of water is inked alongside the lane on the west side, an indication that this is indeed the route of the sewer.

Between the Strand and the Thames were a series of medieval palaces which by the 18th century had been sub-divided into maze-like streets with "slum-like infilling".[2] Strand Lane, and the Ditch underneath, separated Arundel House – a medieval palace to the east built for the Bishops of Bath and Wells – from Somerset House to the west. The latter has a long and complex history. It was built by the Earl of Somerset, Lord Protector while Edward VI was a boy, and taken by the royal family when he was executed. The future Elizabeth I lived there while her sister, Mary, was on the throne. It was rebuilt by Inigo Jones after the Restoration, but the supposed 'Roman Baths' at the far end of Strand Lane date from the Stuart era. The sunken stone pool, visible if you peer through the window, is in fact a cistern built to feed a fountain. Its fake Roman history was apparently devised as advertising when it was run as a public plunge pool during the early 19th century. The story stuck, to the extent that the site is now owned by a slightly embarrassed National Trust.

• *Follow Strand Lane as far you as can, then retrace your steps, and turn left then left again into Surrey Street.*

The Arundel Great Court development on the right side of Surrey Street is on the site of the medieval Arundel House, demolished in the 1680s. It had belonged, after the Bishops of Bath and Wells, to the Howard family. The collector Thomas Howard housed the ancient Greek Arundel Marbles there, now in the Ashmolean Museum in Oxford, as well as his map maker Wenceslaus Hollar, a Bohemian who etched some of the first representations of London.

Surrey Street and Strand Lane both lead uphill, away from the Thames, their slopes taking the Southampton Sewer to the river. Before the Victoria Embankment was built, reclaiming land from the Thames,

---

2 Inglis, Lucy, *Georgian London*. Penguin Books, 2014, p130

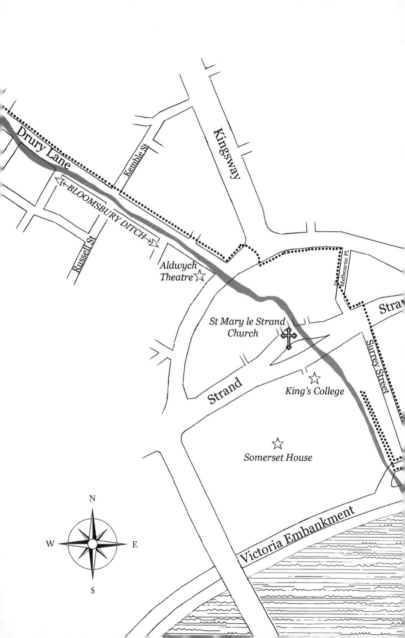

Surrey Street ended at a river wharf called Surrey Stairs, at the place where it now meets Temple Place.

Where Strand Lane meets the Strand, a bridge crossed the Ditch. According to historian Walter Thornbury, "the characteristic features of the Strand [during the 17th century] were the bridges that spanned the various water-courses flowing from the meadows and open fields on the north."[3] A now-gated alley, called Ivybridge Lane, to the west of the Strand marks the site of another crossing – the Ivy Bridge – but it is not clear where the water that ran under it came from.

On the left is the side entrance to the closed Aldwych underground station, now used extensively as a film location. The one-stop Piccadilly Line shuttle service from Holborn to Aldwych never made much sense, as it was generally quicker to walk, and it was eventually closed in 1994.

• *At the T-junction, cross both carriageways of the Strand.*

The Ditch crossed the Strand to the left, passing the east end of St Mary-le-Strand Church and continuing ahead under what is now the Aldwych, below Bush House.

The Strand seems a street that has forgotten why it was important. For one of London's ancient routes, it is a little underwhelming and it is hard to avoid the impression that the action is elsewhere. The 18th century Strand, in common with other main West End thoroughfares such as Piccadilly, was well-known for its prostitution to the extent that, as historian Lucy Inglis writes, "no woman would loiter making willful eye contact if she did not want to be picked up."[4] James Boswell, as she reports, wrote about his many encounters with prostitutes in the vicinity. This makes more sense when the Strand – its name meaning shore – is seen as the riverside street it was before the Thames was embanked in 1870. Linked to the river by numerous small side streets, it was much closer to the water and the wharves, and was notorious for the poverty of the courts that led directly on to one of the capital's showpiece streets.

3 Thornbury, Walter, *Old and New London Vol.3*. Cassell, Petter & Galpin, 1878, p60
4 Inglis, Lucy, *Georgian London*. Penguin Books, 2014, p148

• Walk ahead along Melbourne Place.

A large grille on Melbourne Place gives off a distinct whiff of the sewer some distance beneath, reassuring evidence that we are on the right track.

Melbourne Place passes behind Australia House, home to the Australian High Commission. The building, which opened in 1918, is built over a well which can be accessed through a manhole cover in the basement. This is probably St Clement's Well, first recorded in the 1100s and also known as the Holy Well, where on Maundy Thursdays "newly baptized converts appeared, dressed in white robes."[5] It is also on the site of one of the lost Inns of Chancery, Lyon's Inn, which was demolished in 1863 having apparently lost its credibility with the public through shady practices.

• At the T-junction turn left and walk along Aldwych.

We pick up the line of the sewer or ditch at Bush House, where it turned left up Drury Lane, under what is now the street called Aldwych. This is a relatively late development, built during the early years of the 20th century together with Kingsway as a giant urban redevelopment scheme. It was the last of the great Victorian thoroughfares, designed with the dual aims of improving transport and clearing slums. The target here were the winding, disreputable streets of Clare Market and Drury Lane, which had long had a reputation for poverty, and an atmosphere of dirt and dilapidation not helped by the meat market surrounded by slaughterhouses.

The Booth Survey visited the streets around the south end of Drury Lane in the late 1890s, after demolition had begun, and described "A hot thundery day. Sleepy, weedy men in the courts and streets & stout burly Irish women – a few drawn-faced children."[6] The monumental, but bland Edwardian buildings lining the new streets – hotels, theatres and offices – contrast with what they replaced. Several streets were entirely demolished, included Holywell Street, named after the lost well, which

5 Sunderland, Septimus, *Old London's Spas, Baths and Wells*. John Bale, Sons & Danielsson, 1915, p18
6 Booth/B/354 p133

was noted for its "second-hand booksellers and chemists of doubtful reputation"[7] or, to put it less delicately, the centre of pornography in London. It began as a street of radical printers in the years of the French Revolution and later became known for its dirty books and for its Jewish stallholders, lending a double edge to the famous description of it, in an 1857 letter to *The Times*, as "the most vile street in the civilised world".[8] No trace remains of the street, which ran parallel to the Strand between St Mary-le-Strand and St Clement Danes churches, under the Australian High Commission and past the Holy Well.

• *Cross Aldwych at the pelican crossing in front of Bush House and turn left along the opposite side of the road. Turn right on to Drury Lane.*

Drury Lane leads uphill along the Bloomsbury Ditch, back towards the Cock and Pye Ditch. Into the 20th century this route from the Thames along Drury Lane was a constituency boundary, showing that the sewer had local significance and strongly suggesting that its full length was once above ground.

The Ditch continued along Drury Lane, the bottom part of which was demolished for the Aldwych. Until then it was the main route between Holborn and the Strand. It was paved in the Tudor era having "become miry and nearly impassable",[9] so there were evidently drainage problems. In 1671 the Westminster Commissioners for Sewers reported that "from time whereof the memory of man was not to the contrary... a common ditch, sewer, and water-course" had run along Drury Lane. They complained that this had been illegally built over, causing the road at Charing Cross to become "very much overflowed with water, and become exceeding miry, dirty, and dangerous for the royal person of our sovereigne lord the king, and all his leige [sic] people."[10] They imposed a fine of 20 shillings on the landowners responsible.

---

7 Booth/B/354 p129
8 'C.R.T.', Letter to the Editor, *The Times*.1857, p9
9 Parton, John, *Some Account of the Hospital and Parish of St. Giles in the Fields. Middlesex*, Luke Hansard and Sons, 1822, p596
10 ibid, p120

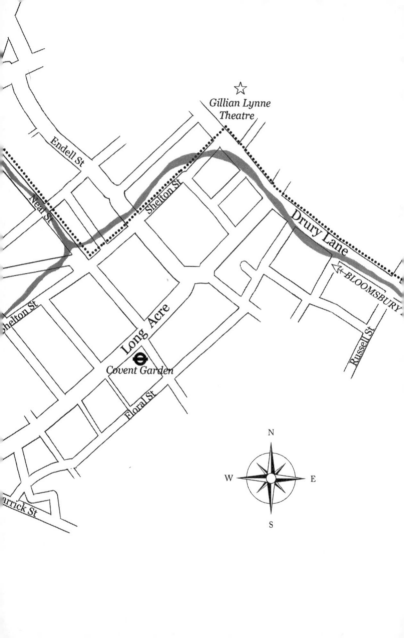

On the right, St Clement Danes Primary School remains in Covent Garden, but its sister grammar school moved out to Hammersmith in the 1920s, and is now in Hertfordshire. Its site, on the other side of Kingsway, is now part of the London School of Economics.

Drury Lane Gardens, on the left, is a former overflow burial ground for St John's Church in Broad Court nearby. The church has been demolished, and the burial ground a children's playground since the 1870s.

Further along, the Peabody Estate on the right is built on the site of the Cockpit Theatre, the first theatre in the Drury Lane area, which opened in 1616. A former cockpit, it was converted into an early indoor theatre, run by actor and impresario Christopher Beeston. After it was attacked by a gang of apprentices, who were possibly angry that it charged more than Beeston's outdoor theatre, it was rapidly rebuilt and nicknamed 'The Phoenix'.

On the right after Peabody Buildings, the Victorian building at 145 Drury Lane is the former Lambert and Butler tobacco factory, which operated until after the Second World War.

• *Where Drury Lane meets Great Queen Street cross, and continue straight ahead along Drury Lane to the Gillian Lynne Theatre. Turn left along the unmarked alley opposite the theatre (Shelton Street).*

The Bloomsbury Ditch crossed the junction with Great Queen Street and continued along Drury Lane, connecting with the Cock and Pye Ditch only a little further on.

The name Aldwych, revived when the road was built, comes from Ealdwic, an Anglo-Saxon word meaning 'Old Settlement'. This was Lundenwic, the Anglo Saxon London, a new town to the west of the abandoned, Roman Londinium. Lundenwic is the first version of Covent Garden, which Peter Ackroyd claims "has always been one of the fiery territories of London... There has never been, and never will be, a place equal to Covent Garden as a market and emporium."[11] Charles Dickens

11 Ackroyd, Peter, *Peter Ackroyd's Historical Tour of Covent Garden*. accessed 22.7.19, online

conjured the fruit, vegetable and flower market in its full glory in *Martin Chuzzlewit*: "Many and many a pleasant stroll they had in Covent Garden Market; snuffing up the perfume of the fruits and flowers, wondering at the magnificence of the pineapples and melons... rows and rows of old women, seated on inverted baskets, shelling peas... fat bundles of asparagus... speckled eggs in mossy baskets, white country sausages... new cheeses... live birds in coops and cages... rabbits, alive and dead, innumerable... cool, refreshing, silvery fish-stalls, with a kind of moonlight effect about their stock-in-trade, excepting always for the ruddy lobsters... fragrant hay, beneath which dogs and tired waggoners lay fast asleep, oblivious of the pieman and the public-house."[12] When the market, which in its modern form dated from the 1650s, departed in 1974 it left a hole at London's centre.

For a few years after the market closed, Covent Garden was a place of unpredictability and cultural experimentation, empty warehouses providing cheap space before development pinned the area firmly on to a tourist itinerary. Theatre director Phelim McDermott, in an anecdote that distils peak 1980s Covent Garden, reported following the impossibly hip composer Philip Glass as he strolled through the back streets from St Martin's Lane, and stopped outside a Shelton Street sushi restaurant – then an entirely new phenomenon in the UK – to inspect the menu. Covent Garden's cutting edge dulled as it became an established shopping destination, and the reminders of its alternative days are becoming harder to find.

• *Continue straight ahead along Shelton Street, crossing Endell Street.*

A small valley can be detected in the gradient along Shelton Street, which is built over the course of the Ditch.

At Endell Street the walk turns right, circling around three sides of the Cock and Pye Ditch and the Marshland field that it drained. The fourth side of the field and the Ditch continues straight ahead along Shelton Street, meeting the walk route again at the end of the road.

---

12 Dickens, Charles, *The Life and Adventures of Martin Chuzzlewit*. Chapman and Hall, 1843, p369

At the Shelton Street junction, the brown brick Odhams Walk development on the left shows how views on the future of post-market Covent Garden changed. In the late 1960s the Greater London Council planned a sweeping redevelopment of the entire district, involving mass demolition and a new international conference centre. After much opposition, led by the Covent Garden Community Association, historic buildings were preserved and new ones, such as Donald Ball's 1979 flats and shops on the site of the Odhams Print Works, added without dismantling the unmistakable streets.

The route also passes around Seven Dials, a junction where six radiating streets converge, built on Cock and Pye Fields at the end of the 17th century. The unusual layout of Seven Dials reflects Covent Garden Market which, as historian Lucy Inglis points out, was unusual for its time in being self-contained – that is, facing inwards towards its Inigo Jones-designed piazza.

Until the walk reaches St Martin's Lane, all roads to the left lead to Seven Dials, the centre of which is marked by a column with only six sundials. The current version is a replica, put up during the 1980s revival of the area. The original was erected in the 1690s and became a London landmark. John Gay, writing in 1730, described how "where fam'd *Saint Giles's* antient limits spread / an inrail'd column rears its lofty head."[13] It was taken down in 1773, and re-erected on Weybridge Green, in Surrey, as a memorial to the Duchess of York. The dial stone was replaced with a ducal coronet and, now called the York Column, it is still there. The story that the column was pulled down by a mob looking for buried gold is an urban myth, and the column was apparently removed to prevent undesirables hanging around it.

In *The Old Curiosity Shop* Charles Dickens described a "Covent Garden Market at sunrise... in spring and summer, when the fragrance of sweet flowers is in the air, overpowering even the unwholesome streams of last night's debauchery."[14] He was probably not referring to the ditches. In fact, according to Inglis, Covent Garden was provided with

13 Gay, John, *Trivia or the Art of Walking the Streets of London*. Bernard Lintot, 1730, pp22-23
14 Dickens, Charles, *The Old Curiosity Shop*. Chapman and Hall, 1868, p2

sewers that were "well-ventilated and not uncivilised"[15], at least until the end of the eighteenth century. Nevertheless, it was a neighbourhood with a dubious reputation from early in its existence. Samuel Pepys recorded his views of the area in the 1660s: "the coachman desiring to go home to change his horses, we went with him into a nasty end of all St Giles's, and there went into a nasty room, a chamber of his, where he hath a wife and child."[16] In 1730, John Gay described St Giles as a "doubtful maze" where "the peasant" "tries ev'ry winding court and street in vain".[17] By 1751 the gin craze had taken over, and Hogarth's etching 'Gin Lane' illustrated the perils of distilled spirits with the social chaos of St Giles, when a quarter of all premises in the parish were gin shops.

• *At the Crown and Anchor pub, turn right along Neal Street.*

The Cock and Pye Ditch turns right at this point, passing along the east side of the Marshland, its route now marked by Neal Street. Excavations at Shorts Gardens have uncovered the remains of whitewashed, Middle Saxon wattle and daub houses. Beneath were remains from further back, in the 8th century, including bones from butchered animals, oyster shells and charcoal preserved in the wet blue clay of the Marshland and the Cock and Pye Ditch.

By the 19th century, St Giles had acquired an even worse reputation than in the gin years. The area to the north of Seven Dials was known as The Rookery and associated with Irish costermongers, who worked in the market and lived in some of the worst conditions in the country. Victorian author Mary Braddon, like many others, used "the worst rookeries about Seven Dials"[18] as the archetype of urban crime and poverty. A Seven Dials alley, Nottingham Court, was described in the 1890s as a place with "all doors open, bird cages at windows, mess, barrows, bread, potatoes, lemons, draggled and hatless women"[19] and was somewhere the police were reluctant to go,

15 Inglis, Lucy, *Georgian London*. Penguin Books, 2014, p129
16 Pepys, Samuel, *The Diary of Samuel Pepys*. Thurs 3 October 1667, online
17 Gay, John, *Trivia or the Art of Walking the Streets of London*. Bernard Lintot, 1730, pp22-23
18 Braddon, Mary, *Lady Audley's Secret*. Virago Modern Classics, 1862 [1985], p46
19 Booth/B/354 p111

after a patrol of four men was attacked. By 1929 the poverty had receded, or at least moved elsewhere, but Seven Dials was still a suitable location for Agatha Christie to set a shady but exotic club run by a Russian and frequented by "a damned funny crowd".[20] However, the space around Seven Dials still gave a hint of the field it had been. A Covent Garden flowergirl yearns, in Richard Whiteing's 1899 novel *No. 5 John Street*, for the open fields and complains "I can't 'ear the birds nowhere but in Seven Dials."[21]

• *Follow Neal Street until it reaches Shaftesbury Avenue.*

The Cock and Pye Ditch turned left to follow the north edge of the Marshland field, along the route of Shaftesbury Avenue. This section was called Dudley Street before it was widened in the 1880s, by demolishing the buildings along its south side, and extended to Piccadilly Circus.

The Marshland was developed by Thomas Neale, a Stuart courtier and developer who, among many other things, set up the first postal service in the Americas. There are detailed records of the works, which explain that in 1670 the Cock and Pye Ditch was cleaned out, and the soil removed heaped on to Cock and Pye Fields. The following year, the Ditch was "partly arched over". Ten years later the locals were allowed to build a gravel cause across the fields, "being still wet and marshy",[22] for easier access to St Giles-in-the-Fields Church.

In the 1890s, Neal Street was home to "many Irish cockneys, costers, roadsweepers & newsvendors" and summed up by the Booth Survey as "rough, poor, working class fling bricks at the police but are not criminal".[23]

• *Turn left, crossing Monmouth Street, to walk along Shaftesbury Avenue.*

A small oblong grille at the entrance to Mercer Street is a sign of water somewhere beneath. John Strype dismissed early 18th century Mercer

---

20 Christie, Agatha, *The Seven Dials Mystery*. Pan Books, 1929 [1962], p94

21 Whiteing, Richard, *No. 5 John Street*. Grant Richards, 1899, p90

22 Parton, John, *Some Account of the Hospital and Parish of St. Giles in the Fields, Middlesex*. Luke Hansard and Sons, 1822, p123

23 Booth/B/354 p107

Street describing it, cuttingly, as "of no great Account for Building, or Inhabitants, who are a great Part French". He does, however, explain its topography: "It falls into Castle-street, against the Dial in the new Buildings in Cock and Pye Field."[24] The street was described in 1650 as having long gardens which reached down to the Cock and Pye Ditch, which had not yet been covered over.

Monmouth Street, which in the late 19th century was Great Andrew Street and Little Andrew Street, was more respectable than the Covent Garden courts and side streets and had small restaurants and a street market selling a good quality of produce – anything from damsons to "hot bullocks cheek".[25]

John Parton, writing in the early 1800s, reports that "At what time the Marshland came to be called Cock and Pye Fields, a name it received from the neighbouring public-house of the Cock and Pye, does not certainly appear"[26] but is first seen in 1666, after the first houses were built on the fields. On a map from 1658, the former Marshland was labelled St Giles Fields, a still-open patch between St Giles Church and the new houses of Covent Garden, to the south. London ended at St Giles and to the west, where Soho would soon be built, were fields and, on Great Windmill Street, a windmill.

The same map shows a small cluster of buildings on the south-east corner of the field, at the top of what is now Upper St Martin's Lane. One of these is the Cock and Pye Inn, "a brick building of two storeys and a garret."[27] Alongside were two small houses, one a wheelwright's shop, a thatched tenement building and a garden "late converted into a garden, beinge very well planted wth rootes."[28]

Tudor St Giles was a village "of a character completely rural".[29] St Giles Hospital owned most of the parish, and people living there as its

24 Strype, John, *A Survey of the Cities of London and Westminster.* A. Churchill, J. Knapton, 1720, p74

25 Booth/B/354 p193

26 Parton, John, *Some Account of the Hospital and Parish of St. Giles in the Fields, Middlesex.* Luke Hansard and Sons,1822, p120

27 Riley, Edward & Gomme, Laurence, *Survey of London: Volume 5, St. Giles-in-The-Fields.* London County Council, 1914, p112

28 quoted in Riley, Edward & Gomme, Lawrence, ibid, 1914, p112

29 Parton, John, *Some Account of the Hospital and Parish of St. Giles in the Fields, Middlesex.* Luke Hansard and Sons, 1826, p597

tenants, their cottage gardens bordered by marshland. Roads through the area were drained by ditches that ran beside them. The hamlet was not considered a healthy place, the marshy country encouraging disease. In 1665 the parish of St Giles-in-the-Fields was the site of the first suspected cases of the Great Plague. The authorities began sealing houses of plague victims to contain its spread but crowds broke down the doors of the first house in St Giles to be closed and released its inhabitants.

The Odeon cinema on the opposite side of Shaftesbury Avenue opened in 1931 as the Saville Theatre, and features a frieze called 'Drama Through the Ages'. The Beatles' manager, Brian Epstein, took a lease on the theatre in 1965 and ran it, until his death two years later, as a theatre and music venue. Bands included the Jimi Hendrix Experience, Cream, Fairport Convention and the original, British, Nirvana.

• *After the Brewdog pub, turn left along West Street.*

The walk follows the Cock and Pye Fields boundary and the route of the Ditch. West Street, which covers the line of the ditch, is apparently so named because it was the western boundary of Cock and Pye Fields. Crown Street and West Street were, when they still crossed fields, together known as Hog Lane. Parish records show a payment in 1662 for maintaining "the ditch at the Town's-end"[30] by a pub on Hog Lane, called the Crooked Billet.

West Street, in the 1890s was, according to The Booth Survey, "a street with a bad reputation" with "a fair smattering of 'snatch' men... & burglars as well as bullies & prostitutes."[31] A wide selection of stolen goods could be purchased "from rusty nails to oil paintings."[32]

St Martin's Theatre, on West Street, is home to Agatha Christie's *The Mousetrap*, which has been running there since 1974. It transferred from the Ambassador's Theatre, where it had been on since 1952. The total run

---

30 Parton, John, *Some Account of the Hospital and Parish of St. Giles in the Fields, Middlesex*. Luke Hansard and Sons, 1822, p241

31 Booth/B/354 p189

32 Booth/B/354 p191

– 67 years at the time of writing – is the longest in theatrical history and testament to an insatiable appetite for undemanding theatre.

• *Follow West Street as it curves left after the St Martin's Theatre to meet Upper St Martin's Lane. Cross Upper St Martin's Lane and turn right.*

The Cock and Pye Ditch continued straight ahead, along Shelton Street, to complete the fourth side of its square course around Cock and Pye Fields. The walk's route, however, turns along St Martin's Lane to follow the course of the St Martin's parish sewer that drained the Cock and Pye Ditch. The street follows a noticeable gradient, sloping downhill towards the Thames, which is still some distance way. It is clear that any water finding its way on to this slope would flow straight ahead, making this route the inevitable course of the parish ditch and of the Marshland waters.

The Cock and Pye Inn itself stood at the south-west corner of the Marshland, roughly where Slingsby Place, an alley straight ahead of St Martin's Lane, is now. The pub, despite stories about elaborate peacock pies, is more than likely to be named after a cock and a magpie. The phrase, which seems to have been a common one, appears in Shakespeare's *Henry IV Part 2* when Justice Shallow, addressing Sir John Falstaff, declares: "By cock and pie, sir, you shall not away to-night."[33]

The pub's popularity was apparently dependent on its semi-rural location. The 1561 Ralph Agas map of London shows St Giles as a settlement in the fields, separated from the nearest buildings, at Charing Cross and on the Strand. To the west of St Martin's Lane, cattle are grazing and a person with a large basket lays out clothes to dry. To the east are more cattle and field paths towards Drury Lane, where a man, a boy and a dog are walking. The building of Seven Dials filled in the last field "and the business of the Cock and Pye was so much injured that the place fell into obscurity."[34] The Cock and Pye was later renamed the Two Angels and Crown, before being demolished.

New Row, to the left, rises relatively steeply away from St Martin's Lane helping to confirm the impression that we are walking along the bottom of a valley.

33 Shakespeare, William, *Henry IV Part 2*. The Arden Shakespeare, 1988, p157
34 Hough Clinch, C., *Bloomsbury and St. Giles's Past and Present*. Truslove and Shirley, 1890, p46

Leicester Square

Garrick St

Upper St Martin's Lane

The Coliseum

Chandos Pl

William IV St

Strand

Charing Cross Rd

Adelaide St

Buckingham St

Duncannon St

Viller's St

Gordon
Wine Bar

Charing Cross

N
W E
S

On the corner of New Row, the pub currently called Mr Fogg's Tavern was, until recently, the Angel and Crown. It is a successor to the original Two Angels and Crown, which sat above the Ditch back along St Martin's Lane. The current pub inherited the old pub's licence when it was pulled down in 1848, and transferred it to a new site further along the street.

Opposite, the Salisbury pub has an impressive Victorian interior and was described by Ian Nairn as "Real West End glitter, with all the stops out... A pint in here is like drinking in one of Inigo Jones's cubes."[35]

Cecil Court, on the right, is the closest modern equivalent to Holywell Street, a 'booksellers' row' since the 1930s. Before then, it was the centre of Edwardian era filmmaking and distribution in London during the early days of cinema, when it was referred to as Flicker Alley. The oldest shop on the street, Watkins Books, is an occult specialist founded in 1901. Aleister Crowley claimed to have made all their books disappear.

Brydges Place, on the left beside the London Coliseum, is a remarkably tight alley – possibly the narrowest in London – between the side wall of the theatre and the backs of the pubs on Chandos Place.

• *Follow Upper St Martin's Lane until it reaches the Chandos pub on the left.*

The modernist monument to Edith Cavell, the British nurse executed by the Germans in 1915 for helping Allied soldiers escape from occupied Belgium, was erected during a popular frenzy over her death. Its location on St Martin's Place was, at the time, next to the headquarters of the British Red Cross.

• *Turn left along William IV Street, then first right along Adelaide Street.*

The gradient becomes steeper on Adelaide Street, and the descent towards the Thames more obvious. The lie of land suggests that is the likely course of the parish sewer, en route to the river.

---

35 Nairn, Ian, *Nairn's London.* Penguin, 1966, p73

The white stucco building on the left, now Charing Cross Police Station, was Charing Cross Hospital for 150 years, until 1973 when it moved to a far larger, modern complex in Hammersmith but retained its name.

Further along Adelaide Street, Maggi Hambling's sculpture 'A Conversation With Oscar Wilde', installed in 1998, is also an indirect tribute to film director Derek Jarman who campaigned for a London memorial to Wilde before his death in 1994. The quirky piece, showing Wilde emerging from his own tomb, is infamous for repeatedly losing the cigarette between the statue's fingers, which is repeatedly stolen, either in protest or tribute.

• *Cross Duncannon Street and then the Strand via pelican crossings ahead, and turn left on the other side.*

The St Martin's parish ditch must have crossed the Strand near Charing Cross Station to reach the Thames, although there is no record of exactly where.

Charing Cross Station was built on the site of Hungerford Market, a long-standing produce market sold to the South East Railway in 1862. It was rebuilt in the 1830s with a new, Italianate building by the Covent Garden Market architect, Charles Fowler. Two square, Venetian-style towers fronted the river, and direct access across the river was added in 1845 with the new Hungerford Bridge for pedestrians, a suspension bridge designed by Brunel. However, attempts to compete with Billingsgate for the fish trade did not succeed and the market was sold after damage in a fire.

Until the First World War, when it was replaced by Victoria, Charing Cross Station was the main departure point for boat trains to the Continent. It has been rebuilt twice, the current Terry Farrell version dating from 1986. In 1905 the roof of the first station failed spectacularly, killing six people, as its western wall collapsed into the next-door theatre.

Opposite the station, the glass-fronted building on the Strand is Coutts, the traditional bank of the extremely wealthy. Its clientele is clearly identifiable from the location of its first out-of-town branch, which was in Eton. It was originally based on the opposite side of the Strand where it took the place of the New Exchange, a proto-shopping centre popular during the Restoration, not least with Samuel Pepys who "laid out 10s. upon pendents and painted leather gloves, very pretty and all the mode" there for his wife.[36] The bank moved over the road in 1904, its new headquarters replacing Lowther Arcade, an enclosed shopping street topped with glass domes which had been almost entirely occupied by toyshops. John Nash's original columned arcade entrance was replaced in the 1970s by the Frederick Gibberd glass front, and the Nash columns were re-erected in the Gibberd Garden, in Harlow.

• *After Charing Cross Station and Villiers Street turn right into Buckingham Arcade, a passageway between shops. Walk down the steps at the end and continue straight ahead along Buckingham Street.*

Buckingham Arcade is, annoyingly, shut outside shopping hours. If it is closed, detour to the right, turn left along Villiers Street and then left again along John Adam Street to rejoin the route. However, it is worth taking the arcade route if possible, as it provides some sense of the steep, narrow passageways that dropped away from the Strand to the old riverfront. The early 19th century riverfront featured passageways under run-down buildings and wharves. As a boy Charles Dickens worked in a blacking factory at Hungerford Stairs, close to where Embankment Station is now. He was a general dogsbody, based in the first floor counting house of a ramshackle building overlooking the Thames, which was overrun with rats.

York Place, on the right, was once called Of Alley. The land was owned by the Duke of Buckingham, who sold it in 1672 to notorious Restoration developer Nicholas If-Jesus-Christ-Had-Not-Died-For-Thee-Thou-Hadst-Been-Damned Barbon, a man with Puritan parents. Apparently, a condition of the sale was that each new street on the site had to be named after the Duke in some way, leading to George

---

36 Pepys, Samuel, *1660-1669. The Diary of Samuel Pepys.* Friday 10 April 1663

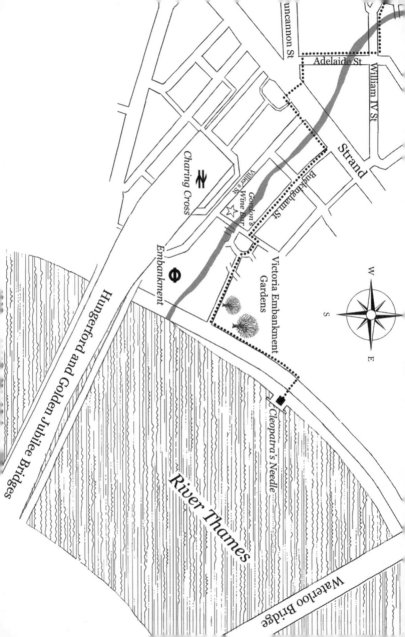

Street, Villiers Street, Duke Street, Of Alley and Buckingham Street. The name disappeared in the 1850s, but Barbon's idea of a joke has not been forgotten.

• *Cross John Adam Street and continue along Buckingham Street.*

Buckingham Street drops down towards the Thames, which once lapped at the watergate at the bottom of the steps. The Ditch will have emptied into the Thames at the bottom of the steps, but the original riverfront was entirely lost when the Victoria Embankment was completed in 1870. Today, the Thames is on the other side of Embankment Gardens.

No.14, on the right, is a house with a succession of famous residents, beginning with Samuel Pepys and including Queen Anne's chief minister, the Earl of Oxford, who employed Daniel Defoe and Jonathan Swift to write his political pamphlets. Opposite, the plaque to William Smith, 'Father of English Geology', is one of eight memorials to him across the country. This is due recognition for the man who produced, in 1815, the first geological map of the entire country: *A Delineation of the Strata of England and Wales with Part of Scotland Exhibiting the Collieries and Mines, the Marshes and Fen Lands Originally Overflowed by the Sea, and the Varieties of Soil According to the Variations in the Substrata.*

• *Walk down the steps at the end of the street, and turn left along Watergate Walk.*

To the right is the York Watergate, built by the Duke of Buckingham in 1626, and possibly designed by Inigo Jones. It was one of many landing stages along the Thames which were an essential form of London transport. There is no water at the gate now, which is marooned 150 yards inland.

Gordon's Wine Bar, at basement level along the alley to the right, occupies a former riverside seed warehouse that is now at some distance from the Thames, with the Embankment in between.

• *Turn right into Embankment Gardens. Bear right, and then left to cross the gardens to reach Victoria Embankment.*

George Borrow, writing in the 1850s, described the riverside at Embankment as a "forest of masts, and a maze of buildings, from which, here and there, shot up to the sky chimneys taller than Cleopatra's Needle, vomiting forth huge wreaths of that black smoke which forms the canopy – occasionally a gorgeous one – of the more than Babel city."[37]

The waters of the Ditch are now swept away into the Low-Level Interceptor Sewer, contained along with the District and Circle underground lines, in the Embankment which is essentially a very large box. A short distance to the east another street that drops from the Strand to the river, Carting Lane, features evidence of what lies beneath the streets in the form of a sewer gas lamp. Now a famous relic of Old London, the Webb Patent Sewer Gas Lamp was designed to run off the methane available below the street available from the tunnels that carry the Ditch. It never really worked though, and is now powered by a standard gas supply.

• *Turn left along Victoria Embankment, cross and walk to Cleopatra's Needle beside the Thames.*

There is no outfall to view, only a lost riverbank to contemplate. However, Cleopatra's Needle is an excellent substitute. According to Alan Moore, "Few symbols match THIS stone in potency."[38] The monument, carved 1500 years ago at Heliopolis and decorated with prayers to Atum, the Egyptian sun god, was brought to London by ship. The journey, naturally, was cursed and the ship sank en route, in the Mediterranean. When the Needle was recovered, a second ship was caught again in a storm in the Bay of Biscay with the loss of six sailors.

The needle comes with its own set of Egyptian-themed Embankment benches, with arm rests in the form of camels and sphinxes. Coincidentally, or not, the exact geographical centre of London has been mapped to one

37 Borrow, George, *Lavengro*. John Murray, 1851, p193
38 Moore, Alan & Campbell, Eddie, *From Hell*. Knockabout, 2000, p20

of the benches to the right of Cleopatra's Needle. The plaque beside the Trafalgar Square statue of Charles II, at the junction with Whitehall, is the main rival candidate and various claims have been made for other spots using different criteria. However, the mouth of the Bloomsbury Ditch seems as suitable a centre for London as anywhere.

The obvious place to toast the river, in sherry from the wood, is Gordon's Wine Bar on Villiers Street, where the subterranean wine cellars feel as though they are built into the ancient river wall.

Counter's Creek

'Counter's Creek, an unmistakable dividing line across West London, lives on and refuses to be buried.'

Counter's Creek

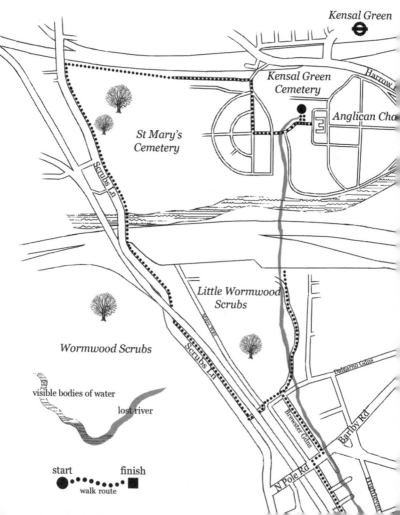

N

W   E

S

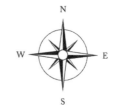

Kensal Green

Kensal Green
Cemetery

Harrow

Anglican Cha

St Mary's
Cemetery

Scrubs La

Little Wormwood
Scrubs

Mason Way

Scrubs La

Wormwood Scrubs

Dalgarno Gdns

visible bodies of water

lost river

Brewster Gdns

Barlby Rd

Highlever

start   finish

walk route

N Pole Rd

Practicalities

Distance – 7 miles
Start – Kensal Green Cemetery
Getting there – Kensal Green
Station
End – Chelsea Creek
Getting back – Imperial Wharf
Station

Note – this walk should be
done during daylight hours, to
allow access to Kensal Green
and Brompton Cemeteries.
Gates at Kensal Green
Cemetery are locked as early as
4.30pm on weekdays, and the
Cemetery closes at 1.30pm on
bank holidays.

Introduction

Although Counter's Creek flows mostly below ground, culverted until
its very last few hundred yards, it remains an unmistakable dividing line.
A railway and road corridor through West London follows its course,
running along the valley of the Creek which separates North Kensington
from East Acton, Holland Park from Shepherd's Bush, and Chelsea from
Fulham. The slopes of Notting Hill rise one hundred feet out of the valley
to the east, and the waters of its high ground drain into Counter's Creek,
where the notorious Notting Dale slum was located beside the river.

The river is named after a bridge – Counter's Bridge – which carried
Kensington High Street across its waters. The current name has developed
from Countessesbrugge or Countess's Bridge, which probably referenced
Matilda, who was a 15th century Countess of Oxford. As owner of the
manor of Kensington, she is likely to have been responsible for the bridge's
upkeep. However, as with other buried London watercourses, different
names have been used by the various neighbourhoods along its banks for
their stretch of river. Between Olympia and Earl's Court it was known as
Bull Creek, named after a nearby pub. Billingswell Ditch was the name
used near Earl's Court, derived from local wells. At the point where the
river crosses King's Road it became the Stanford Brook, a name which is
very easily confused with Sandford Creek, which is another name for the

lower reaches of Counter's Creek, or with the nearby Stamford Brook, a separate river. The lowest part, still open today, is called Chelsea Creek or even New Cut Creek. The section between Olympia and the Thames even became, for a short time in the 19th century, the Kensington Canal. It is likely that the river was never consistently called Counter's Creek, because the name is notable by its absence and, unlike other lost London rivers, is not to be found in place or street names anywhere along its route. In fact, virtually the only contemporary reference to Counter's Creek comes courtesy of a folk band of the same name.

Before it was culverted for the construction of the West London Railway in the late 1830s, Counter's Creek was an open sewer, supposedly draining only surface water but carrying, in reality, a whole lot more. Once placed underground, it became the main outlet for West London's sewage which it carried directly into the Thames. Only when the London sewerage system was completed in the 1870s, with the construction of Chelsea Embankment, was sewage diverted away through the new Northern Low-Level Sewer. Counter's Creek now runs through a storm sewer, but continues to exercise its influence over the surrounding floodplain. During the heavy rains of Summer 2007, the sewer system flooded basements in much of the area along the river's course. Flooding on a smaller scale was already common and Thames Water, eventually deciding against building a new storm relief tunnel, has carried out extensive, smaller scale engineering works across Fulham and Chelsea to protect, they say, 1,700 basements. The paving over of gardens means that the Counter's Creek catchment area, which extends from Brent to Camden, collects much more water, much faster than it did fifty years ago. The Creek lives on and refuses to be buried.

Route

• Starting point: Anglican Chapel, Kensal Green Cemetery, closest to the West Gate on Harrow Road.

All Souls' Cemetery, Kensal Green is the likely source of Counter's Creek. Evidence of a spring can be detected in the depths of the cemetery hidden among 19th century tombs. The stream appears to have formed the original western boundary of the cemetery which, when it was consecrated in 1833, extended only as far as the north-south path that is now called Cambridge Avenue. The old cemetery boundary has now been absorbed by an extension, laid out in the 1880s, but its line still forms the boundary between the London Boroughs of Kensington and Chelsea to the east, and Hammersmith and Fulham to the west, marked by boundary stones along its route. The boundary, which continues all the way to the Thames, follows the route of the buried Counter's Creek.

The cemetery today is a combination of two adjoining burial grounds. The distinction between All Soul's, the Anglican Cemetery, and St Mary's Catholic Cemetery, which dates from 1858, is not obvious, although the two are operated separately. All Soul's is generally known as Kensal Green Cemetery. It was at the vanguard of the movement to improve burial hygiene by opening new cemeteries beyond the city edge to relieve crowded churchyards. It opened following the cholera epidemic of the late 1820s, and became the ultimate gallery of Victorian funerary monuments. Its status as the place to be seen in death was sealed with the burial of royalty in the form of the Duke of Sussex, a son of George III, in 1843.

The cemetery contains an unrivalled collection of notable graves from multiple eras. Just two examples of many are the Victorian superstar tightrope walker 'Blondin', whose tomb is topped with a life-sized female figure of 'Hope'; and, a century later, Shoreditch art curator Joshua Compston, who drifts into the afterlife laid on a stone version of the small Thames boat he owned. The proportion of monument to accomplishments is sometimes inverse. Quack doctor John St Long, remembered for killing his patients with lethal remedies, has one of the finest monuments in the most prominent location, while the ashes of Freddie Mercury were scattered, unmarked, in an undisclosed location. The cemetery also contains the mausoleum of Imre Kiralfy, the producer, with his brother Bolossy, of stage spectaculars and founder of a lost landmark along the Counter's Creek route: the Earl's Court Exhibition Centre.

The detailed directions below lead to a well which is located on a path between Squares 142 and 143 (as shown on cemetery maps). This is the only visible indication of the river's source.

• *Stand at the back of the chapel, at the bottom of the steps, facing away from it along the main path that leads west, towards the West Gate. To your right is the tomb of Major General Marcus Waters. Walk along the path ahead a short distance, then take the second path on the right through the graves, between a red marble memorial to Christian Paton and Thomas Cardwell and a light grey one belonging to William Smellie Graham. Turn left after the eighth grave, beside a small oak tree. A small square slab in the centre of the path covers a well.*

The source of Counter's Creek is a well, entirely unmarked and a truly hidden spot. The stone slab closes a brick-lined well shaft, surprisingly deep, with water at the bottom. This seems to feed the river, and is the only visible evidence of a source for the lost river. The slab is not secured and can be lifted, but it is heavy and the well shaft underneath unguarded.

Counter's Creek flows south, passing straight ahead under the Grand Union Canal, but has left little sign in the cemetery. The view beyond the cemetery contains the gasholders of the Kensington Gasworks, of which there were once five. They are closely identified with Kensal Green and are still in operation, although their working lifespan is limited. The smaller was designed by the impressively named Vitruvius Wyatt, while the larger is known as 'The Colonel' after Colonel Sir William Makins, Chairman of the Gas Light and Coke Company.

Coffins occasionally arrived by barge at gates which gave access to the Grand Union Canal, but they are no longer used and there is no pedestrian route out of the cemetery along the route of the Creek, which passes under the canal. The walk therefore takes a substantial detour to leave the cemetery. It then loops around, via Scrubs Lane to reach the line of the Creek again at Little Wormwood Scrubs.

• *Return to the main path and follow it west across the Cemetery, following signs to the Crematorium. Turn right at the open stone colonnade along the path to the West Gate. Immediately after the West Gate, turn left through another set of gates into St Mary's Cemetery. Leave the cemetery via the Scrubs Lane Gate. Turn left along Scrubs Lane.*

On the right-hand side of Scrubs Lane, the Car Giant second hand car emporium sprawls across multiple industrial buildings, including the modernist former Rolls Royce factory which closed in 1992 and is hidden behind blue metal cladding. The building beneath was a repair works, where the Rolls Royce Phantom was also made in very small numbers. This entire industrial neighbourhood is due to be replaced, if plans come to fruition, by a new town surrounding a station for HS2 and the Elizabeth Line at Old Oak Common.

• *Follow Scrubs Lane for ¾ mile, passing under a railway bridge and passing an area of scrub until you reach an unlabelled turning to the left under a railway bridge (Dalgarno Gardens).*

The railway bridge provides views out over the course of Counter's Creek, the land dropping towards the Thames under the big skies of Wormwood Scrubs.

The area around Little Wormwood Scrubs, ahead, was originally known as St Quintin Park when houses were first built here in the 1890s, on fields that belonged to Notting Barn Farm. The aspirational name is now largely forgotten because St Quintin Station, which was originally called Wormwood Scrubs, was destroyed in the Blitz. A wooden platform on top of the railway embankment, it extended between Dalgarno Gardens and North Pole Road but, despite discussions over reopening, has never returned.

• Turn left in Dalgarno Gardens, and then left into Little Wormwood Scrubs. Turn right to follow the path around the edge of the park, to the north-west corner.

Counter's Creek used to flow above ground across Little Wormwood Scrubs, running along the far (eastern) side of the open space. There is now little sign of the river, which is surprising because in the early decades of the 20th century it was landscaped as a park feature. The path in the north-east corner of the park crossed the river on footbridge, and it then formed a sequence of ponds linked by six separate weirs, with two further footbridges. Where the park ends at Dalgarno Gardens, the stream dived underground again. This elaborate celebration of the Creek was entirely gone by the 1930s, and the ponds filled in. The borough boundary, however, continued to follow its line for leaving a narrow strip of the park in Kensington and Chelsea until the 1960s.

• Retrace your steps to Dalgarno Gardens, cross over, and walk ahead down Brewster Gardens.

The river flows behind the houses on the right-hand side of Brewster Gardens, forming their rear boundaries.

The unresolved character of St Quintin Park in its early days was captured by the Booth Survey, which reported that the Charity Commissioners, who owned the land, refused to build the smaller, working class houses that were in great demand and insisted on larger, more expensive houses which no-one wanted. The estate was still on the edge of London with open space on one side of St Quintin Avenue and on the other "a field used for grazing purposes, let to a horse dealer."[1] The name of the now-closed North Pole pub reflects the remoteness of this edge of London, viewed from the centre.

---

1 Booth/B/359 p105

• *Cross North Pole Road, turn right and then left along Latimer Road.*

The river continues to flow behind the buildings on the left, all the way along Latimer Road. Its course can be seen clearly on maps in the boundary line between properties, which undulates in contrast to the straight streets on either side.

Latimer Road still retains the small, industrial buildings once found along more of the Creek's route. Sites backing on to the railway line, in the damper areas at the bottom of the river valley, were ideal for businesses such as engineering, dyeing and laundry which provided employment in the working class neighbourhood of North Kensington. It was only in the late 20th century that the property values in this area began to rise, and its ordinariness to erode.

The continued existence of Latimer Road is thanks to the cancellation of the notorious Ringway 1 scheme for an inner London motorway ring road. Only two sections – the East and West Cross Routes – were built, and the latter stops at the bottom of Latimer Road, where an elevated roundabout connects it to the Westway link road. The roundabout has only three exits, with a stub on the north side showing where the overpass would have continued along Latimer Road and through Little Wormwood Scrubs. The destruction came to halt in 1973, when Ringway 1 was cancelled, leaving the roundabout unfinished and saving Latimer Road.

• *Follow Latimer Road until it reaches the Westway Flyovers. Walk around the left side beneath the elevated roundabout then near right towards the tower blocks. Walk along a path with tennis courts on the right, then bear left to reach Freston Road.*

The river continues straight ahead, but the road no longer does. Latimer Road was cut short when the Westway junction was built, and the walking route therefore curves round to the left through the cavernous motorway undercroft.

On the other side of the Westway, the river flows to the left of Freston Road, under the Silchester Estate to the left, built in the 1960s and 1970s. The Lancaster West Estate immediately behind became known around the world in 2017 in the worst possible circumstances, when 72 people died in the disastrous Grenfell Tower fire. The greatest loss of life in a residential fire since the Second World War uncovered deep flaws in 21st century British society that remain unreckoned with and unresolved. The location of the fire was highly symbolic, as North Kensington had been known as the poorest place in London from its earliest days. A little way to the west of the walk route, a back street called Pottery Lane is a last reminder of when this part of North Kensington was known as The Potteries, a nickname for the Notting Dale slum. The Counter's Creek valley, which had already been dug for the bricks used to build the streets such as Ladbroke Grove, also provided stiff clay that was ideal for the trade, which grew up from the 1830s. The pig-keepers of Tyburnia had also moved out here when their fields, near Paddington, were developed and a shanty town sprang up amid appalling conditions. Thousands of pigs were kept among the houses, which were drained by a system of open ditches that polluted drinking water, leading to disastrous cholera outbreaks the extraordinarily high death rates. Avondale Park is on the site of the largest of the many stagnant pools created by brick-earth excavation, which was known as 'The Ocean'. The Metropolitan Commission for Sewers investigated, but the pig-keepers resisted change and conditions continued to worsen, as people flooded in from areas of London cleared for the railways. The pigs were eventually removed in 1878, but migrations to the area continued and its reputation endured.

At No.10 Rillington Place, renamed Ruston Mews and now beside the Westway, multiple murderer John Christie encapsulated the rotting post-war city, hiding bodies under the floorboards and in the walls. Colin MacInnes' *London Trilogy*, set at the end of the 1950s, captures Notting Hill as the fundamental shifts of the 1960s began to gather, poised to engulf an unsuspecting society. The neighbourhood was "clean, new concrete cloud-kissers, rising up like felixes from Olde English squares".[2] The squares were, however, full of sub-divided Victorian stucco terraces. Notting Hill was the territory of slum landlord Peter Rachman, who became notorious for his exploitation of the tenants he packed into

2 MacInnes, Colin, *Absolute Beginners*. New English Library, 1959, p5

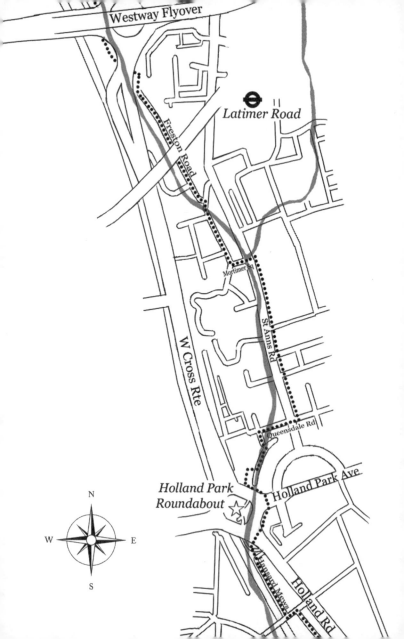

semi-derelict Victorian houses, many of whom were immigrants from the West Indies. Naturally enough, he owned the properties at the centre of the Profumo Affair, which wired West London sleaze directly into the national narrative.

Amid the poverty of what MacInnes described as 'Napoli', youth culture, drugs, sex, celebrity and race boiled up. Notting Dale had been cleared, but conditions in the surrounding area remained grim for most of the 1960s. Long-term resident Carol Meehan described how "You'd rob your own gas meter, or cut off pieces of lino to shove in the meter until there was nothing left covering the floor."[3] The Notting Hill riots of August 1958, the worst racial violence seen in Britain at the time, were caused not just by the conditions people were living in, but by provocation from racist groups, including Oswald Mosley's Union Movement.

The riots are said to have begun when a group of white youths attacked a woman called Majbritt Morrison who later wrote a book, *Jungle West 11*, about the times. They had started a fight the night before, offering unwanted protection during an argument with her Jamaican husband, Raymond Morrison, outside Latimer Road Station. Soon, mobs of up to 400 white youths were attacking black homes, mostly in North Kensington which was the part of Notting Hill with the fewest black residents. The riots peaked over three days, but the attacks continued for another two weeks. The first version of the Notting Hill Carnival took place the following year, organised by local activist Claudia Jones, to help defuse tensions. Mosley stood as a parliamentary candidate for North Kensington in 1959, and lost his deposit.

• *Walk straight ahead along Freston Road. At the T-junction, turn right (still Freston Road).*

Freston Street is the southern end of Latimer Road, renamed when the Westway cut it off, leaving Latimer Road Station at some distance from the road it was named after. During the 1970s the street was heavily squatted, with condemned Victorian terraces occupied by protestors,

---

3 Meehan, Carol in Oldham, Mark, *White Riot: The week Notting Hill exploded*. Independent, 29 August 2008

who organised themselves to defend the neighbourhood from the demolitions planned by the Greater London Council (GLC). In 1977 they declared the Free and Independent Republic of Frestonia, and issued a formal appeal for help to the United Nations. The organisers were writers Nick Albery and Heathcote Williams of the Ruff Tuff Cream Puff Squatting Agency. David Rappaport, later famous as an actor, was Foreign Minister.

During the 1980s the scene developed a home-made cyber-punk aesthetic, with bands characterised by World Domination Enterprises whose single 'Asbestos Lead Asbestos' targeted council leader Dame Shirley Porter, responsible for gerrymandering and for housing families in dangerous, asbestos-ridden accommodation. Another local band, Transvision Vamp, sang about "Walking down the line / heading for the Grove" in 'W11 Blues'. Anarcho-rave took over in the late 1980s, with Mutoid Waste Company parties and collectives such as Spiral Tribe and Transglobal Underground playing at a venue next to Latimer Road Station. The Republic of Frestonia eventually formed a housing co-op with Notting Hill Housing Trust and, while traces of the alternative scene have dissipated, an annual Frestonia party still takes place in their communal gardens.

• *Beside a blue corner house, turn left (Mortimer Square), then right on to St Anne's Place. Follow St Anns Road, which becomes St Anns Villas.*

By turning left, the walk rejoins the line of the buried Creek which flows under the middle of St Anns Road. The terraced houses on the left by the junction were described by Jerry White as "the tiny remnants of Notting Dale... a faint echo of fifty years ago."[4]

Further along, the tower and low rise blocks on the left belong to Henry Dickens Court, built during the 1950s to replace the Bangor Street area, described as "perhaps the worst slum in London."[5] Its reputation as the worst part of Notting Dale could be traced back to the late 19th century, when the Booth Survey described Bangor

---

4 White, Jerry in Whitehead, Andrew & White, Jerry, *London Fictions*. Five Leaves Publications, 2013, p189
5 ibid, p173

Street as "streets of unenviable notoriety all over London".[6] Four or five streets north of St James's Gardens were known as "streets of casuals, thieves and prostitutes,"[7] many of whom were passing through or had relocated from slum demolitions elsewhere in the city. Rooms in houses were cheap and extremely low quality, hence the attraction. Not everyone was a criminal of course, and Booth records local occupations as being rag, bone and bottle collecting, organ grinding, wood chopping and flower selling. Notting Dale was a bad place to live, and "there were years when half of all the babies born here would be dead of hunger, disease and neglect before their first birthday."[8]

At the open space on the left before the Mortimer House shops, the Creek turns to the right, away from St Anns Road, to flow behind the buildings.

A bespoke coal hole cover in the road outside No.17 claims, defensively, that the Victorians did not approve of the exuberant, neo-Jacobean houses, built in the 1840s. The house in question has a blue plaque in memory of music hall comedian Albert Chevalier, born here, whose Cockney costermonger character was famous for songs including 'My Old Dutch' and 'Knocked 'em in the Old Kent Road'. His full name, remarkably, was Albert Onésime Britannicus Gwathveoyd Louis Chevalier.

• *After the mock Jacobean villas, turn right along Queensdale Road.*

The walk rejoins the line of the Creek again at the junction with Norland Road. The underground river crosses Queensdale Road, where Thames Water has recently expanded the sewer capacity to prevent Counter's Creek flooding basements, and continues between Norland Road and Royal Crescent Mews. At the junction of the two roads a drain cover in front of the Edward Woods Estate marks its course.

---

6 Booth/B/359 p157
7 Booth/B/359 p157
8 White, Jerry in Whitehead, Andrew & White, Jerry, *London Fictions*. Five Leaves Publications, 2013, p173

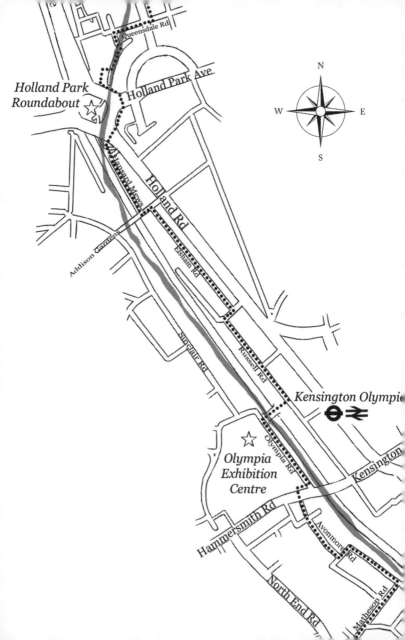

• *Turn left into Royal Crescent Mews.*

The Creek's valley can be seen, running to the left of Norland Road, and the walk descends into the dip along Royal Crescent Mews. While the course of the river passes this way, the sewer carrying it was realigned to match the new road pattern when the Norland Estate was built in the 1830s. The Westminster Commissioners of Sewers insisted that the West London Railway Company, building a new railway to the west of the Creek, should pay to divert the open sewer into a covered channel all the way from North Kensington to Cromwell Road, in South Kensington. The river was moved to the east and, as a result, the sewer runs under the centre of Royal Crescent.

• *Turn right past the vehicle barrier to leave the Mews, then left on to Norland Road.*

At No.22, the Honorary Consulate of Mali is in an impressively obscure location that, nevertheless, is still part of Kensington.

A twelve-sided concrete shaft gives access to the London Ring Main, a 16-mile long tunnel loop, 130 feet below ground, carrying drinking water from reservoirs to the west of London, at Shepperton and Walton-on-Thames. It opened in 1994, with a new pumping station under Holland Park Roundabout.

• *Turn left at the barriers alongside the roundabout. Turn right at the lights to cross Holland Park Avenue at a two-stage pelican crossing. Turn right again to cross Holland Road at another two-stage crossing. Follow the pedestrian path on the other side across a grass area to Hansard Mews.*

Thames Water's 1990s London Ring Main tower is the main feature of the Holland Park roundabout and is functional rather than decorative, containing a surge pipe that provides extra capacity during high rainfall. The roundabout is perhaps the least accessible public space in London. Although it is landscaped, actually reaching it would involve a sprint across six lanes of relentless traffic.

To the left, on the opposite side of the road, Clearwater Terrace, which runs beside the Hilton hotel, is a late 20th century renaming and probably has more to do with the Ring Main than the Creek.

• *Walk down Hansard Mews to a T-junction.*

The realigned Counter's Creek sewer follows the line of Holland Villas Road and Holland Gardens to the east, but the walking route instead follows the original route of the river, which is also the borough boundary, to the west of the railway lines. Before Hansard Mews was built in the 1870s, it was an unnamed back lane. Maps showed a well in the gardens of its only two houses.

• *Turn left along Lower Addison Gardens, then right on to Elsham Road.*

The river ran on the east side of the railway, but crossed over to the west side at the junction of Hansard Mews and Lower Addison Gardens, before returning again to the east side. The railway lines that occupy the river valley were completed in the 1840s, an attempt to make the failing Kensington Canal viable. We reach the site of the canal further along the river's route, but the West London Railway was conceived to connect the canal basin, beyond what is now West Cromwell Road, to the railway network at Wormwood Scrubs. The railway company also bought the canal, but the combination was no more of a success than the canal had been. The railway was unreliable, trains having to wait to cross the Great Western mainline, and was little used. It was seized by the courts against unpaid debt after only a few months, and it was ten years before the London and North Western Railway took it over and began to run trains again.

• *At the T-junction turn right along Russell Road, and follow it as it turns immediately left.*

On the corner to the left is the Georgian Embassy, which employs similar locational tactics to the Mali Consulate. On the opposite corner, a new building replaces the Kensington Hotel, demolished in the early 2010s, which was a jazz pub in the early 1970s, and then a pub rock venue frequented by the likes of Dr Feelgood and Eddie and the Hot Rods.

• *Turn right at the Kensington Olympia Station sign and cross the tracks on the footbridge to Olympia Way and the Olympia Exhibition Centre. Turn left along Olympia Way.*

Kensington (Olympia) Station, which was originally called Kensington (Addison Road), now has regular trains as part of the Overground loop around London. For many years it was officially a London terminus, but was oddly underused. Its quietness was convenient: General Eisenhower used it to visit the troops on the South Coast before D-Day and it was to be used, in the event of a nuclear attack, to evacuate civil servants to Central Government War Headquarters in a Wiltshire bunker.

Directly ahead at the footbridge is Blythe Road, with George's Cafe at No.36. The address was, in 1900, the headquarters of the Second Order Vault of the Adepts, a branch of occult secret society The Order of the Golden Dawn. A split in the order – with W.B. Yeats among others on one side and founder Samuel MacGregor Mathers and 'The Beast' himself, Aleister Crowley, on the other – culminated in the 'Battle of Blythe Road'. Crowley occupied the premises and changed the locks but, while he was out, the rival faction changed them back. Crowley, incensed, hired an 'enforcer' from Leicester Square and arrived to demand entry "with a mask of Osiris, a dirk of 'cold steel', and a MacGregor tartan".[9] His way was barred by Yeats, who supposedly chained himself to the door, accompanied by the landlord and a police constable. Crowley's heavy turned up late, having got lost, and they beat a retreat. Crowley left the Order of the Golden Dawn not long after to strike out on his own, but Yeats complained to friends that wax images were being made of him, and pins stuck into them.

Olympia was built on the former Vineyard Nursery where, in the 1780s, fuchsias were commercially grown for the first time, having been discovered in a sailor's garden in Wapping. He had brought

---

9 Sutin, Lawrence, *Do What Thou Wilt: a life of Aleister Crowley*. St. Martin's Griffin, 2000, p77

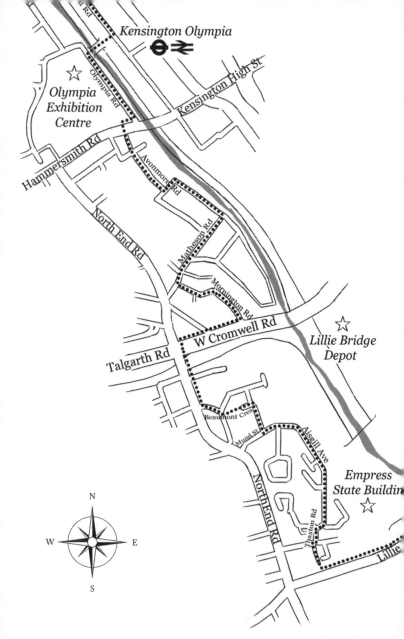

them from the West Indies as a present for his wife. Olympia was called the National Agricultural Hall when it opened in 1886, but the name was soon upgraded to something more impressive, suited to the largest venue in the country. A huge glass and iron structure, it combined ethnographic trade exhibitions of the kind popular at the turn of the century – such as the 1888 Irish Exhibition – with circus spectaculars including Phineas T. Barnum's "Greatest Show on Earth", which arrived in 1889, and Charles Cruft's dog exhibitions. It was requisitioned as an internment camp for enemy aliens during the First World War, and as a prisoner of war camp in the Second World War. In between, it hosted an infamous 1934 Black Shirt rally. For most of its existence it struggled for West London exhibition supremacy with its nearby rival at Earl's Court, but the battle is now comprehensively won.

To the right, beyond Olympia, a set of reflective glass offices on Hammersmith Road occupy the site of Cadby Hall. Demolished in 1983, this was the enormous Joseph Lyons food manufacturing complex which employed 30,000 workers in the post-war years, including Margaret Thatcher who worked there as a chemist in the early 1950s. It was also the home of the first computer used by a business, introduced in 1949.

• At Kensington High Street cross at the lights, turn right on the other side, then left along Avonmore Road.

Counter's Creek crosses straight ahead under Kensington High Street and continues along Addison Bridge Place which, incidentally, contains houses once inhabited by W.S. Gilbert, by Samuel Taylor Coleridge and by Harold Laski, political philosopher and former chairman of the Labour Party. The river follows the railway line for much of the rest of its route. The walk takes a through route along Avonmore Road to stay as close to the railway and the river as possible.

This crossing point is where the Countess Bridge was located, marking the point where Hammersmith Road becomes Kensington High Road. Despite the presence of the river that is named after this spot, there is no sign that it was ever here. Counter's Bridge is last shown on maps in 1813. It was recorded at various points, with several variations on its name appearing during the 15th century: Contessesbregge in 1421, Contassebregge in 1422, Cuntassebregge in 1445, and Countesbregge in 1475, when it was said to be in ruinous condition.

The basin of the Kensington Canal was located on the other side of the railway, on a site being substantially redeveloped. It was the terminus of a short canal which opened in 1828, connecting this part of West London to the Thames. Conceived by local landowner Lord Kensington, the canal scheme made Counter's Creek navigable by widening it from Kensington to the Thames. At the opening, Kensington sailed up the canal in a barge, the National Anthem was played on board, and the workforce of 200 was given a grand dinner with a butt of porter. However, the project was a commercial disaster and attracted very little traffic, apparently because it was tidal and could therefore only be accessed during short windows which changed every day. Plans to extend it further north along the Counter's Creek route therefore came to nothing, and the West London Railway took over instead. After it, too, had failed to make the canal pay it was filled in during the early 1860s and built over with a railway extension over the Thames to Clapham Junction. The basin was replaced by a coal depot. The end of the canal also meant the end of Counter's Creek, which was almost entirely eliminated above ground.

• *At a T-junction, turn left (still Avonmore Road). Follow the road around to the right. Turn first right (Matheson Road).*

The direct route ahead is blocked, and the walk therefore detours to the right. The blockage is Kensington Village, a gated housing estate with public access. It is a redeveloped 1880s complex that once belonged to Whiteley's Department Store. Some of the buildings were used as laundries but most were furniture depositories for storing the belongings of people who had left to work in the colonies.

• Turn second left along Mornington Avenue.

Mornington Avenue ends at a wall, beyond which is the multi-laned West Cromwell Road. This is now the main route from central London to the west along the A4 but, until the 1940s, the road ended around this point and went no further east. It was extended with a bridge over the railway in 1941, against much local opposition and later widened, with significant demolition, at the end of the 1960s to create the current expressway.

• When Mornington Avenue reaches the West Cromwell Road, turn right between walls to walk alongside the main road. At the junction opposite the Famous Three Kings pub, turn left to cross both carriageways of West Cromwell Road and walk along North End Road.

The Famous Three Kings is another former music pub. It began as a country music venue, but its heyday was in the 1970s and 1980s when, as The Nashville Room, it hosted new wave bands including Joy Division, Elvis Costello, The Undertones and The Selecter.

To the right, Castletown Road is another location where Thames Water has carried out engineering work to protect houses against the Creek in flood.

• Turn second left along Beaumont Crescent. Turn first left past the vehicle barrier into the Gibbs Green Estate, then bear right along a footpath between housing blocks and past a playground.

The walk route now turns right in the direction of the railway and the river. No.2 Beaumont Crescent has a plaque commemorating the Universal Negro Improvement Association, the black separatist organisation founded by Marcus Garvey which was based here during the 1930s. Garvey, who died here in 1940, is buried in St Mary's Cemetery at Kensal Green.

Behind Beaumont Crescent, the Gibbs Green Estate was built in the 1960s, replacing badly bombed streets. The Gibbs Green Bridge crossed Counter's Creek near here, recorded during the Middle Ages. The Gibbs

Green and West Kensington Estates, the latter next door, have been the subject of controversy after the then Conservative-run council submitted plans in 2009 to demolish and redevelop them as part of the Earl's Court development. Concerted local opposition focused on plans to make new homes available to only a quarter of estate residents. The estate was sold to developer Capital and Counties (Capco) in 2012 but nothing has happened, and Capco is said to be trying to sell the land, leaving the area in long-term limbo.

• *Turn right into Dieppe Street, then next left at Fairbairn House (Mund Street). Continue straight ahead through a low fence along Aisgill Avenue.*

The streets at this end belong to the adjoining West Kensington Estate, built in the 1970s on the West Kensington Coal and Goods Depot. This, in turn, was built between the wars on pleasure gardens which had been part of the original Earl's Court development. They included a switchback railway and a bandstand, apparently the largest in London, which operated into the 1920s.

Counter's Creek flowed across the land where the Empress State Building now sits, at the corner of the estate. It ran above ground across the site until the plot was first developed in the 1880s, for the Midland Railway's sidings and the Lillie Bridge Works.

The tower, completed in 1962, was one of London's first seriously tall buildings. It was built on the site of the Empress Theatre, developed in the 1890s by showman Imre Kiralfy as part of the Earl's Court Exhibition site. In the First World War it housed Belgian refugees (part of Britain's largest ever immigrant population) and was then used for building railway station mock-ups. In 1935 it became an arena, renamed the Empress Hall, specialising in musicals on ice. It staged the boxing events at the 1948 Olympics, but was demolished at the end of the 1950s.

The Empress State Building, although originally designed as a hotel, has been occupied by various branches of state security including the Admiralty's communications and Government Communications Headquarters (GCHQ), and is now used by the Metropolitan Police.

• Follow the road as it curves right then immediately left, then right again to follow what is now Thaxton Road. Turn second left soon after along an unnamed path beside a new, dark brick block surrounded by a green fence. Follow the alley between fences to the left to reach Lillie Road. Turn left along Lillie Road.

Lillie Road is named after one of the investors in the Kensington Canal, Sir John Scott Lillie, a commander in both the British and the Portuguese armies during the Napoleonic War who was wounded three times during the Peninsula War and left for dead on the field at the Battle of Toulouse in 1814, lying undiscovered for 48 hours. He was also, remarkably, a friend and supporter of radical Irish politician Daniel O'Connell, and an anti-vivisection campaigner. Lillie donated land beside Counter's Creek, now the site of West Brompton Station, to enable the building of wharves as part of the doomed canal project. The Lillie Langtry pub was, until recently, named The Lillie after him, but has been rebranded to imply more glamorous associations.

This section of Lillie Road has been relabelled West Brompton Crossing, and is the point where the road crossed Counter's Creek and, subsequently, Kensington Canal. The land on the west side of the railway has been recently developed but, until it was incorporated as landscaping for the newly built flats, was a section of the filled canal that was prone to flooding in wet weather. Part of a bridge that once crossed the Kensington Canal could also be seen here before the development, incorporated into the station's passenger bridge.

When West Brompton Station was bombed in the war, its buildings were demolished, the West London Line was closed, and it became an underground station only. Like Kensington (Olympia) it came back to life in 1994, when the West London Line reopened again after a hiatus of more than 50 years.

The vast empty site opposite the station was occupied by the Earl's Court Exhibition Centre until its closure in 2014 and demolition. The site opened in 1887, but its art deco halls dated from the 1930s. Earl's Court was particularly known for popular events of the second half of the twentieth century such as the Royal Tournament, Cruft's, the Ideal

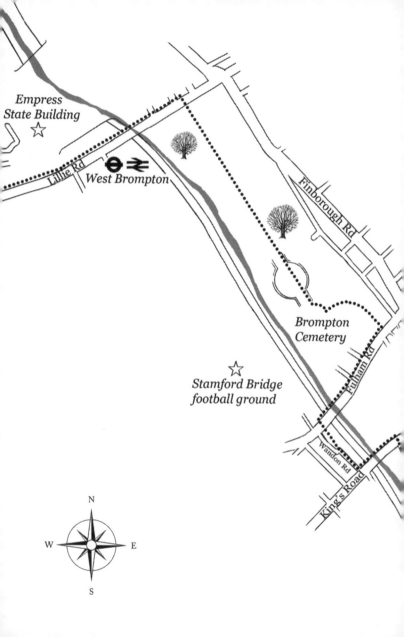

Empress
State Building
☆

Lillie Rd

West Brompton

Finborough Rd

Brompton
Cemetery

Fulham Rd

☆
Stamford Bridge
football ground

Wandon Rd

King's Road

N
W   E
S

Home Show, the London Boat Show and the British International Motor Show. A second hall was built over the railway lines in 1985. The site, along with neighbouring estates and the Lillie Bridge Depot, forms part of the Capco-owned development which, at the time of writing, shows no signs of taking place.

A little further along Lillie Road is Earl's Court Road, where the pioneering 18th century surgeon and anatomist, John Hunter, lived in the village of Earl's Court. Here he had a large house with a menagerie in its grounds, which featured lions, buffaloes, a zebra, a jackal, an ostrich, and eagles chained to an artificial rockscape, among other wildlife. He was a formidable character who was once observed grabbing two leopards, which had escaped and were fighting the dogs, by their collars and marching them back to their enclosures. He also owned a bullock, presented by Queen Charlotte, which he was said to enjoy wrestling.

• *Follow Lillie Road over the railway bridge past West Brompton Station to Brompton Cemetery.*

There was what an account from 1900 describes as "a very old footpath"[10] connecting Fulham Road and King's Road, beside the Creek. It was called Bull Alley, after The Bull Inn at the King's Road end, which is also the reason that this section of the river was sometimes known as the Bull Creek.

The railway and the river separate West Brompton Cemetery from sites on the opposite bank that were once sports grounds. Chelsea Football Club's Stamford Bridge Ground remains, but the Lillie Bridge Grounds have disappeared. They did not last long, opening in 1866 as part of the railway extension, and closing after a riot in 1887 which destroyed the grandstand. In between it was the home of Middlesex County Cricket Club, before it moved to Lord's. The first amateur boxing matches using Queensberry rules took place here. It was also the home of the Amateur Athletics Club, and was used for the 1872 FA Cup Final between Wanderers, a team of ex-public schoolboys who did not have a

---

10 Feret, Charles James, *Fulham Old and New.* The Leadenhall Press Ltd., 1900, p224

home ground, and Oxford University. The Grounds were replaced by the Brompton and Fulham Goods and Coal Station, and the site was being redeveloped again at the time of writing.

The land between the Grounds and Stamford Bridge stadium was occupied, from 1877, by the Western Hospital for Infectious Diseases, which was first built to treat smallpox. After evidence that the disease was spread to neighbouring streets, and public panic across London about the risk of infection, smallpox treatment moved to a hospital ship moored in the Thames, at Deptford and later Dartford. The hospital specialised in polio during the 20th century, and was eventually demolished in 1979.

• *Turn right through the gates to follow the main path through the cemetery.*

Brompton Cemetery, like Kensal Green, is one of the Magnificent Seven London cemeteries. It opened in 1839 on what had been market gardens and was equipped with long, distinctive colonnades with catacombs beneath. It contains the graves of many notable people, including Emmeline Pankhurst, whose cross is located on the main path with purple and green tributes at the foot. Elsewhere in the cemetery are the graves of both the composer Constant Lambert and his son Kit, manager of The Who. John Wisden, of cricketing almanack fame, can be found here, with actor Ernest Thesiger, actor-manager Sir Squire Bancroft and journalist Bernard Levin. The cemetery also contains the graves of a number of people, including Mr Nutkins, Mr McGregor, Mr Brock, Mr Tod, Jeremiah Fisher and Peter Rabbett, whose presence suggests that Beatrix Potter, who lived nearby, may have walked here.

In the middle of the cemetery is the Egyptian-style mausoleum of Hannah Courtoy and her daughters Mary and Elizabeth. Courtoy, who died in 1849, was friends with Egyptologist Joseph Bonomi, who designed her tomb. It is also depicted on Bonomi's own headstone, also in the cemetery. After Courtoy's relatives lost the key to the mausoleum in the 1980s an urban myth developed, enabled and possibly created by musician Stephen Coates, that Courtoy and Bonomi had accessed lost ancient technology and that it was, in fact, a teleportation chamber forming part of a system that allows instant travel between the Magnificent Seven. As the key remains lost, no-one has been able to verify this theory.

• *At the chapel turn left, then left again to follow the path out of the cemetery. Turn right along Fulham Road. Cross at the zebra crossing and continue along the opposite side.*

The section of Fulham Road to the west of the cemetery was sometimes called Bridge Street. Where the river and the railway pass under Fulham Road, Sandford Bridge was located. Stamford Bridge, the name used for the football ground, is a version of this original name. The first recorded reference, in 1410, called it 'Samfordbregge' – 'the bridge at the sandy ford'[11]. However, the name as used today is based on confusion between two bridges over the Creek, relatively close to one another, at Fulham Road and King's Road. The former was Sandford Bridge while the latter was 'Stanbrigge' or Stambridge – the stone bridge. The two became conflated and, with the bridges themselves forgotten, today's Stamford Bridge actually refers to two different places at once. The current bridge dates from the 1860s, when the railway was extended.

The streets to the right, between the cemetery and Fulham Road, are a small 19th century estate called The Billings. It consists of Billing Place, Billing Road and Billing Street and its name refers to Billings Ditch, an alternative name for Counter's Creek, which dates back to the 17th century. A Billings Well was still here in the 1820s, a medicinal spring "much frequented for its virtues, though now scarcely known in the parish".[12] This, in occult London lore, was a well associated with the Celtic sun god Belinos.

The chapel and the hexagonal building on the left are remnants of St Mark's College for Boys, founded in the 1840s by the National Society for Promoting Religious Education. Its first principal was Rev. Derwent Coleridge, estranged son of Samuel Taylor Coleridge, who

11 ibid, p224-5
12 Faulkner, Thomas, *History and Antiquities of Kensington*. T. Egerton, Payne & Foss and Nichols & Son, 1820, p26

was known as a linguist. He spoke Arabic, Coptic, Hawaiian and Zulu amongst other languages, and was particularly fond of Welsh poetry. The school, on the banks of the Creek, was surrounded by market gardens when first founded, and pupils looked after livestock and the kitchen garden as part of their education. In the 1920s it merged with St John's College, Battersea and, in the 1990s, the institution moved, surprisingly, to Plymouth where it is now known as Plymouth Marjon University.

On the left under Stamford Bridge, traces of the former Chelsea and Fulham Station on the West London Line can be spotted. The station was apparently the reason the football club, founded in 1905, was named Chelsea rather than Stamford Bridge. It closed after bombing in 1940, although damage was relatively minor, and lay derelict into the 1960s before being demolished.

Counter's Creek runs behind the East Stand at Stamford Bridge, Chelsea FC's home ground. As the ground is on the west bank of the river, it is actually in Fulham rather than in Chelsea. Stamford Bridge Athletic Grounds opened on this site in 1877, used by the London Athletic Club. The football ground was designed in 1905 by Archibald Leitch, the architect also responsible for the Craven Cottage football ground, and had a capacity of 100,000 when it first opened. B.S. Johnson described the "ad hoc, piecemeal construction of the terrace: a huge earth mound formed from the excavated centre with a steeply cantilevered shell on it."[13] It was built without a team to occupy it so, when Fulham FC turned it down, its promoter Guy Mears founded Chelsea FC to play there instead. The London Athletics Club carried on using the stadium too, until the 1930s, and it also featured greyhound racing in the mid-20th century.

• *After the railway bridge turn first left along a path that leads to Wandon Road and walk straight ahead.*

Lynne Banks describes the seedy lodging house territory at the Fulham end of the King's Road in the early 1960s. "My room was five flights up

---

13 Johnson, BS, *Albert Angelo*. Picador, 1964 [2004], p25

in one of those gone-to-seed houses in Fulham, all dark wallpaper inside and peeling paint outside… The landing lights were the sort that go out before you can reach the next one… There were a couple of prostitutes in the basement."[14] Cheap lodgings were available, and artists of various kinds spent time in the vicinity. In the early years of their career Mick Jagger, Keith Richards and Brian Jones lodged not far away at No.102 Edith Grove, where Keith's mother Doris collected their washing and where "they survived the freezing 1962 winter by staying in bed all day."[15] The writer Katherine Mansfield had lived at the same address in 1919, with her husband John Middleton Murry.

• *At King's Road turn left.*

The bridge taking King's Road over the river was called Stanley Bridge, another name apparently designed to be confused with Stamford Bridge. The undistinguished turn of the century Plaza building on the right-hand side of the road, by the railway bridge, is built over the buried river. Counter's Creek became Chelsea Creek at this point, and the Kensington Canal was open to the Thames from this point until the late 1990s, when it was filled in and built over between King's Road and Lots Road. The bridge still crosses the Creek as well as the railway, but only the latter is now visible.

To the right, further along New King's Road, is Eel Brook Common. In the 1860s, the Eel Brook could be seen flowing above ground along the west side of the common, along the line of what is now Favart Road. This small watercourse drained into the Thames to the south of Chelsea Creek but, before the Thames was embanked, the tidal mudflats along this stretch of the river connected numerous small channels. As well as following its current course along Chelsea Creek, Counter's Creek also ran to the south through the mud along the line of what is now Townmead Road. It linked with the Eel Brook near where Imperial Park is now sited, to the south of Chelsea Harbour.

14 Reid Banks, Lynne, *The L-Shaped Room*. Chatto & Windus, 1960, p7
15 Unsworth, Cathi, *Lynne Reid Banks: "The L-Shaped Room"* - 1960, in: *London Fictions* in Whitehead, Andrew & White, Jerry, 2013, p185

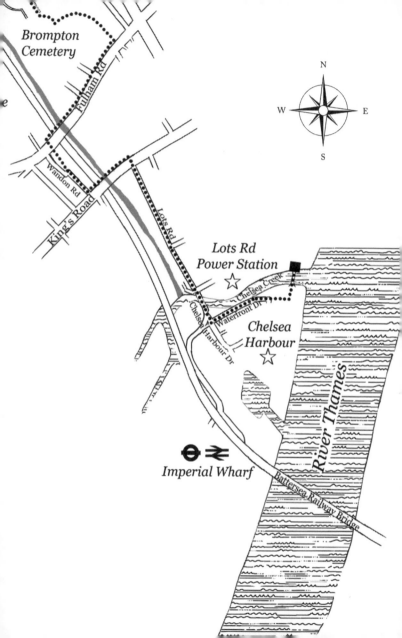

The Creek passes through the wrong end of Chelsea, beyond even World's End which is further up King's Road to the left. The area, known as Sands End, was a working-class enclave dominated by the giant Fulham Gasworks. The Booth Survey claimed in the 1880s that, while families of gasworkers were respectable, there was an area of streets on the other side of the site around Langford Road with a "monthly average of one to two policemen injured". People did not have regular work and were "casual class, many from the courts of central London, round Drury Lane".[16] Samuel Beckett lived nearby in 1934-5, writing his novel *Murphy*. It is set very precisely in the streets around the Creek, where his character Celia can smell the river: "She had turned out of Edith Grove into Cremorne Road, intending to refresh herself with a smell of the Reach and then return by Lot's Road..."[17].

• *Cross at the green Furniture and Arts Building and turn right down Lots Road.*

The change in social tone that has come over Sands End since the 1960s is exemplified by the 1980s houses on the left in Poole's Lane, where cricket commentator and Chelsea denizen Henry Blofeld lived. Bomb damaged terraces along this side of the road were cleared to make room for Westfield Park and new houses. Opposite, garages, timber yard, auction rooms and an ambulance station concealed Chelsea Creek, running behind.

Chelsea Creek Highways Depot and Hammersmith and Fulham Vehicle Pound on the right is the last vestige of the industrial sites that were once the sole occupiers of the Creek. It is on the site of the last canal wharf, Christian Wharf, which closed in the 1960s. On the opposite side of the railway, the Fulham Gasworks has been dismantled, with the exception of a single gasholder, and a high density housing development will be built on the site, due for completion in 2036. The gasworks were built on the grounds of Sandford Manor House which survived, surrounded by gasholders, until the early 20th century. It 1905 it was

16 Booth/B/361 p221
17 Beckett, Samuel, *Murphy*. Calder and Boyars, 1970, p11

"still in existence but fallen on evil days".[18] It had been used for industry for a more than century when the gasworks opened, as a saltpetre factory and as a cask works, making army canteens for the 1815 Napoleonic campaign. It had also been a pottery and later, in 1888, arts and crafts potter William De Morgan moved his business from Merton Abbey to a new factory by the river at Sands End, where it operated until 1907.

Lots Road, further along to the left, is named after a common meadow called The Lots, divided into portions, on which it was built. The narrow band of alluvium – clay, silt and sand deposited by the river – that marks the course of Counter's Creek, widens south of Lots Road, explaining the sandy place names at this end of the river, and suggesting it may have once had a delta.

The street is dominated by Lots Road Power Station, which is derelict and roofless but being developed as part of the surrounding, glassy-towered scheme. Penelope Fitzgerald described it in her river novel *Offshore*: "The mist had cleared, and to the north east the Lots Road Power Station had discharged from its four majestic chimneys long plumes of pearly white smoke which slowly drooped and turned to dun."[19] The power station, which had four chimneys until the 1960s, may have been the first steel framed building in Britain when it opened in 1904. It was the world's longest operating power station, eventually closing in 2002 and, until the end of the 20th century, it powered the Underground network. When an obsolete component failed in the late 1990s, the entire tube system was brought to a halt and Londoners waited in all-night cafes and bars until the early hours for the power to come back on. The tube system was subsequently switched to the National Grid. When the National Grid supply failed in 2003 and cut power to the underground again, Lots Road was no longer available to provide back-up.

Beyond the power station, Cremorne Gardens is the site of a 19th century pleasure garden which opened in 1845 and stretched between King's Road and the Thames. Its attractions included a circus, a bowling

18 Webb, W. Arthur, *Survey of London Monograph 8, Sandford Manor, Fulham*. Guild & School of Handicraft, 1907, p11

19 Fitzgerald, Penelope, *Offshore*. 4th Estate, 1979, p24

hall, two indoor venues, a hotel, a 'stereorama', and gardens with fountains, walks, a fernery, a maze and a 'Gypsy's Grotto'. Cremorne Gardens was the subject of James McNeill Whistler's 'Nocturne' paintings of the 1870s, its glimmering lights viewed across the Thames at Battersea. These included 'Nocturne in Black and Gold: the Falling Rocket', which became the subject of the 1878 libel trial in which Whistler sued John Ruskin, who had called him "a coxcomb" who charged 200 guineas for "flinging a pot of paint in the public's face". By then the Gardens had closed, and were built over with houses and wharves. Some of the latter were demolished in the 1960s to carve out Cremorne Gardens, a much smaller area than the original site. It is now a work site for the Thames Tideway sewer, being constructed along the Thames to intercept storm sewers, including the one that channels Counter's Creek.

• *Cross the bridge over Chelsea Creek. Turn left along Waterfront Drive to reach another bridge over Chelsea Creek, to the left.*

On the other side of the power station Counter's Creek is at last revealed, in the form of Chelsea Creek which runs the short distance to the Thames. On the right-hand side of the bridge to Chelsea Harbour, the Creek continues for a short distance before disappearing under the gasworks site beyond. The transition from riverside industry to riverside apartments is particularly extreme around the mouth of the Creek. The 1980s mini-Monaco of Chelsea Harbour, one of the first developments of a type that has become ubiquitous beside the Thames, is charmless and designed for the convenience of residents who come and go via underground car parks. It was built on former railway sidings around Chelsea Basin. The newer Chelsea Waterfront development around the Creek will, presumably, attract the same hyper-rich residents but does, at least, improve access to the river.

In the industrial era Chelsea Creek's surroundings were much less polished. John Le Carré's 1961 book *Call for the Dead*, the first George Smiley novel, has its denouement in the thick fog by the river at Chelsea Creek. The area, characterised by "the smell of tar and coke" is "the dividing line between the smart and squalid, where Cheyne

Walk meets Lots Road, one of the ugliest streets in London."[20] Sidney Lumet's 1967 film of the book, *The Deadly Affair*, was made in the same locations, including the former Balloon Tavern on the corner of Lots Road (now the Lots Road pub) where Roy Kinnear's scrap dealer, petty criminal and drinker spends his time. Later his character meets his end in the mud and dirty water of Chelsea Creek as does the villain, played by Maximilian Schell.

Counter's Creek, having been muscled out of sight by heavy infrastructure for most of its route, finally becomes a river again in its final moments. Its route, once full of edgeland uses – industry, institutions, cemeteries and sports grounds – now links hot spots of post-industrial rebuilding, a 7-mile strip that reveals the 21st century version of London being squeezed into leftover spaces. The closest option for a post-walk drink is the Lots Road pub, where the process of lost river gentrification can be contemplated close-up.

20 Le Carré, John, *Call for the Dead*. Penguin Books, 1961 [2016], p157

Falcon Brook

‘ *The Falcon flows below the radar, its shifting identity, changing names and hazy sources making it a tricky river to find and follow.* ’

Falcon Brook

Practicalities

Distance – 4¾ miles (Route 1) or 4½ miles (Route 2)
Start – Tooting Graveney Common (Route 1) or Streatham Hill (Route 2)
Getting there – Route 1: Streatham Station, followed by a 15 minute walk. Turn left out of Streatham Station; take the second left along Gleneagle Road, then the first right up Ambleside Avenue. Turn second left along Mitcham Lane, cross the railway bridge, then take the second right turn along Thrale Road after the Furzedown pub. Walk all the way up Thrale Road to Furzedown Road, and turn left to the junction with Furzedown Drive to begin the walk.

Route 2: Streatham Hill Station followed by a 5 minute walk. Turn left out of the station, cross Streatham High Road, and take the second right and follow Barcombe Avenue to the starting point.

End – Thames at Battersea between Wandsworth Bridge and Battersea Railway Bridge
Getting back – a 10 minute walk to either Clapham Junction Station or Wandsworth Town Station

Introduction

Despite its audible presence under the side streets of Streatham, Balham, Wandsworth and Battersea, the Falcon Brook flows below the radar. Its shifting identity, with different names along its upper reaches and hazy views on its sources makes it, at times, a tricky river to find and follow. The valley of "the soughing Falcon,"[1] as Christopher Fowler describes it, runs across South West London and across the tides of people travelling to and from central London. Its alignment follows an older logic, stitching Streatham back into the Borough of Wandsworth where it belonged before 1965, when local government reform removed it to Lambeth, breaking its links along the lost river valley.

Three streams, branched like a lightning strike, meet to become the Falcon. The Streathbourne and the Hydeburn arc across Streatham and

---

1 Fowler, Christopher, 2006, *The Water Room*. Bantam Books, p385

Balham, combining near Wandsworth Common. They are joined by the Woodbourne – although the names Streathbourne and Woodbourne seem interchangeable – a distinct stream between the two branches tracked by this walk. Its source, harder to trace, is thought to be in the vicinity of the Sackville Estate; the stream then crosses Streatham High Road, where a valley can clearly be seen, flows along Woodbourne Avenue and crosses Tooting Bec Common and the railway line to join the southern, Streathbourne stream. This walk follows the other two source streams – Route 1, described here as the Streathbourne, which rises in Streatham Park, and Route 2, the Hydeburn with its source on Streatham Hill.

The ridge of higher ground above Brixton that forms Brixton and Streatham Hills is the watershed between the Falcon and its near neighbour, the Effra. Once its source streams meet in Balham, the Falcon Brook flows among the houses of Wandsworth Common and under the full length of Northcote Road, hitting the Thames at Battersea. However, the clarity of its lower course is a relatively recent phenomenon. As the Thames has narrowed, the marshes on its southern banks have been drained and riverside places become solid ground. Battersea was once surrounded by water, and traces remain of the channels that made it an island, at least at high tide.

The name Falcon is probably drawn from the crest of the 16th century St John family, lords of the manor in Battersea. A much earlier reference is to the Hidaburna, in a gift of land from 693, when England was still divided into Saxon kingdoms. The presence of a buried river may have slowly faded over the intervening millennium, but it still offers a key to its neighbourhoods. While we can reconstruct its course, the lack of visible sources for the river is now an inherent part of its character. As the poet of South London rivers Allen Fisher puts it, "it is also that the course of the Falcon / is all that need concern us / as its source / or the source / it will create / is already part of it".[2]

2 Fisher, Allen, *Place*. Reality Street, 2005, p41

Route 1: Streathbourne/Woodbourne

• *Starting point: the roundabout at the junction of Furzedown Road and Furzedown Drive.*

Stink pipes, venting the sewers, are to be found beside the route from Streatham Station to the walk's starting point, on both Faygate Road and Thrale Road. They indicate the line of a sewer which probably collects Streathbourne headwaters and delivers them into the buried stream further ahead.

The southern branch of the Falcon is a stream referred to both as the Streathbourne and the Woodbourne. It divided Tooting Commons into its two adjacent parts – Tooting Graveney Common and Tooting Bec Common, the boundary between the two ancient Tooting manors. The stream being long buried the two commons are now a single area of open land, but they retain separate names. Graveney is also the name of Tooting's river, the next stream to the south, which is mostly still above ground, although hidden behind houses.

The wooded southern section of Tooting Graveney Common contained three small streams in the 1860s, but none are now visible. Two of them, which met and ran along the east side of the Common, disappeared when Tooting Bec Athletics Track was built over their source in 1937. The third flowed on the west side of this section of common, from a point close to where the path meets Church Lane. There is no clear sign on the ground, and it was no longer recorded on maps by the 1890s. It could have been seasonal, but the pattern of water flows is likely to have been altered by the extensive building that took place all around as the Victorian suburb was built.

The three streams were not the only nearby water. The grounds of Thrale Hall, to the right, contained a particularly large fish pond which reached up to Tooting Bec Road. On the opposite side of the common, on the corner of Church Lane and Tooting Bec Road, a similarly sized fish pond belonged to another large house, Tooting Lodge. The latter on maps linked to the Streathbourne by a small stream. Both were filled in before the end of the 19th century, but are likely to have been fed by springs which were sources for the river.

The houses of Streatham Park, to the right, were built on the grounds of Thrale Hall, which was demolished in 1863. The hall was a famed 18th century landmark, owned by the Thrale family who made their fortune from brewing in Southwark. They bought land and a medieval house from the Dukes of Bedford, who owned the manor of Tooting Bec. It first came into the family under John, Duke of Bedford, brother of Henry V and recurring character in Shakespeare's history plays.

The shadow of Thrale Hall and its grounds is now hard to detect but, during the late 18th century, it was known as the salon of Hester Thrale and as Samuel Johnson's favourite place. Between 1763, when Hester married Henry Thrale and 1781, when he died, Johnson frequented Thrale Hall with the cultural elite of his age, including James Boswell, Edmund Burke, Fanny Burney, David Garrick, Oliver Goldsmith and Joshua Reynolds. Hester's marriage was tempestuous, and the Thrales competed for Johnson's attention. Johnson, an undoubted genius and notoriously rude, is now thought to have suffered from Tourette's Syndrome among many other conditions. He took regular breaks from his hard-drinking city life with trips to the country at Streatham. Thrale Park's glory days ended when Henry died, and the house was sold. Hester caused a scandal by marrying an Italian music teacher, and eventually returned to her home territory in Wales. *Thraliana*, her diaries, show her as shrewd, entertaining and direct. In a typical aside she complains about constant trips to Bankside to deal with the sale of the brewery after her husband's death, wishing she could "defecate my Mind of Borough Dirt".[3] One disciple was Samuel Beckett, whose early unfinished play *Human Wishes* was to have been about the relationship between Hester Thrale and Dr Johnson. He only completed two scenes in which Johnson's lodgers, perhaps inevitably, wait while he fails to arrive.

---

3 Thrale, Hester Lynch, *Thraliana, The Diary of Mrs Hester Lynch Thrale 1776-1809. Volume 1 1776-1784*. Oxford University Press, 1942, p492

• Follow the tarmacked footpath through the woods. After passing three lampposts, bear right into a clearing with a lone tree and along the path through the woods lined with logs. Follow the path as it bears right and crosses a clearing. At the athletics track fence, turn left and follow the path around the fence to the right.

On the left-hand side of this section of Tooting Bec Common, housing built in the late 1990s fills the site of Tooting Bec Hospital, which closed in 1995. It was an asylum, mainly for people with dementia, which opened in 1903. It was built closer to central London than the existing asylums beyond the city's edge, so inmates could be visited by relatives. The huge site included ward blocks connected by high-level bridges, and looked like the archetypal Victorian locked ward complex. It was completely demolished except for its spiked iron perimeter fence, which now surrounds a housing estate.

• At the main road – Tooting Bec Road – cross via the lights to the right. Cross Doctor Johnson Avenue at the water fountain and turn right to walk along the left hand side of the road.

A valley runs on the left hand side through the Common, parallel to Doctor Johnson Avenue. Its course is still clearly visible from the air in dry weather, but not so apparent at ground level.

On the right is Tooting Bec Common, from where another stream joined the Streathbourne, still partly visible in the 1860s. It ran at least as far as the railway line and may have been the remains of a longer branch, with its source in the higher ground on the far side of Streatham High Road. There were a number of ponds in the area, as well as the Streatham Mineral Wells off Valley Road, which were part of Streatham Spa.

Woodbourne Road meets the common on the east side, suggesting that a stream continued on the far side of the railway. The route of this branch would pass under Tooting Bec Lido, to the right, which opened in 1906 but acquired its distinctive, Art Deco look when it was refurbished in the 1930s.

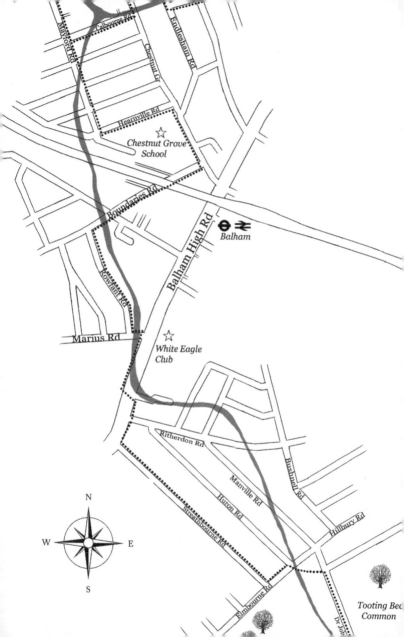

The London Ring Main passes under Tooting Graveney Common and the Streathbourne. In 1988 work was halted for more than a year by a "catastrophic inundation". Water and silt burst into the tunnel, which could only be rescued by freezing the surrounding soil to stabilise the saturated earth.

• *At the end of the Common, turn left through a black and white vehicle barrier, then right on a tarmacked path to Elmbourne Road.*

To the left a jubilee oak planted in 1939 commemorates the 50th anniversary of the London County Council, long abolished. It follows a tradition of planting symbolic trees on the Common, which goes back to an avenue planted for Elizabeth I's visit to Tooting in 1600. She probably came to visit Sir Henry Maynard, Secretary to her Secretary of State Lord Burghley, and owner of the manor of Tooting Bec.

The river crosses Elmbourne Road, which has a name suggesting another stream. However, it seems more likely to be a Victorian creation, describing the river marked by elm trees, now lost along with the stream.

• *Turn left, then second right along Streathbourne Road.*

In the 1880s, the river was redirected along Streathbourne Road as part of the development of the area. Before it was culverted, the river ran along a line between Manville Road and Bushnell Road, through the grounds of Bedford Hill House, which belonged to William Cubitt, brother of the builder Thomas. He landscaped the gardens to create a large fish pond, fed by the river, complete with an island containing a small, man-made hill.

Streathbourne Road was probably named by its Victorian developers after the river underneath it. However, as there seems to be no record of the name in use before it appeared here, there is also a possibility that they made it up. When these streets were laid out in the 1880s they were known as the Elms Estate, after Streatham Elms, an 18th century mansion on Tooting Bec Road. The latter was the home of Alfred Heaver, a housebuilder who shaped much of south-west London, was responsible for the surrounding streets and much else along the course of the Falcon, in Battersea, Tooting and Wandsworth. Heaver was shot dead in 1901 by his brother-in-law, James Young, while walking to church with his wife in Westcott, near Dorking. Young, who had a long-standing grudge against Heaver and his own sister, then killed himself. The area is now known as the Heaver Estate.

On the right, a block called Streathbourne at Nos.111-117 has its own swan logo. Further along the road at No.31 there is an earlier Streathbourne, one of the original Victorian houses, with its own decorative brick sign.

• *At Balham High Road turn right, cross at the lights.*

Balham High Road is part of the Roman Stane Street, which ran from London to Chichester. Between Argos and Tesco on the right, an insignificant looking side road is called Brook Close. This follows the course of the river, which crossed Ritherdon Road and flowed behind houses to reach the High Road. It then ran along the other side of the road for a short distance.

On the right, the White Eagle Club is a local institution dating from the 1980s, reflecting the Polish population that settled in this part of London from the Second World War, before the new arrivals who came to the same area after Poland joined the European Union in 2006. In the 1960s it was the 211 Club, owned by a friend of the Kray twins called Billy Foreman. When, in 1967, Jack 'The Hat' McVitie drunkenly threatened to wreck the place, the Krays were highly displeased.

Next door, Rutherford House School, which opened in 2012, is named after the actor Margaret Rutherford, who lived in Balham. Its two school houses are Heaver, after Alfred Heaver, and Ransome, after the writer Arthur Ransome. The latter lived briefly on Huron Road, parallel to Streathbourne Road, and is not usually fêted in Balham after supposedly describing it as "the ugliest and most abominable of London's suburbs".

Du Cane Court, the large block of flats further along the High Road, was completed in 1937. The timing of its construction, and its good fortune in avoiding bomb damage, has led to a persistent urban myth that it was spared by the Luftwaffe because it was intended for use as Nazi headquarters or that it is shaped like a swastika when seen from the air. Disappointingly, neither of these stories are true, but its 600-plus flats do seem to make it one of the largest blocks in the country.

Opposite, Italian restaurant Bucci opened in 1985 and is still operating, despite the imprisonment of its then owner in 2018. He was, it was revealed in court, using the business as a front to launder money for the feared 'Ndràngheta organised crime network, based in Calabria.

• *Turn second left along Marius Road. Turn first right along Rowfant Road.*

The stream follows the back fence of the houses on the right-hand side of Rowfant Road which turns slightly left and then right, reflecting the course of the river beneath. At the junction with Boundaries Road, the river continues straight ahead along a route that is crossed by the railway. It is therefore necessary to detour around Balham Station to pick up the river on the other side.

• *Turn right along Boundaries Road. After the railway bridge, turn left along Chestnut Grove.*

Along Boundaries Road a loud rushing sound comes from beneath a series of drain covers which, although the street is not on the direct route of the river, demonstrates that there is plenty of water passing through the vicinity.

The 1950s building before the railway bridge, set back from the road, is Irene House, owned by the Department of Work and Pensions. In 1976 it was the target of an IRA bomb, which was placed in a rubbish bin outside and damaged the chapel next door instead. More recently it has been the target of protests against the disability benefit assessments carried out here by US contractor, Maximus.

Chestnut Grove School, which stands beside the course of the river, was originally Balham Secondary School. It was expanded in 1975, with the demolition of two entire streets – Kate Street and Dendy Street – and renamed Hydeburn School. The name did not last but it shows that,

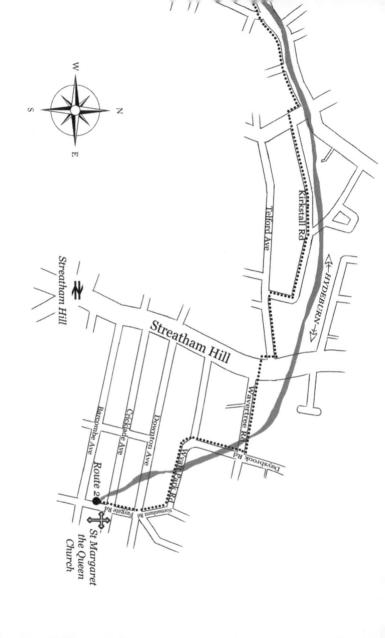

although the Hydeburn branch joins a couple of streets further along, it is still the name for the river associated with Balham.

• *Turn left along Hearnville Road, then right along Mayford Road.*

Where Hearnville Road drops away towards the corner with Ravenlea Road, we pick up the river's route again. On the left, a gap between No.165 and No.167 reveals the railway embankment behind and the point where it emerges from under the tracks.

There are prominent drain covers in the middle of Mayford Road, at the junction with Tantallon Road and at Calbourne Road (another suggestive, rivery name). Water is both audible and visible flowing under both, if you peer through the grating. The Streathbourne meets the Falcon's other branch (Route 2: Hydeburn) at the Calbourne Road junction.

Route 2: Hydeburn

• *Starting point: St Margaret the Queen Church, junction of Barcombe Avenue and Faygate Road.*

The source of the Hydeburn is debatable, but it seems likely that it was among the multiple ponds and springs once found on the ridge which rises on the east side of Streatham Hill. Drain covers are prominently located along Faygate Road in the centre of mini-roundabouts at the junctions, pointing at drainage under the road. The area now occupied by the church and surrounding houses were the extensive grounds of Leigham Court until the late 19th century. Leigham Court was a long-standing manor, created when the lands of Bermondsey Abbey were divided up under Henry VIII. Just to the south of the current church were fishponds, large enough to incorporate a boathouse, suggesting significant streams, while the gardens also included two separate fountains.

The estate built on the gardens is officially the Leigham Court Estate, usually known as the 'ABC Roads', after Amesbury, Barcombe, Cricklade and Downton Avenues. The combination of houses, maisonettes and flats, noted for their Arts and Crafts design and decoration, was built between 1889 and 1928 by the Artizans', Labourers' and General Dwellings Company, and bought by the Borough of Lambeth in 1966. The estate was designed as a self-sufficient community of 2,500 people and comes with its own parade of shops on Streatham Hill and a bespoke church, St Margaret the Queen. The Company built three other large London estates – Noel Park (see Chapter 7: Moselle), Queen's Park and Shaftesbury Park, in Battersea.

• *Standing in front of the church facing away from it, turn right along Faygate Road. At a mini-roundabout, fork left along Normanhurst Road. Turn first left along Wyatt Park Road, then first right along Daysbrook Road.*

The roundabout is on the site of a well, marked on pre-development maps, at the edge of Leigham Court's gardens.

Daysbrook Road is the first suggestion of a stream, and runs behind reservoirs, now covered. They date back to 1832, when the Lambeth Waterworks Company built its first reservoir here, to provide an alternative to the supply they extracted from the Thames. The reservoir is likely to have incorporated the existing watercourse and the streams that feed it, taking over the Hydeburn's source and removing further traces of its headwaters.

Off to the right on Daysbrook Road, a large round pond occupied the playground of Streatham and Clapham School, before houses were built. On the left-hand side of the road were the only houses in the neighbourhood, large villas facing Streatham Hill. Their long gardens contained several fountains.

• *Turn first left along Wavertree Road.*

At the junction with Streatham Hill, the Corner Fielde block on the right is typical of the development of the 1920s and 1930s, when Streatham High Road came into its own as a modernist destination, with serviced blocks attracting the middle classes and driving the growth of the department stores, theatres and cinemas that, for a time, made

Streatham South London's prime town centre. The ultimate example is Frederick Gibberd's Pullman Court, a 1930s estate a little further to the right on Streatham Hill, one of the first International Modern buildings in Britain. It has emerged that the sharp, white blocks were originally much more colourful – highlighted in pink, blue, grey and brown – something invisible in black and white photographs.

• At the T-junction with Streatham Hill cross at the pedestrian lights to the left. Turn right along the opposite side of the High Road, then turn first left into Telford Avenue.

The Hydeburn crosses Streatham Hill just after Telford Avenue, passing under the bus garage and then under the bus stop and behind the Conway House flats on the corner. The two houses next door, which date from the early 19th century, are the last traces of the Paragon, villas along the west side of Streatham Hill that were the first serious housing built in the area. They were bombed, and replaced after the war by the housing blocks of Staplefield Close.

• Turn first right along Kirkstall Road, continuing to follow the street as it turns to the left.

The river flows behind the houses on the right-hand side of Telford Avenue as their garden boundaries, and continues as the back boundary of the houses on Kirkstall Road.

There is evidence of springs among the streets to the left, between the Falcon and Streatham Hill Station, and a small fragment of unidentified stream remains on late 19th century maps, behind the pavilion at Telford Avenue Tennis Club.

• At the T-junction, turn right on Thornton Road, then first left along Emmanuel Road. Cross Rastell Avenue to Tooting Bec Common.

The Hydeburn is now the borough boundary, with the houses on the right in Lambeth, while Tooting Bec Common is in Wandsworth. The section

of stream between Streatham Hill and the Common was previously the boundary between early 19th century parliamentary constituencies in the 19th century.

• *Walk alongside the Common along Emmanuel Avenue.*

The Hydeburn runs along the Emmanuel Avenue and then across the top of Tooting Bec Common through what were the fields of Hyde Farm. The street was called Bleakhall Lane until the end of the 19th century, and was the farm lane. The open area, separated from the rest of the Common by the railway embankment, is the remainder of the farm. The streets to the right were built on the rest of its fields, also covering the short lived Hyde Farm Athletic Grounds. Set up in the early 1890s the grounds achieved a lot in a short time, hosting cricket, football, rugby, athletics, lacrosse, and even baseball, which had a brief moment of popularity in Britain. A velodrome was built and a cycling club formed, but the track was suddenly sold in 1896 and demolished for the streets that now cover the site.

• *When the Common ends, turn right along Cavendish Road.*

Cavendish Road was once called Dragmire Lane, no doubt thanks to the river which turns north here. Two very short tributaries join from the south and from south east, from the direction of the common.

• *Follow Cavendish Road for half a mile.*

The industrial estate, behind a wall on the right-hand side of the road, is the Zennor Road Trade Park. The houses of Zennor Road were demolished in the 1970s to expand it. However, the balance has shifted in the now-desirable, Victorian back streets of Balham. In 2019, a furore erupted over plans to convert the Grange Mills office building at the back of the site into twenty-six 'studio flats', each smaller than a budget hotel room. Permitted development rights, allowing offices to be converted to residential use, meant planning permission might not be needed.

Weir Road on the right sounds as though it should be related to the river, but is in fact named after Dr Benjamin Weir, founder of the former Weir Maternity Hospital a little way along the road. The original Weir Hospital, one of the most modern of its time in the early 20th century, was also used as a First World War military hospital. When the NHS was formed it was merged with the Wandsworth War Memorial Maternity Home next door to become a maternity hospital, and eventually closed in 1977 when the era of specialist maternity hospitals ended.

Further along on the right La Retraite, a Roman Catholic Girls' School, was set up in the 1880s by an order of nuns from Brittany, called Les Dames de la Retraite. It occupies houses that belonged to society portrait painter Philip Alexius de László and music hall comedian Dan Leno.

Opposite La Retraite, Kenilford Road was built in the 1880s, when the Streathbourne still ran along the left side of Cavendish Road and was still above ground for a short stretch between Balham New Road and Kenilford Road. It is possible that the rivery name refers to the adjacent stream. This is still a point where flood waters collect during heavy rain. Honeybrook Road, further along on the right, also has a suggestive name, but there is no apparent link with any tributary stream.

Between Kenilford Road and Dinsmore Road the stream makes a sharp turn to the left. It flows behind the houses to the left on Dinsmore Road, forming their rear boundaries all the way through to Balham High Road.

• *When you reach Dinsmore Road, turn left. At Balham High Road turn right to cross at the pedestrian lights, turn left on the other side of the road, then turn right into Oldridge Road.*

To the left, a low point can be seen on Balham High Road where the valley of the river crosses the street. The next turning to the right off the High Road, Alderbrook Road, marks the presence of a short stream that flowed into the Hydeburn from the north.

The river continues behind the buildings to the left on Oldridge Road. It then crosses Lochinvar Street and Caistor Road before joining Oldridge Road. This part of the river is marked as the York Sewer on

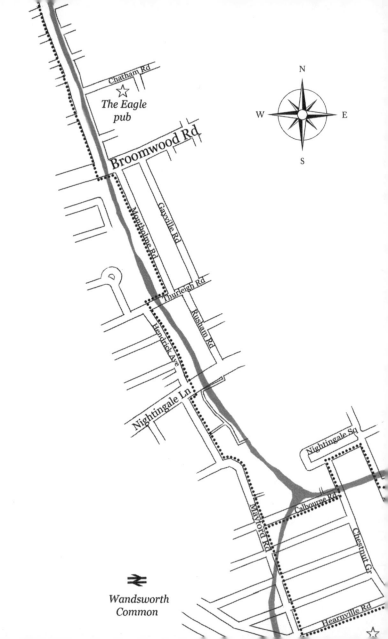

19th century maps, having been culverted, for reasons that are not entirely clear. This has led to confusion with York House, which stood by Battersea Creek, and inaccurate claims that the Creek was also called the York Ditch.

• *At a T-junction, turn right along Endlesham Road. Take the next left on Nightingale Square, left again on to Chestnut Grove, then first right on to Calbourne Road.*

The Hydeburn continues straight ahead, marked by a drain cover, under the school site, but the walking route has to skirt around the block to rejoin the route. On the other side, it runs to the right of Calbourne Road, which has a street name that is river-related, although the name is not used elsewhere. It meets the Streathbourne branch of the river (Route 1) at Mayford Road, where a bridge crossed the river and the junction was marked by a boundary stone before the houses were built. It indicated the parliamentary constituency boundary between Battersea and Clapham, which followed this short section of the Hydeburn.

Combined Route

• *Continue along Mayford Road. When it turns to the left, turn right on to Birchlands Avenue.*

Before houses were built at the turn of the 19th century, a large boating lake lay along the line of the Falcon, in the grounds of Fernside House, between Gosberton Road and Calbourne Road. Mayford Road runs through the middle of the lost lake.

• *Cross Nightingale Lane to walk straight ahead along Hendrick Avenue.*

The large institutional building to the right is Nightingale House Home for the Aged Poor of Jewish Faith. It has a blue plaque to Ted 'Kid' Lewis,

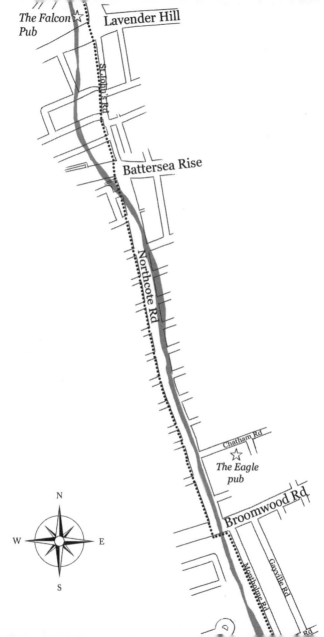

who spent the last years of his life there. A world welterweight champion during the First World War, he was a boxer from the Jewish East End, whose reputation has outlasted his ill-advised associations with Oswald Mosley and, later, the Krays. He was both a bodyguard and parliamentary candidate for the British Union of Fascists. When he finally understood their anti-Semitism, Lewis was said to have punched Mosley and his two bodyguards to the ground.

The slight curve of Hendrick Avenue matches the curve in the river as it passes behind houses to the right.

• *At the T-junction turn right along Thurleigh Road, then first left along Montholme Road.*

The line of the river passes straight ahead, between No.29 and No.31 Thurleigh Road, while the walk follows Montholme Road which runs parallel to its course.

• *Turn left on Broomwood Road, then right along Northcote Road.*

The line of the river reemerges to the left on Broomwood Road, where No.57 appears to have been built directly over the course of the river.

At the end of the streets to the left, Bolingbroke Grove runs parallel to Northcote Road, beside Wandsworth Common. The street was previously called The Five Houses, reflecting the number along its entire length in the 1860s, when it was a particularly isolated spot. It retains some of the isolated atmosphere recorded in the Sherlock Holmes adventure The Greek Interpreter, in which a character is dumped from a carriage, late at night, on "some sort of a heathy common mottled over with dark clumps of furze-bushes."[4]

One of the five houses was Bolingbroke House, and development began on its grounds in the 1870s, moving north alongside the Common. Clapham Junction Station had opened in 1863, setting the scene for new suburbs. The population of Battersea increased twenty-five fold in the

---

4 Doyle, Arthur Conan, *Sherlock Holmes: The Complete Stories.* Wordsworth Editions, 2006, p793

second half of the 19th century, and much of the new housing around Northcote Road was built by Alfred Heaver.

The streets either side of Northcote Road have been respectable, middle-class houses since their earliest days. The 1890s Booth Survey of poverty identified a single street between Clapham and Wandsworth Commons that it felt could be described as poor. This was Chatham Road, still the only patch of council housing in the immediate area. The four beer shops that the Booth surveyors saw as a sign of social depravity have gone, but the pub remains.

It soon becomes apparent that Northcote Road runs along a valley. The Falcon is routed directly beneath the road to allow the way to Clapham Junction Station, ahead. Streets to the right, in particular, such as Kelmscott Road, rise fairly steeply up the slope towards Lavender Hill and Battersea Rise. The local centre is lined up along the buried river. As poet Allen Fisher says, "take your place from the little hills / rising about Clapham / view the pleasant villages".[5]

Northcote Road has been extensively dug up in the recent past for sewer improvement works. The whole street remains vulnerable to flooding and, in 2007, Northcote Library was inundated by the Falcon. Before the street was built in the 1870s there was no road, only a substantial stream flowing along its route. It is shown as relatively wide in parts, and several 'waterfalls' are marked – at what are now the junctions with Belleville Road, Salcott Road, Mallinson Road, Shelgate Road and Abyssinia Road. There was a single footbridge over this section of the river, just before Shelgate Road.

• *Continue straight ahead as Northcote Road becomes St John's Road.*

When Northcote Road becomes St John's Road, the Falcon swings away from the line of the road and flows behind the shops on the left-hand side. The line of the river can still be detected in the property boundaries along this section. Behind their façades, the red-brick Victorian shops to the left on Battersea Rise are sharply angled along the river's route.

---

5 Fisher, Allen, *Place*. Reality Street, 2005, p74

Battersea Rise was also known as The Washway in the mid-1800s, showing that it carried surface water into the Falcon.

Further along at the junction of St John's Road and Lavender Hill, the former Arding & Hobbs on the corner, currently owned by Debenhams, is one of the last of London's grand, suburban department stores. It opened in the early 1880s and, with its local landmark corner turret, was described by *Buildings of England* as possessing "similar Edwardian magniloquence"[6] to central London department stores. Arding & Hobbs were Wandsworth drapers who decided to scale up. The original building was destroyed in a 1909 fire, in which 8 people were killed, but was immediately rebuilt in its current Edwardian baroque.

• *Cross Lavender Hill and continue straight ahead along Falcon Road.*

The Falcon crosses St John's Hill to the left, emerging alongside the single-storey nightclub at No.1. The Falcon pub on the corner of St John's Hill and Falcon Road was once a riverside inn. It is first mentioned in 1756, as 'The Falkeon'. However, the name may go back further, as the Manor of Battersea was owned by the St John family from the early 17th century. The family crest, which features as a stained glass window in the pub, is a falcon perched on top of its coat of arms. Specifically, it is a 'falcon rising' – in profile – an appropriate symbol for the river. The falcon crest seems to have retrospectively given its name to the Falcon Brook which, being associated with this part of Battersea, came to describe the entire river.

The current version of the Falcon was said to have the longest bar in Britain until the 2000s, when other bars noticed and built longer ones. It is a purpose-built hotel, constructed in the 1880s in a "debased Italianate"[7] style. Before it was rebuilt, the pub was located next door, where the Slug and Lettuce can now be found. The corner site was empty because the Falcon was an open stream separating the pub and Falcon Road. It continued above ground behind the buildings fronting Falcon Road, forming their rear boundary. It then rejoined the Falcon

6 Cherry, Bridget & Pevsner, Nikolaus. *London 2: South. Buildings of England.* Penguin Books, 2001, p678
7 ibid, p678

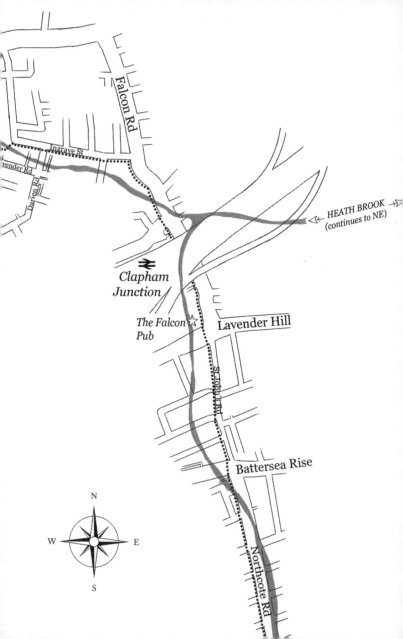

Falcon Rd

Ingrave St

vender Rd

Darien Rd

HEATH BROOK →
(continues to NE)

⇄
Clapham
Junction

The Falcon ☆
Pub

Lavender Hill

St John's Rd

Battersea Rise

Northcote Rd

N

W ⊕ E

S

Road just before the railway bridge, where it disappeared underground. This section of the river was culverted during the 1880s, when the pub was moved to the corner and a tramway depot built on its site. This was later replaced by the Empire Hall theatre, and is now a stretch of featureless 1980s frontage.

An article from 1883 mourns the replacement of the "very picturesque" old Falcon, with "a modern gin palace". It records that "The old wych-elm, with a cupboard made of its hollow trunk, and a door hanging on old fashioned rusty hinges, was a striking feature."[8] The old pub, complete with elm, is depicted in an 1811 engraving by John Nixon, called 'Drinking at Death's Door'. The river does not feature, but it shows a group of undertakers making merry outside the pub, a pun on the name of the landlord, Robert Death, known for his jovial demeanour. This seems to have been a great joke of the time and, while its hilarity has faded over the centuries, "many a doggerel rhyme was penned on the landlord"[9] who apparently liked to tell his guests that if they did not pay their bills, Death would stare them in the face. Edward Walford helpfully recorded, in 1878, that "Mr. Death has long since submitted to his mighty namesake".[10]

On the corner opposite the Falcon, the Party Superstore was rebuilt after the original shop was burnt out during the 2011 London riots. It took over the premises of Dub Vendor, described as "the most famous reggae record shop in the UK",[11] which never reopened after it was also torched.

Clapham Junction Station was called Falcon Bridge Station when it first opened in 1863. Its name was changed in an attempt to reflect the social status of Clapham, but is highly misleading as the station is in Battersea, a mile from any part of Clapham. Describing itself as 'Britain's Busiest Station', twenty railway lines are carried over Falcon Road on a 'crushing bridge' which packs the lines close to one another

8 J.F.B. The Old Falcon Inn, Battersea. *Notes and Queries. 6th Series Vol. VIII.* John C. Francis, 1 November 1883, p421

9 Ibid, p421

10 Walford, Edward, *Old and New London*. Cassell, Petter & Galpin, 1878, p467-479

11 Goodwin, Tom. Reggae record shop Dub Vendor to close after 35 years due to riot damage. *New Musical Express*, 1 September 2011

as they cross the road and the buried river, before splaying them back out into the station platforms. In the other direction, the railway lines open out to plunge into a web of interwoven lines known as 'the Battersea Tangle'.

As soon as the river crosses reaches the Falcon pub, it becomes suddenly central to the identity of the area. As well as Falcon Road, which follows the route of the river, there is Falcon Lane to the right and, on the other side of the railway bridge, Falcon Grove, Falcon Terrace and a small open space called, unconvincingly, Falcon Glade. Iain Sinclair writes of Falcon Road that "even under the hoot and snarl of cars and white vans the falcon can still, if he works at it, hear the falconer."[12]

The supermarket and newer buildings on the right, before the bridge, are built on the site of the Falcon Lane Goods and Coal Depot, which closed in 1968 and was eventually redeveloped in the 1980s. It was built on the site of Lavender Lodge, where there was a lavender nursery in the early 19th century and a street, which no longer exists, called Lavender Sweep.

Falcon Road is prone to flooding from the buried river, particularly under the railway bridge where what is described as 'ponding' takes place, with waters reported up to five feet deep. In 2007, during the worst floods for decades across much of the country, the Falcon flooded a much wider area than usual, cutting off the back entrance to Clapham Junction Station.

• *After the railway bridge and the tower blocks, turn left along Ingrave Street.*

The Falcon flows to the left, where it formed the boundaries between houses on Ingrave Street and those on Lavender Street. These houses were demolished in the late 1960s, and the line of the river has been lost.

The Falcon runs through a patchwork of interlocking council estates which are difficult to navigate. They combine several different eras, all courtesy of Wandsworth Borough Architects Department. The first towers on the left belong to the Falcon Estate, built between 1959 and 1963. The York Road Estate, next door, dates from 1969-1973. The Kambala

---

12 Sinclair, Iain, *London Overground*. Hamish Hamilton, 2015, p119

Estate, on the right-hand side of Ingrave Street, was built from 1975 onwards. The Winstanley Estate, closest to Clapham Junction Station, is the earliest. Construction began in 1953 and lasted throughout the 1960s. Ken Loach's 1965 film, *Up the Junction*, features the half-built estate and the Victorian terraces alongside. By the time of Douglas Hickox's 1972 film *Sitting Target*, the estate was complete and its windswept plazas provided the perfect setting for Oliver Reed to scream "You bastards! You bloody bastards!" into the shopping precinct void.

Allen Fisher describes how "I retraced my steps / took the Ditch at Nine Elms / which forms a communion with the Falcon Brook / making an island of Battersea / inside a tidal loop".[13] He neatly summarises the change in the landscape around Battersea which was once, it is thought, an island. The ending 'ea' is Thames language for island, with several existing examples and others, such as Bermondsey, no longer surrounded by water. It is thought that the Falcon split into two channels around this point. The walk follows the route west to the Thames, where the culverted Falcon still flows. However, another route to the east is thought to have passed through Falcon Park and around Battersea Park, entering the Thames at Nine Elms and surrounding Battersea.

A watercourse, the Heath Brook, still exists along this route and is contained in the Heathwall Sewer. The culverted stream, which connects to the Falcon near Ingrave Road, runs east behind Battersea Arts Centre, where Heathwall Road is located. The sewer passes around the Battersea Tangle, near Heath Brook Passage and Brooklands Avenue, and connects to the Thames at two places: Heathwall Pumping Station, west of the US Embassy, and near the New Covent Garden Market site on the other side of Nine Elms. Its name comes from the flat heath land on the higher ground above the Battersea marshes, of which Clapham Common is a remnant.

To the west of Battersea Park, other watercourses can be detected – possibly the Rowditch that has given its name to Rowditch Lane. A stream could be seen crossing Latchmere Recreation Ground above ground in the 1950s, and the nearby Culvert Road also indicates water.

13 Fisher, Allen, *Place*. Reality Street, 2005, p46

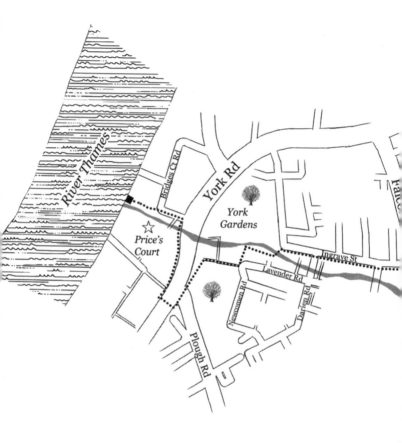

River Thames

Bridges Ct Rd

York Rd

York Gardens

Ingrave St

Lavender Rd

Newcomen Rd

Darien Rd

Falc...

Price's Court

Plough Rd

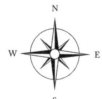

N
W   E
S

• Where Ingrave Road turns right to become Wye Street, walk ahead along a pedestrian path beside Battersea Chapel. Turn left across the shopping precinct. Walk ahead into York Gardens and turn right.

York Gardens was created by demolishing a number of streets, including Creek Street which led directly to Battersea Creek, the final section of the Falcon. Footage from the early 1960s shows that the demolished street featured tall stink pipes, venting the Falcon beneath.

The Falconbrook Pumping Station was first built in the 1950s, and then rebuilt in the 1970s on a much larger scale, with a confident, brutalist design. It is an important construction site for the Thames Tideway, which will divert most of the storm water and sewage it currently projects into the Thames along with the waters of the Falcon. The pumping station and Falconbrook Primary School, further to the right, seem to be the only places where this particular version of the name is used.

• At York Road turn left to cross Plough Road and then immediately right to cross York Road at the lights (York Road is difficult to cross anywhere more convenient). Turn right on the other side.

The streets on the opposite side of Plough Road were recorded in the Booth Survey as the poorest part of the area: "no doubt this area is rough and troublesome to the police".[14] However, the Survey also notes "the number of beautiful cottage gardens. Nowhere else in London have I seen so many on which time and money had evidently been lavishly spent".[15] Ken Loach was back in the area for his 1967 film *Poor Cow*, shot partly among the sooty houses and derelict plots of Plough Road, as well as the WInstanley Estate, the new social housing already shorthand for urban poverty.

---

14 Booth/B/366 p213
15 Booth/B/366 p215

• *After the single storey, brick former factory building, turn left along Bridges Court to reach the Thames.*

York Road is a thin dividing line between ostentatious Thames-side apartment blocks and working class Battersea, on the opposite side of the street. A road bridge, marked as York Bridge on early 19th century maps, carried York Road across the river. The final section of the Falcon, known as Battersea Creek, was open between York Road and the Thames until the 1960s. When Price's Candle Factory to the south expanded, the Creek was covered over. Bridges Court runs to the north of the line of the river which runs under the green space and the car dealership. A large, green stink pipe on the left of the street makes it clear what is happening beneath.

Bridges Court is a reference to the original name for York House, which was Bridgecourt Manor before its acquisition by the Archbishop of York. Timbers belonging to the palace, built in 1474, have been uncovered by archaeologists on the south side of the Creek. Demolished in the late 18th century, it was a moated building which made use of the Creek as part of its defences.

Price's Court, on the right, is part of the former Price's Candle Factory, which diversified into soap when electric lighting cut the market for candles. The factory, officially called the Belmont Works, opened in 1830. Its riverside location gave it access to palm oil, imported from West Africa, but the Creek was not big enough and lack of wharf space led the company to move its main manufacturing to the Wirral. In its heyday Price's was said to be the world's largest candlemaker and their candles were in the background of historical moments including the wedding of Victoria and Albert, the coronation of Elizabeth II, the funeral of Winston Churchill and Scott's final expedition to the Antarctic, for which they supplied edible candles. The Battersea site closed in the 1990s, although the firm continues elsewhere.

The river path to the left, Clove Hitch Quay, is lined with early riverside development from the 1980s including Calico House, Ivory House, Molasses House and Plantation Wharf. The exotic names, which sound more like unwitting references to slavery than the developers perhaps intended, replaced rather more prosaic uses. There had been a sugar works nearby since the 1670s, processing imports from the West Indies, but the development is on the site of the Garton's glucose factory. It made sugar for the brewing process, and apparently smelled of rotting animal hooves. This section of the Thames was characterised, until the 1980s, by a series of semi-noxious industries, including the Grove paint works, two chemical works, the Gargoyle Wharf Shell oil terminal, a distillery and a starch factory. The latter was accessed via a now vanished road called Starch Factory Road. When a steel plant moved in during the 1950s, it was renamed Steelworks Road.

Further along the river to the right is the London Heliport, which opened in the 1960s, an early sign of riverside social change which still transports people who are too wealthy or too unpopular to travel at ground level. The developments between the former Creek and the Heliport occupy a location-free world of international asset flows, down to the bespoke luxury river boats moored at Oyster Pier.

Retrace the route to the Falcon pub, the most convenient and appropriate place to drink to the river that runs past its back wall.

Hackney Brook

' Entirely buried in storm sewer tunnels, the Hackney Brook echoes loudest in the imagination. '

Hackney Brook

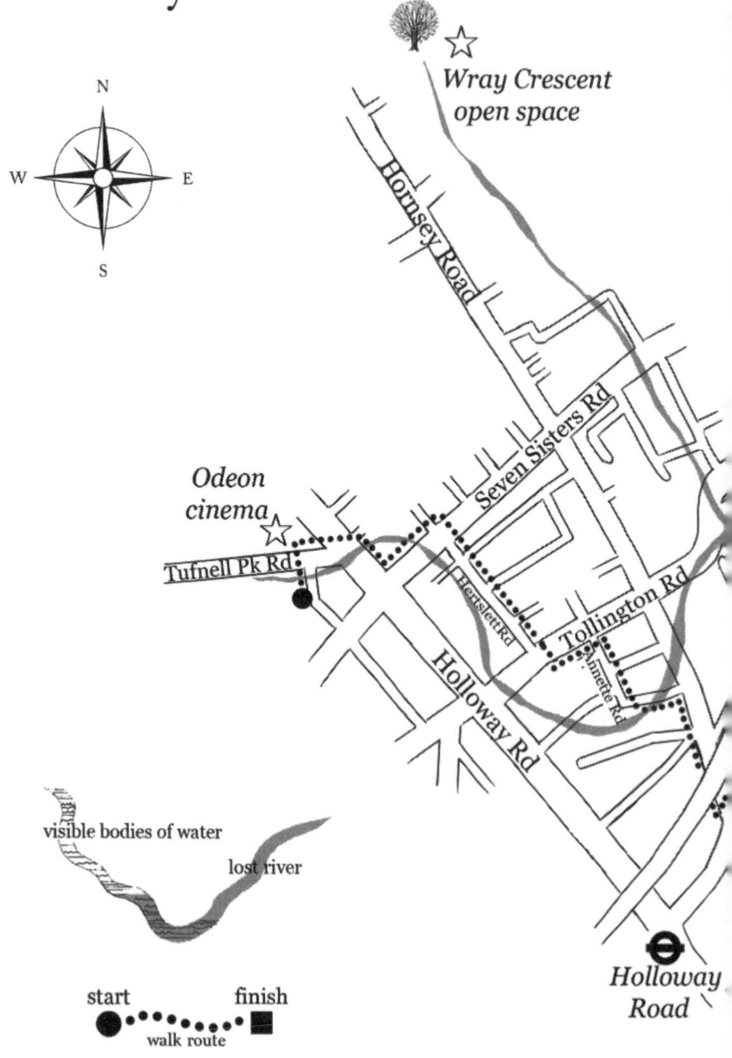

N
W · E
S

Wray Crescent
open space

Hornsey Road

Seven Sisters Rd

Odeon
cinema

Tufnell Pk Rd

Hertslett Rd

Tollington Rd

Annette Rd

Holloway Rd

visible bodies of water

lost river

Holloway
Road

start   finish
walk route

Practicalities

Distance – 7 miles
Start – Holbrooke Court, Holloway
Getting there – Holloway Road Station, then a 10 minute walk along Holloway Road

End – Old Ford Locks, Hackney Wick
Getting back – Hackney Wick Station
Note – this walk should be completed during daylight hours, as Clissold Park closes at dusk.

Introduction

The Hackney Brook might seem to be just another local stream, buried by the growth of 19th century London, but is a cultural focus like no other lost river. In recent decades it has received an unexpected level of creative attention, largely due to its location in the Borough of Hackney, the troubled heart of alternative 21st century London.

The Brook boasts dedicated work from twin London mages, writers Iain Sinclair and Alan Moore. When the former, a long-term Hackney resident, wrote that "London is a labyrinth… You feel the gravity, the insistent pull of the Northwest Passage, the whisperings of hidden rivers,"[1] he was talking about the Hackney Brook. Likewise, when graphic novelist and hidden London enthusiast Alan Moore intoned "When we excavate the place we excavate ourselves: the inside is the outside",[2] it was the Hackney Brook echoing in his imagination.

The river, entirely buried in storm sewer tunnels, runs from west to east, from higher ground in Holloway across Hackney to the marshes of the Lea Valley. Alan Moore and Tim Perkins' album *The Highbury Working* conjures up Joseph Bazalgette's sewer system, "One pig iron colon, winding under Highbury Hill to swallow Hackney Brook in giant acoustics."[3] It rises from two springs or, as Alan Moore explains "two

---

1 Sinclair, Iain, *London's Lost Rivers: The Hackney Brook and other North West Passages*, Gresham College, 22 June 2009

2 Moore, Alan & Perkins, Tim, *Highbury Working, A Beat Seance*. RE:. 2000, 'Lady, That's My Skull'

3 Moore, Alan & Perkins, Tim, *Highbury Working, A Beat Seance*. RE:. 2000, 'A Skeleton Horse'

heads better than one... dual currents plaited in a cold, chrome braid."[4] However, its upper course is hard to trace. Barton and Myers track the source of its main stream to a location at the south side of Whittington Park, and there are ponds and fountains both here and further south, near Mercers Road. This walk begins further along the Holloway Road, where signs of a river become more definite.

Iain Sinclair thinks that the river is "a kind of repository of dreams... outside of time" and that it "definitely haunts the poets."[5] Hackney is an island, or at least it was. The 'ey' or 'ea' suffix is a giveaway, referring in London to islands, generally tidal and surrounded by marshes. Hackney was therefore a raised area of ground surrounded by land that was wet, either some or all of the time, possibly belonging to an ancient landowner called 'Haca'. The water was supplied in part by the Hackney Brook which, joined by tributaries in central Hackney, fed into what must have been a semi-permanent flooded area beside the River Lea. Even in more recent times, the Hackney Brook was much wider than seems possible. At Clissold Park it was said to be 30 feet wide, at Hackney 70 feet wide and, by the time it reached Hackney Wick, 100 feet wide. Now, the route it takes across London often seems to be swimming against the tide, favouring back streets over main roads and the suburban over the spectacular. It is a surprise, then, that it offers such a dense and varied version of London.

4 Moore, Alan & Perkins, Tim, *Highbury Working, A Beat Seance*. RE:. 2000, 'A Skeleton Horse'
5 Sinclair, Iain, *London's Lost Rivers: The Hackney Brook and other North West Passages*, Gresham College, 22 June 2009

Route

• *Starting point: Holbrooke Court.*

Holbrooke Court, its name strongly suggestive of flowing water, is hiding in plain sight. A low point in the back street next to a whitewashed electricity sub-station indicates the presence of an underground stream that feeds the Hackney Brook.

To the right, behind Holbrooke Court, is a large drill ground space at the back of the former Territorial Army Centre which, in the 19th century, was the garden of a house with a large pond, big enough to include a small island. It sits at the head of a small valley, which can be detected on a contour line that surrounds the site of the pond, opening out to the east in the direction in which the stream flows.

Contour maps show that the Hackney Brook has a double-headed source, with two small valleys running either side of Tufnell Park Road. The broader valley runs behind Holbrooke Court, while a narrower one joins from the north side of the road, behind the Odeon cinema. This branch originates a short distance away in the vicinity of Mercers Road, on the north side of the block.

On the other side of Tufnell Park Road, at the corner with Holloway Road, is a 1930s mansion block development called Northview, grouped around a green. The southern source of the Hackney Brook runs underneath the block at the rear and the parade of shops facing Holloway Road. In the past, the road outside Barclay's Bank at the south end of the parade has collapsed, suggesting that the ground conditions in the vicinity are unstable.

• *Facing the small electricity sub-station, turn left, then right along Tufnell Park Road. Cross Holloway Road at the pedestrian lights.*

The Holloway Road is a 'hollow way' first recorded in 1307, the route north that has become the A1. It follows a gentle gradient down towards a low point at the junction with Tufnell Park Road. Water is close to the surface in this part of Holloway, and the Odeon Cinema ahead has a pump that keeps the ground waters of the Hackney Brook out of its basement. Until the mid-19th century there was a moat on the cinema site, just to the east of the current building, that surrounded what was known as the manor house. In the 1720s a moated house on this site had been rebuilt by the carpenter who owned it. The 1930s Odeon was designed by the same architect, the American C. Howard Crane, responsible for the now-demolished Earl's Court Exhibition Centre.

• *Turn right on the opposite side of Holloway Road. Cross Seven Sisters Road, then turn left along it.*

Seven Sisters Road was a shopping street in the 1890s, and the Booth Survey described its coffee houses as being of good repute, "with no beds let out to chance customers as is sometimes done."[6]

To the left, a plaque on a house in Bowman's Mews marks the site of the house, later demolished, where artist and nonsense poet Edward Lear was born. He wrote that his earliest memory was of being held up to the window to see the fireworks celebrating victory at the Battle of Waterloo in 1815. Lear was the youngest of twenty-one children, and the economic turmoil that followed the end of the Napoleonic Wars caused his stockbroker father to be declared bankrupt. The four-year old Lear was taken away to be cared for by his sister, twenty years older, who acted as his surrogate mother for the rest of her life.

• *Turn right along Hertslet Road.*

"The infant brook is teasing and hard to trace",[7] according to Iain Sinclair. The signs of its course are not yet easy to distinguish from the solid 19th century city built over its course. The Victorian suburbs of Holloway were never quite as grand as other options, a characteristic that was permanently fixed in the general consciousness by George and Weedon Grossmith's comic novel, *The Diary of a Nobody*, published in

6 Booth/B/349 p5
7 Sinclair, Iain, *Hackney, That Rose-Red Empire – A Confidential Report*. Penguin Books, 2010, p552

1892. The Pooters, Charles and Caroline, live at a fictional house called The Laurels at Brickfield Terrace, Holloway in what Alan Moore calls "the suburbs of oblivion".[8] The Pooters, fortunately, are happily unaware of this. The Booth Survey, meanwhile, which was conducted around the same time, describes the houses in these streets as middle-class but "all taking in lodgers".[9]

• *At the T-junction cross and turn left along Tollington Park, then take the next right on to Annette Road.*

By the 1890s Holloway Road was known as a Welsh neighbourhood. It possessed two Welsh chapels and the Jones' Brothers department store, a block away to the right, where the proprietor "favoured his fellow countrymen".[10] The store finally closed in 1990 although its fine building, complete with tower and clock, remains next to the Art Deco Coronet cinema, which is now one of the more dramatic Wetherspoon's conversions.

Nearby, at No.304 Holloway Road, record producer Joe Meek recorded the era-defining instrumental 'Telstar' in his flat, which was equipped as a studio like no other, full of home-built innovations that would change music. Unfortunately, most of Meek's influence came after his death. He made little money despite hit record sales and, as a gay man in the early 1960s, became the victim of blackmail. He grew increasingly paranoid, a heavy amphetamine user, and in 1967 shot his landlady dead before killing himself. The flat is marked with a black plaque.

• *Turn second left along Caedmon Road.*

At No.3 a plaque marks the birthplace of 'Christian fantasist' novelist and poet Charles Williams, a member of C.S. Lewis's Oxford writers group The Inklings, with other writers who included J.R.R. Tolkien and Roger Lancelyn Green.

---

8 Moore, Alan & Perkins, Tim, *Highbury Working, A Beat Seance*. RE:. 2000, 'Lady, That's My Skull'
9 Booth/B/349 p1
10 Booth/B/349 p5

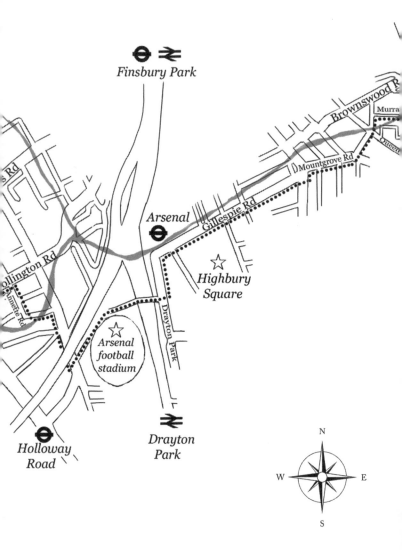

• *Turn right along Hornsey Road.*

The Harvist Estate, on the other side of Hornsey Road, has experienced the full range of problems associated with modernist social housing. The towers were built using prefabricated slabs, a system shown to be disastrously vulnerable when the Ronan Point tower in Canning Town partially collapsed in 1968, so the towers had to be strengthened before they could be occupied. All the buildings were later reclad to deal with chronic damp problems, and the low-rise blocks had their flat roofs replaced after they began to leak.

There was originally a pub called The Monarch on the corner of Citizen Road, on the left before the railway bridge, and the unusual road name seems to be a response to the pub.

• *After the railway bridge, turn left up the ramp between the railway line and the Arsenal Stadium.*

The Arsenal Stadium is a point of convergence for railway lines and for sewers. A tributary joins the Brook here, the second of its two headwaters, passing under the railway lines somewhere towards the north end of the stadium, having passed through the streets west of Hornsey Road, from Wray Crescent open space where it is believed to rise.

The Holloway Storm Relief Sewer carries the headwaters of the Hackney Brook, crossing the High Storm Relief (Camden Branch), North London Storm Relief and High Level Interceptor sewers somewhere nearby. Intrepid underground adventurers from Guerrilla Exploring walked some of the High Interceptor sewer here, which they described as "Directly built by Sir Joseph Bazalgette's team in the middle 1800s. It starts on Holloway Rd from a local sewer, and eventually it passes Gillespie Park, near Arsenal Football Ground."[11] They found a maze of calcium-encrusted tunnels lined in glazed brick, and deep concrete chambers.

---

11 'GES262', 8 September 2014

The stadium was known as Ashburton Grove before the decision was taken to rename it after its sponsor. It opened in 2006, replacing the club's historic Highbury ground, just around the corner. The site was industrial, squeezed into a corner between railway lines and, until the 1960s, the LNER's Goods and Coal Depot. It later housed the Islington Council rubbish dump. Queensland Road, the street that runs past the far side of the ground to the right was, according to the Booth Survey, "the most vicious place in the [police] subdivision… noted for thieves, prostitutes, rag pickers and common labourers". Lodging houses for women were on the north side of the street and for men on the south, and the survey claimed that "women troop home between 1 & 2 am from the neighbouring streets and also as far off as King's Cross." Both prostitutes and police were regularly visited by a London City missionary known as 'The Bishop of Queensland Road'.[12]

The stadium walls are decorated with posters of past players, not least 1950s Welsh international goalkeeper Jack Kelsey who is described poetically as having "cat like reflexes and velcro hands from the Valleys." Around the corner, a statue makes Tony Adams look like a Subbuteo player.

• *Walk around the stadium and cross the Ken Friar Bridge over the railway to Drayton Park. Take the stairs to the left, walk along Drayton Park, and follow the road as it turns right to become Gillespie Road.*

Up on higher ground to the left, where the road turns right, is Gillespie Park and Ecology Centre. There are ponds in the grounds, but these are separate from the Brook, and are fed by recycled waste water.

Further along on the right is Highbury Stadium Square, a gated housing development occupying the site of the ground that was Arsenal's home from 1913 until 2006. B.S. Johnson described it as "older-looking in its outdated modernity than last century's houses."[13] A rumour persisted that a horse was buried under the North Bank stand having toppled in during construction, along with the coal merchant's cart it was pulling, in

12 Booth/B/348 p237
13 Johnson, B.S., *Albert Angelo*. Picador, 1964 [2004], p47

an echo of the supposed custom of burying an animal in the foundations of a new building for luck – in the words of Alan Moore, "A bone mare, rattling loose beneath the Arsenal ground... a skeleton horse!"[14] When the ground was converted for housing workmen found horseshoes and timber from a cart, suggesting the story might have some truth.

Late 19th century living conditions in the Gillespie Road neighbourhood were summed up by the Booth Survey, which described how families would effectively store their Sunday clothes at one of the many local pawnbrokers, buying them out of pawn for the weekend and then putting them back in to raise money for the rent collector, who visited on Monday or Tuesday. The boys who worked in the pawn shop storage rooms suffered badly from flea bites.[15]

• *When Gillespie Road reaches Blackstock Road, cross and continue ahead along Mountgrove Road.*

The Brook was known as the Black Ditch where it crossed Blackstock Road, above ground until the mid-19th century. Alan Moore claims that there is "above the Black Ditch over Blackstock Road, an astral Highbury of the air, the element of mind, a stratosphere in which rarefied intellects might dance."[16] He is referring to the connection between Aleister Crowley and Blackstock Road. Crowley took a brief sojourn from the Abbey of Thelema in Cefalù, Sicily, the ritual commune he was struggling to fund, to publish his novel *Diary of a Drug Fiend* through an engraver based on Blackstock Road, with whom he may have stayed. More than fifty years later, famed blues keyboardist Graham Bond threw himself under a train at Finsbury Park Station, nearby, having lost his grip on reality via an obsession with Crowley and, like his idol, heroin addiction.

The photographer Don McCullin, brought up in Finsbury Park in the 1930s and 1940s, writes that it was "then known as the worst area in North London."[17] He returned to the area in the late 1950s, after

14 Moore, Alan & Perkins, Tim, *Highbury Working, A Beat Seance*. RE:. 2000, 'A Skeleton Horse'
15 Booth/B/348 p225-22
16 Moore, Alan & Perkins, Tim, *Highbury Working, A Beat Seance*. RE:. 2000, 'Opium Nights'
17 McCullin, Don, *Unreasonable Behaviour: an autobiography*. Vintage, London, 2002, p7

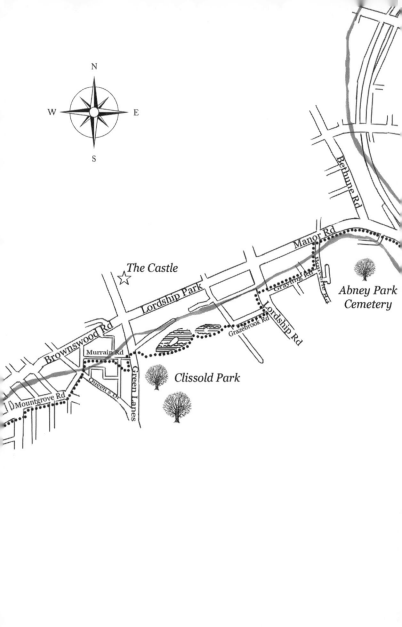

his national service, where he hung around with and photographed the gang of young men who met in a cafe on Blackstock Road, in their suits and ties, Dillinger hats and cigarettes. McCullin's picture of 'The Guvnors' posing on the first floor of a derelict building nearby, arranged across its exposed wooden frame, was published in the *Observer* in 1958 after a policeman had been stabbed to death in the area, and made his name. The Guvnors look good in black and white, but it was an extraordinarily violent scene and McCullin describes gaining someone's respect by smashing him repeatedly in the face with a brick for damaging his wing mirror.

The Sylvanian Families shop at No.68, located here for no obvious reason, brings children to Finsbury Park from far and wide.

• *Take the third left along King's Crescent. At the next junction, after the traffic barrier, turn right on to Queens' Drive.*

In front of the traffic barrier, in the centre of the road, a drain cover sits over the course of the Brook.

• *Take the next left under Bramfield Court. At the next junction turn right along Murrain Road to reach Green Lanes.*

The Clissold Quarter replaces the 1970s King's Crescent Estate, much of which was demolished in the late 1990s. It then sat derelict and fenced off for more than 15 years while rebuilding proposals came and went, before work finally began in 2015.

• *Turn left along Green Lanes and cross to enter Clissold Park.*

The unlikely building to the left is the former pumping station for the New River waterworks, converted into a climbing centre in 1995. It was completed in 1856 in a style that is properly fantastical, described by *The Buildings of England* as "beyond belief",[18] featuring three towers, each in

18 Cherry, Bridget & Pevsner, Nikolaus, *London 4: North. Buildings of England*. Yale University Press, 2002, p540

a different architectural style. The cinema was disused for 25 years and under threat of demolition, hosting avant-garde cinema nights before it was eventually rescued.

• *Walk into Clissold Park, bear left to walk along the left bank of the lakes.*

The two lakes are, rather fancifully, named Becksmere and Runtzmere after Joseph Beck and John Runtz who saved the park from development in the 1880s. The Hackney Brook once fed the lakes but, as with culverted rivers in parks all over London, it was separated to allow cleaner water to be fed in separately from springs that would otherwise have flowed into the Brook. The Hackney Sewer now carries the river under the northern edge of the park.

A section of curved stream at the south end, to the right, is all that remains above ground in the park of the New River, built in 1613 to carry drinking water to London from Hertfordshire. It ran through Clissold Park above ground in a loop, passing under Riversdale Road a little way to the south of the Hackney Brook. It then linked north to the New River Company's filter beds at Brownswood Park, built over in the 1990s, and the two reservoirs next to The Castle. The loop was straightened out and culverted in the 1860s, and remained in Clissold Park until the 1970s when it was almost all filled.

• *Leave Clissold Park, cross Queen Elizabeth's Walk and continue straight ahead along Grazebrook Road.*

At the far end of Runtzmere, water can be seen flowing out through a drain towards the buried Brook. Where the sewer leaves the park it turns right along Queen Elizabeth's Walk for a short distance, then left along Grazebrook Road. A valley can be seen along the line of Grazebrook Road, which sounds like a name used for this section of the Brook. In fact, the street was called Brook Road until the late 19th century, and 'Graze' was probably added to distinguish it from the many other Brook Roads in London.

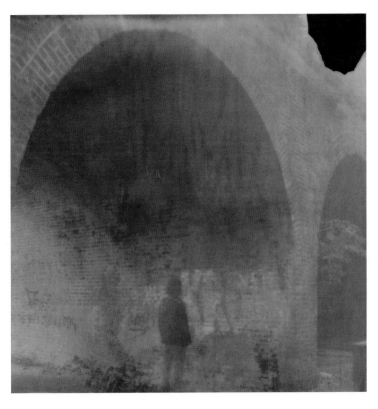

i • Black Ditch

ii • Bollo Brook

iii • Cock & Pye Ditch

iv • Counters Creek

v • Falcon Brook

vi • Moselle

vii • Stamford Brook East

viii • Stamford Brook West

• At the T-junction turn left along Lordship Road, then right along Grayling Road.

The Brook continues straight ahead to the right of Grayling Road, beside Grazebrook Primary School.

• At the T-junction turn left along Bouverie Road, then right along Manor Road.

In the 19th century, Hackney Brook was also called Manor Brook. The line of the river valley continues straight ahead, passing beneath the 1990s terraces to the right on Bouverie Road, specifically under No.92, heading towards Abney Park Cemetery, marked by a line of trees. Further along, off Manor Road to the right, Listria Park drops down into a clear river valley. The river runs along the cemetery boundary to the right. Abney Park is one of the London's Magnificent Seven Victorian burial grounds built to relieve pressure on over-stacked city churchyards. It is a non-denominational cemetery, which reflects the dissenting character of Stoke Newington in the 19th century. William and Catherine Booth, founders of the Salvation Army are buried there, as are missionaries, Chartists, peace campaigners and a number of anti-slavery activists. William Wilberforce asked to be buried here, but was claimed by Westminster Abbey instead.

Iain Sinclair writes that "There is a magic place, close to Abney Park Cemetery, that no-one can find twice."[19] He claims this myth, originating with writer Arthur Machen, encourages the inhabitants of Stoke Newington in a belief that their place is exceptional. Machen, a local resident, wrote a story called 'N' about a hidden paradise, a garden in the fictional Canon's Park, "a neighbourhood laid out in the twenties or thirties of the last century for City men of comfortable down to tolerable incomes." The garden, "a panorama of unearthly, of astounding beauty", can only be visited once. If you try to return, you will find that the roads no longer lead where they did before. Those

---

19 Sinclair, Iain, *Hackney, That Rose-Red Empire – A Confidential Report.* Penguin Books, 2010, p552

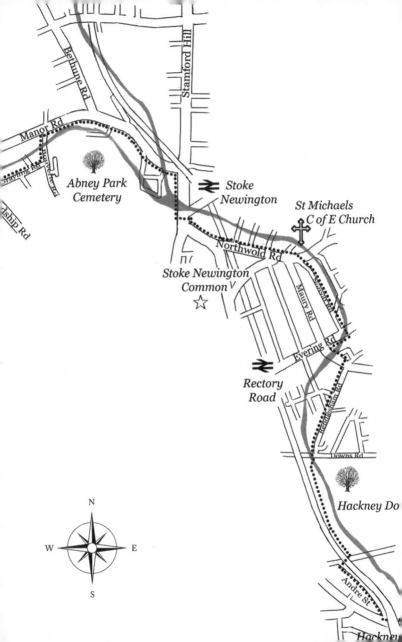

Bethune Rd

Stamford Hill

Manor Rd

Harrington

Abney Park
Cemetery

Iship Rd

≥ Stoke
Newington

St Michaels
C of E Church

Northwold Rd

Stoke Newington
Common
☆

Maury Rd

Evering Rd

≥

Rectory
Road

Sandringham Rd

Downs Rd

Hackney Do

N
W E
S

Andre St

Hackney

who keep on searching will not find the garden again but may find themselves "lost... forever".[20]

The teasing concept of a parallel world around the corner suits the atmosphere of Abney Park Cemetery, an overgrown, enclosed landscape of austere tombs. Its separateness also means that a detour is needed to reach the line of the river, and the walk therefore skirts its northern edge. The cemetery can be accessed a little further along the route.

Through the gates of Royal Close, to the left off Manor Road, the railway embankment can be glimpsed. The line opened in 1872 and was built along the route of a lost Hackney Brook tributary, which disappeared in the process. Pre-railway maps show a string of four ponds on Amhurst Road and Dunsmure Road, connected by a stream that reached Stamford Hill near the point where the railway now tunnels underneath. A name for the tributary has not survived. However, there is tangential evidence of its presence. Persistent damp problems in the 1990s on the Holmleigh Estate, which is next to its route, may have been connected, and some maps show a surviving section of water on railway land west of South Tottenham Station, where the source may have been.

• *When Manor Road reaches Stamford Hill, cross the road and turn right.*

Stoke Newington has a long-standing reputation as "the village of visionaries",[21] a retreat for those with unorthodox political and religious views and, although this has been diluted by 21st century prosperity, Stamford Hill is still London's Hasidic Jewish centre. It has also attracted writers and artists who share a certain detachment from the mainstream. Edgar Allan Poe went to school here; Mary Wollstonecraft founded a school; Joseph Conrad lived off the high street when not at sea; and former resident Daniel Defoe, a Puritan, has a pub named after him.

---

20 Machen, Arthur, *N*. Published for the Stoke Newington Literary Festival by the Friends of Arthur Machen and Tartarus Press, 1936 [2010], p33
21 Morgan, Frances, The Village of Visionaries, in: *Time Out Book of London Walks. Volume 2*. Time Out Guides Ltd., 2002, p38

A valley can be seen where the Brook crosses Stamford Hill, at the junction with Cazenove Road. This is the point where the Old North Road, now the A10, crossed Hackney Brook on Stamford Bridge, not to be confused with the bridge of the same name in Chelsea, which crossed the buried Counter's Creek. The name Stamford may refer to a sandy ford over the Brook on what is a Roman road. In the late 20th century there was a 'Riverside Shoe Shop' on Stoke Newington High Street. Just beyond, go through the neo-Egyptian gates on the right to detour into Abney Park Cemetery.

When Stoke Newington really was a village George Grocott, reminiscing about his 1860s childhood, described the White Hart pub, which still exists a little way south on Stoke Newington High Street, as "an old-fashioned hostelry, with a lay back for waggons and country carts, which came up from Enfield and elsewhere with agricultural produce for Spitalfields Market."[22]

At No.25 Stoke Newington Common, to the right, a plaque marks the house where Marc Bolan grew up as Mark Feld. His father, from an Eastern European Jewish family, was typical of the diaspora who arrived in Dalston, Hackney and Stoke Newington during the late 19th century.

• *Take the second left along Northwold Road.*

Gibson Gardens, the cobbled street, on the left is a philanthropic Victorian development, built in 1880 by The Metropolitan Association For Improving The Dwellings of the Industrious Classes. The flats were built for families, and smaller cottages around the corner for aging parents. Future Russian spy Anna Chapman (nee Kushchyenko) lived here in 2002, with her husband Alex. She later left him and moved to New York, where she was arrested with the Russian network to which she belonged and, later, returned to Russian in a prisoner swap. The street was also a location in the video for Amy Winehouse's 'Back to Black', where a funeral procession gathers before heading to Abney Park Cemetery.

22 Grocott, George, *Hackney Fifty Years Ago.* Potter Bros, 1915, p7

The row of shops on the right once included local favourite Sellfridges, a shop that sold second hand fridges and is now, sadly, closed. Behind the shops, the Smalley Road Estate is built on the site of "The Rookery", an area of alleys described by Grocott as "colonised by the roughest characters... where the police dare not venture."[23] However, the Booth Survey reported in the 1890s that these streets had improved since the London County Council took over the management of Stoke Newington Common.

Stoke Newington Common was originally called Cockhanger Green a name that, for some reason, dropped out of use. It was then Shacklewell Common, and Newington Common, only becoming Stoke Newington Common in the 20th century, suggesting that this side of the High Street has an uncertain identity. The Hackney Brook ran along the south side of Stoke Newington Common, to the right, crossed by a bridge that linked it to market gardens on the other side, before development, described by Grocott as "picturesque".[24]

• *After the Common, at St Michael and All Angels' Church, turn right along Norcott Road.*

On the south side of the junction two bridges crossed the Brook to give access to a large house called Elm House, which was demolished and replaced by houses in the 1870s. Brooke Road, which references the river, was known as World's End Path before it was upgraded in the 1870s, and links Stoke Newington to Clapton. There was a "rustic bridge and a small waterfall"[25] where the path met the Brook, which crossed an area of brickfields surrounding Elm Lodge. Draper's Court on Stoke Newington High Street, which was demolished to make way for Brooke Road was a cobbled courtyard described by Grocott as "a 'scolding yard'", a term for tenement blocks that were the domain of washerwomen.

Development changed the area rapidly and, in an echo of complaints that continue to float around Stoke Newington, rents rose rapidly in the

23 ibid, p8
24 ibid, p8
25 ibid, p8

late 19th century. The Booth Survey reported that "Rents are going up all round. Anything will let or sell in Stoke Newington now."[26]

• *At the T-junction, turn right along Evering Road, then first left on to Maury Road.*

To the right, at No.97 Evering Road, the Kray twins carried out the 1967 killing of their trilby-wearing associate Jack 'The Hat' McVitie, which triggered their arrest and imprisonment and ended their criminal careers. McVitie, a Kray drug dealer and hit man, had started taking the drugs he was selling and double-crossing the Krays. He was said to have been murdered after embarrassing the Krays once too often, asking singer Dorothy Squires, loudly in their club, what Roger Moore was like in bed. According to Alan Moore's re-imagined version, "The twins feel bad, an entertainer of that calibre. The Hat's already on a warning."[27] He was stabbed to death after being invited by the Krays to a fake party, and his body eventually dumped at sea, off Newhaven.

• *Turn first right along Rendlesham Road.*

Before development, there were market gardens on the site of Rendlesham Road, which disappeared during the 1870s, and watercress beds beside the Brook.

The housing to the right, along Ottaway Street, was built in the 1970s on the site of a self-enclosed area known as 'Navvies' Island' or 'The Island'. The Hackney Brook ran through the site beside the railway line, making the surroundings damp and the houses sometimes unstable. In the 1890s it was described by the Booth Survey as "the roughest quarter of the district… inhabited by low-bred English… of no particular occupation."[28] The Island was oddly cut off, with no public access from the north or the west, unless you were willing to pay to enter via someone's house in Evering Road, climbing over the back wall of their

26 Booth/B/348 p9
27 Moore, Alan & Perkins, Tim, *Highbury Working, A Beat Seance*. RE:. 2000, 'Hat-Trick'
28 Booth/B/348 p7

garden. Although very poor, The Island was remembered in the 20th century as a place with Arthur Machen-style qualities of an alternative reality. Apparently, circus elephants were stabled there, women "curled feathers with a flame for the circus performers" and houses were painted in different colours depending on which street they belonged to. Local history project *A Hackney Autobiography* reports that "Ottaway Street was pale green, Mellington Street was dark tangerine, Stellman Street was yellow, Landfield Street was bright emerald. Only Heatherly Street was plain brick". [29]

• *Cross Downs Road and walk into Hackney Downs. Walk straight ahead to cross the park on the path beside the railway viaduct, on your right.*

A valley crosses Downs Way on to Hackney Downs beyond. The Brook ran along the west side of the park on the right, on the line now occupied by the railway viaduct which carries the line towards Enfield. Where a path leads under the viaduct to Amhurst Terrace, a bridge once crossed the Brook. Grocott records a spring next to this bridge which took the form of an iron pipe, constantly spouting water, "slightly mineralised"[30] into a stone tank.

Mossbourne Academy, which opened in 2004, was an early example of a school run on the 'academy' model. The school sounds as if it offers a clue to a lost tributary of the Hackney Brook but, in fact, it is named after Moss Bourne, father of Sir Clive Bourne, a businessman who bought the site and founded the academy.

The Academy occupies the site of Hackney Downs School, which had a deep influence on London culture before entering a terminal decline that led to the Conservative government of the 1990s describing it as "the worst school in Britain". It was closed by the Education Secretary in 1995, and its building and name symbolically erased and replaced. However, as Hackney Downs Grammar School it had an important influence on 20th century English literature. Pupils included Hackney writers Alexander Baron and Roland Camberton, as well as Harold

---

29 https://www.ahackneyautobiography.org.uk/trails/the-island/6
30 Grocott, George, *Hackney Fifty Years Ago*. Potter Bros, 1915, p9

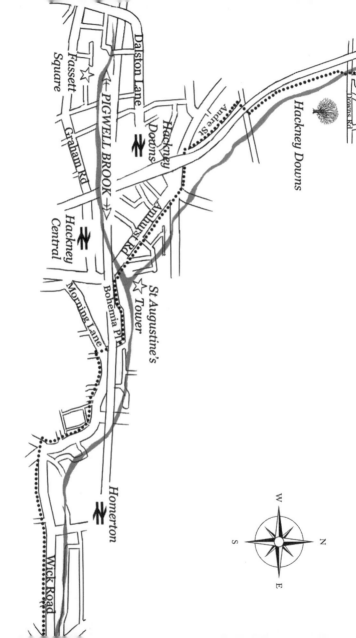

Pinter and Steven Berkoff and, in the 1940s, half of the school's intake were Jewish boys. Teaching staff included the restless imaginations of dislocated ex-servicemen such as Joe Brearley, the English teacher who inspired Pinter, who belonged to the half of the school's intake that was Jewish. Brearley introduced Pinter to the riches of language, and he and a group of close friends would walk the streets of Hackney declaiming "passages from Webster into the wind, or at passing trolley-buses."[31] Meanwhile, Baron's 1963 novel of dog tracks and bookies, *The Lowlife*, is set close by on Ingram's Terrace off Stoke Newington High Street, full of Victorian houses divided into tenements after the war and occupied by a mixture of Cockneys, Jews, West Indians and Cypriots.

• *Leave Hackney Downs, cross Downs Park Road and turn right under the railway bridge, then first left along Andre Road beside the railway arches.*

In the middle of Downs Park Road, after the railway bridge and a short distance past the Andre Road turning, a round grating in the centre of the road offers the rare sight and sound of the Brook, flowing in the storm sewer below.

Andre Road is almost entirely occupied by car repair workshops, with perhaps the odd evangelical church. These occupy the railway arches, once the standard use for arches across London, but an increasingly rare sight in post-gentrification Hackney.

• *Turn left along Amhurst Road under the railway bridge. At the five-way Pembury Tavern junction, follow Amhurst Road as its bears right.*

The green triangle to the left, on the corner of Amhurst Road and Pembury Road, is the site of the Clapton Congregational Church. By the 1860s the Brook was below ground from this point under the centre of Hackney. It entered a culvert which passed under the railway line and emerged again on Morning Lane, ahead.

---

31 Billington, Michael, *The Life and Work of Harold Pinter*. Faber and Faber, 2000, p11

At the other end of Amhurst Road, close to Stoke Newington High Street, the Angry Brigade were arrested in 1971. When police burst through the door of No.359 they were surprised, and pleased, to find a machine gun, revolvers, ammunition, a bag of gelignite sticks and the children's printing set used to issue Angry Brigade communiqués. The small left-wing cell, described as the British Baader Meinhof, created a mini wave of terror in 1970 and 1971, carrying out 25 bomb attacks on targets that included the homes of the Employment Secretary, the Business Secretary and the Attorney General, and on a BBC outside broadcast van transmitting the Miss World contest. Of the Stoke Newington Eight, as they were known, four were given 15 years and four acquitted.

Although Hackney has become the spiritual home of the early 21st century hipster, like Stoke Newington it has a lingering reputation as a place of retreat, a village far enough away from the city to hide in. As Iain Sinclair points out, "Hackney has a very peculiar status because as everyone says, it's not really the East End, and it's not really North London."[32] It fills a gap between through routes, making it hard to visit unthinkingly.

Hackney continuing separation is partly due to a relative lack of public transport. Hackney Central Station is now busy and connected via the Overground but the section of North London Line east of Highbury and Islington was closed to passengers in 1944, and the station did not reopen until 1980. Before then, "Hackney was a surprisingly remote place" mostly reached by buses on "long, heroic journeys"[33], and the borough still has no tube station, although the Overground is a reasonable substitute.

The new, brick block on the right-hand side of Amhurst Road, after the turning to Hackney Central Station, sits over the Hackney Brook culvert. Part of a Victorian terrace of shops, with flats above which occupied the north end of the site, had to be demolished after sudden subsidence in 2014 caused, it is thought, by the collapse of the culvert beneath.

32 *Hackney Citizen*, 28 Nov 2008
33 Elks, Laurie, *Hackney: Portrait of a Community 1967-2017*. Hackney Society, 2017, p74

• *Cross Mare Street and walk along Bohemia Place, with the railway viaduct on your right.*

The Tudor tower of St Augustine's Church appears beside the Brook in an illustration from the 1730s, which shows a stone and brick bridge carrying Mare Street (originally Mere Street, suggesting a pond) over the Brook, with a ford alongside. The remainder of the church was demolished in the 1790s, replaced by the new St John's Church on Morning Lane. The Brook was culverted here in the 1860s, marking a point of transition for Hackney from a village on its own to a part of London.

A short distance to the west of Mare Street a tributary stream called the Pigwell joined the Hackney Brook. The full stretch of the Pigwell was still above ground in the 1830s. Its source was half a mile away at Dalston Lane, and the stream met the Brook at a pond behind the Hackney Empire. The street that is now called Wilton Way was previously Pigwell Path.

• *Follow the road to the right under the railway. Turn left along Morning Lane.*

The Brook ran through the garden of the Black and White House, a large Tudor family house on the corner of Mare Street and Morning Lane which became a girl's school, before being demolished in the 1790s. The Brook emerged from its Hackney culvert here and was briefly visible above ground. There was a small pond or lake on the south side of the gardens, according to 19th century historian 'F.R.C.S', and another pond on what is now the bus station, to the north of the railway viaduct. In the 1870s the area between the railway viaduct and Morning Lane was still filled with watercress beds and the gardens of a nursery. F.R.C.S. asserts, unverifiably, that "watercresses… were first artificially cultivated on this site."[34]

The nursery disappeared when the site was developed, and Chalgrove Road built in its place. The terraces, which surrounded a brush factory, were in turn demolished in the 1970s, having been described by the 1890s Booth Survey as "the abode of prostitutes and street hawkers".[35]

34 'F.R.C.S.', *Glimpses of Ancient Hackney and Stoke Newington*. A.T. Roberts & Co, 1893, p50
35 Booth/B/346 p197

Further along, the 'fashion hub' development beside the railway and the Brook, has turned Morning Lane into an unlikely destination for Chinese tourists.

Morning Lane, called Money Lane in the 18th century, was also sometimes known as Water Lane and "was often underwater through overflowing of the brook."[36] In the 19th century the Woolpack Brewery operated beside the Brook, where Morning Lane turns south with the river, opposite the school. The brewery made use of its water which, at least in the 18th century, was "sweet and clear enough to brew from."[37] The brewery was reached by a bridge with "a centre pier and two arches, all of brick."[38]

The school and the housing to the south are on the site of Berger's Colour Works, a long-standing paint factory founded by Lewis Berger, a German immigrant, who arrived from Frankfurt in 1770, bringing his formula for Prussian Blue paint. The Brook passed around the factory perimeter, crossed by a bridge that led to the front door of the caretaker's cottage. Berger's Paints was a major local employer although, with its extensive use of lead, not a healthy place to work. The Homerton factory closed in 1960, although the main building was only demolished in 2010. The company now operates from Kolkata. The writer and art critic John Berger was, appropriately, a descendant.

• *After Cardinal Pole School and a housing block, turn left along Wick Road.*

On the right-hand side of the road, the Wyke Estate rises up on a bank. The road now runs through a clear valley, the land sloping away on both sides. At the junction with Cassland Road, 'F.R.C.S.' describes how, in 1805, a stage coach missed the road and crashed down the banks of the Brook into the water. He points out that "the brook had a freshet [was in flood], and whether fenced in or no, would render deviation from the

---

36 'FRCS', *Glimpses of Ancient Hackney and Stoke Newington*. A.T. Roberts & Co, 1893, p164
37 ibid, p188
38 ibid, p188

beaten track most dangerous."[39] The Brook ran parallel to Wick Road on the north side, to the left and, until the Victorian houses were demolished in the 1970s, the line of the river was reflected in the undulating back fences of their gardens.

Another small tributary is sometimes mentioned, joining the Brook at the junction with Wick Road, its source not far to the south, in Well Street. An underground stream has been reported flowing under the buildings on the corner of Well Street and Terrace Road, and the water table is high under nearby properties, just below basement level.

• *Continue to follow Wick Road as it crosses Kenworthy Road, and then under a road bridge and a railway bridge.*

On the corner of Wick Road and Kenworthy Road there was a large house, known at different times as Sidney House or Ballance Park, pulled down in the 1880s. The Brook passed through its extensive gardens. A street to the right is called Brookfield Road. In the early 19th century a row of shanties here was known as Botany Bay, a reference to its isolation beyond the edge of Homerton towards the marshes of the River Lea.

Further along on the right is the northern entrance to Victoria Park. The now-demolished Victoria Park railway station was on the far side of the railway bridge. It closed in 1943 when bombs cut the North London Railway to the east, where it ran to Poplar and Millwall Docks, and it never reopened. When the eastern stretch of the North London Line to Silvertown finally opened again in 1980, Victoria Park Station was replaced by Hackney Wick Station, to the east.

The road bridge carries the East Cross Route, once part of the terrifying plan for a motorway box around London, carving its way through neighbourhoods and town centres. This section is unusual in that it was completed by widening the existing road. However, it still succeeds in creating a landscape of J.G. Ballard-esque automobile dystopia. Iain Sinclair writes of "a community of people actually living under the

---

39 ibid, p164

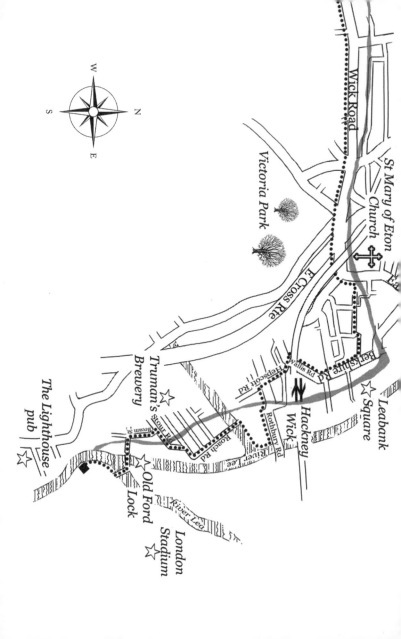

motorway there. As if there was actually a river they could draw on, even though they could not get at it." He adds "I think these are the kind of things that happen with lost rivers."[40]

• *Cross Eastway, turn left, and then right along a footpath beside a small park.*

St Mary of Eton Church is flanked by aggressively polychromatic housing blocks. The church was the unlikely location for the founding of the 59 Club, a biker club at the centre of 1960s Rocker culture. It was set up in 1959 by the church's curate, John Oates, who persuaded Cliff Richard to perform on its first night. A motorcycle section was added in 1962 by another St Mary's clergymen, Father Bill Shergold, who later took the club with him when he moved churches to Paddington. The club, which is still going, is said to have had 20,000 members in its 1960s heyday.

Until it closed in the 1980s, the church was surrounded by the railway lines of the Hackney Wick Goods and Coal Depot. The railway bridge over Wick Road was built with space for the goods lines just as the depot closed, and has therefore never been fully used.

Beyond the church, the Victory Works was a shellac factory. Further beyond Eastway to the left, the National Projectile Factory produced 16,000 shells per week during the First World War, and occupied a full square mile of land, which is now the Mabley Green open space.

• *Continue straight ahead along Beanacre Close. Where the road turns to the right, turn left on to a paved pedestrian area, then immediately right along a paved path between bungalows.*

The low-rise housing around Beanacre Close is built on the site of the demolished Trowbridge Estate, which consisted of seven tower blocks, each 22 storeys high. The first to be dynamited, Northaird House, was one of the first demolitions of post-war council housing when it came down in 1985. After occupation it gradually became apparent that the

40 Sinclair, Iain, *London's Lost Rivers: The Hackney Brook and other North West Passages*, Gresham College, 22 June 2009

estate had not been built to the official design specifications, and crucial, structural steel elements were found to be missing. In 1983 the local MP described the estate as "a wilderness that no-one deserves to call home",[41] and the towers were condemned.

• *Turn right along Berkshire Road. Follow the road as it becomes Wallis Road.*

The Brook makes a sharp turn to the south near Berkshire Road, flowing parallel to the street under buildings to the left, where it was above ground, although surrounded by factories, in the 1870s. It was joined by a channel from the marshes to the north, where a series of drainage ditches crossed largely empty land. The Brook from this point was enlarged to connect into this drainage system.

Hackney Wick was an industrial centre throughout the 20th century and numerous well-known firms were based there. The isolated location, which remained little known until the arrival of the 2012 London Olympics, was ideal for noxious industries, with transport nearby via the River Lea, although less than ideal for the people who worked in the factories and lived in the neighbourhood. In the late 19th century factories here made waterproof cloth, varnish, blood manure, plastics, iron, dye, printing ink, 'tar and chemicals' and 'lucifer matches'.

The 1990s housing on the left is Leabank Square which, despite being somewhat featureless, was designed by noted architects CZWG. It was built on the site of the Atlas Works. Until the 1980s the factory was the home of the British Perforated Paper Company, manufacturers of Bronco toilet paper for a century, perhaps the first toilet paper to be made in Britain, which was introduced in 1880.

Both petroleum and plastic – together, the basis of 20th century society – were invented in Hackney Wick. On the corner with Wallis Road, low rise industrial buildings mark the site of the factory where 'parkesine', the world's first plastic was made in 1866, named after its inventor Alexander Parkes. Carless, Capel & Leonard, the firm that coined and trademarked the word 'petrol', was based nearby.

---

41 Sedgemore, Brian, *Trowbridge Estate, Hackney Wick*. Hansard, 11 November 1983

By the 20th century, factories in Hackney Wick included Lesney's, where Matchbox toy cars were made, Algha, the firm which made the wire-rimmed granny glasses worn by John Lennon and a generation of imitators, and Zamo's bleach. The largest employer in the area was the family confectionery firm Clarnico, which eventually sold up to Cadbury's in 1999.

• *After a railway bridge, turn left along Hepscott Road.*

The Brook makes a double curve, to the east under the railway, and then back to the south again. This final stretch flows through Tower Hamlets, leaving the Borough of Hackney just south of the railway bridge. Before the Olympics Hackney Wick was "a kind of strange community of artists and anarchists and squatters"[42] according to Iain Sinclair, and evidence remains of the repurposed industrial buildings that characterised the place. However, it is midway through a transformative series of housing developments, aftershocks from the Olympic development, that are ending its status as peripheral place.

• *Turn second left along Rothbury Road, continuing to follow as it becomes White Post Lane.*

The river flows straight ahead, crossing Rothbury Road, but there the route is blocked by industry so we detour around. To the left on White Post Lane is Queen's Yard, which was the home of 'Printer's Paradise', a pre-Olympics cluster of printing firms. During the 1970s it was, apparently, known for "knocking out counterfeit £20 and £50 notes by day, hardcore porn by night."[43]

• *At the River Lea, turn right along the towpath. Follow the path around the corner and cross the Hertford Union Canal on the pedestrian suspension bridge.*

We pick up the route of the Brook again at the bridge, close to the point where it crosses under the Hertford Union Canal. This short canal, just

42 Sinclair, Iain, Hackney, *That Rose-Red Empire – A Confidential Report*. Penguin Books, 2010, p7
43 Elks, Laurie, *Hackney: Portrait of a Community 1967-2017*. Hackney Society. 2017, p96

over a mile long, is a link between the River Lea and the Regent's Canal, which it meets at Victoria Park.

On the opposite bank is Fish Island, sandwiched between the canal, the Lea and the A12. Its name comes from streets named after a selection of freshwater fish – Bream, Dace, Monier, Roach and Smeed. The neighbourhood developed with a combination of housing and industry in the 19th century. The Booth Survey noted that the "The whole district is very poor & looks as if were likely but to become poorer." This, it claimed, was because although there was plenty of work in jam, rubber and plastic factories, this was only available to women and boys, leaving the men of the area "to odd jobs or work as scavengers on the dust chute."[44] Nowadays, development marketing proclaims 'Fish Island Village' as 'authentic, vibrant, eclectic'.

The Hackney Brook was routed beneath the Hertford Union Canal when it was completed in 1830 but flowed above ground across Fish Island in the 1870s, to be covered over shortly afterwards by development. It entered a network of drainage channels around the site of the Wick Road Paper Staining works, south of Dace Road, leading to its outlet on the Lea Navigation at Old Ford. Its route crosses Roach Road near the junction with Wyke Road, passes under Monier Road, then turns back east towards the Lea.

• *Follow Roach Road as it turns right, becoming Beachy Road, then take the first left along Stour Road.*

On the right Forman's, a fish smokery, was based in Queen's Yard before the wave of development that came with the 2012 Olympics. Forman's was set up in 1905 and was the first London firm to produce smoked salmon, using what it describes as 'the London cure'. The Courage Brewery distribution centre was located on Fish Island until the late 20th century, supplying most of London with beer. A smell of malt lingers thanks to Truman's Brewery, a revived version of the original firm. Further along Beachy Road are the offices of the *Morning*

---

44 Booth/B/346

Star newspaper, originally the official organ of the Communist Party of Great Britain.

The neighbourhood, which offered cheap premises for creatives as the traditional industries declined, still houses a significant range of artists, including the studios of veteran painter Bridget Riley on Smeed Road.

• *Turn first left along Bream Street. At the T-junction turn left along Dace Street to reach Old Ford Locks.*

Old Ford, now a set of locks where the River Lea Navigation meets the River Lea, is a long-standing crossing place. It was part of an ancient, pre-Roman cross-London route that ran via Oxford Street to the east, all the way to Colchester.

The waterways here are part of a baffling system of natural rivers and artificial channels called the Bow Back Rivers, which date back to at least the 12th century. Diversions were constructed to power tide mills along the course of the Lea, to drain nearby marshes and to help navigation along the river, which was an important industrial artery. Among the sudden tangle of waterways, the Hackney Brook is not the only lost river. Under the Olympic Stadium on the opposite bank lies the short Pudding Mill River, which was filled in during construction of the Olympic Park.

• *Cross the lock and turn right on the opposite bank. Follow the towpath over a pedestrian bridge and, a little further along, under a bridge. On the far side of the bridge an outfall can be seen on the opposite bank.*

The former lock-keeper's cottage behind hedges on the far bank was known during the 1990s as the location for Channel 4's *Big Breakfast* show.

The outfall of the Hackney Brook can be seen from the far bank of the canal. To the right the towpath leads under The Greenway, the footpath along the line of Joseph Bazalgette's Northern Outfall Sewer. Just beyond the sewer pipes that cross at bridge height, a small brick arch in the river wall shows where the remaining waters of the Brook finally reach the River Lea. The outfall formed an inlet, Old Ford Wharf, which served the factories clustered beside the Lea until the end of the 19th century, when it was filled in.

Cross back over the Lea to Wick Lane for the Lighthouse bar, a very convenient place to end the walk.

Moselle

‘ *Partly lost and partly missing in action, the Moselle is under-appreciated to the extent that people from outside the area seems to doubt its very existence.* ’

Moselle

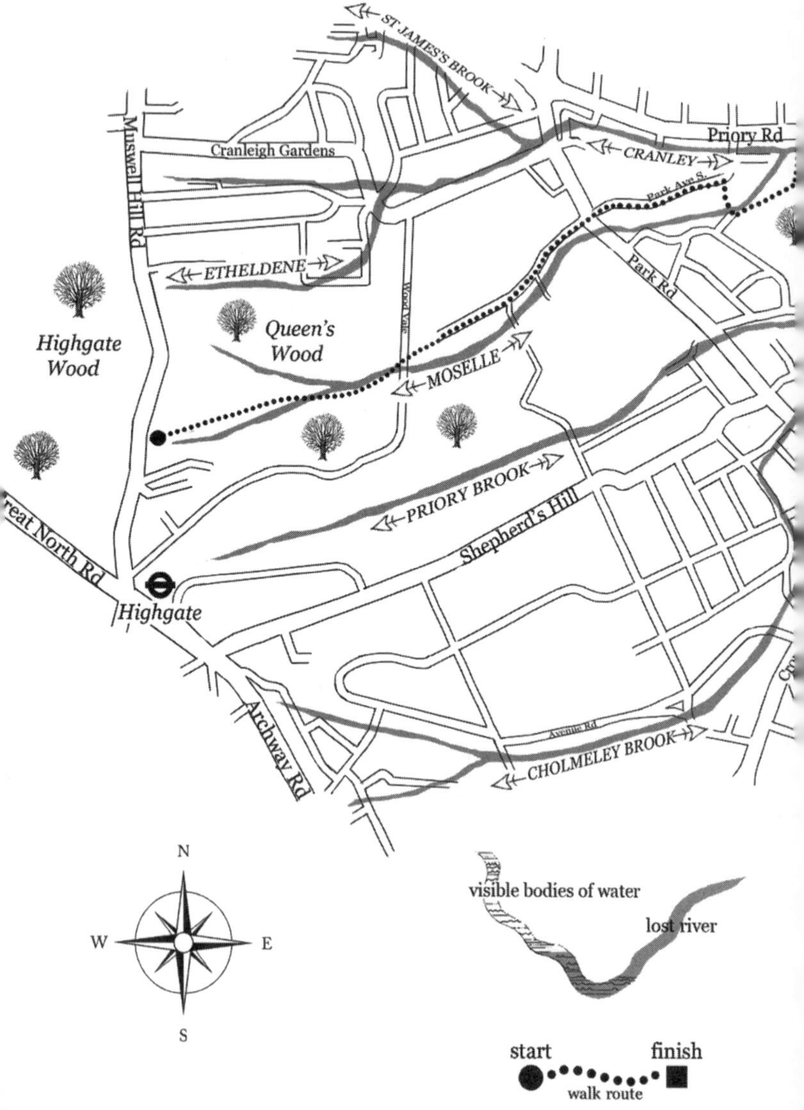

St. James's Brook

Cranleigh Gardens

Priory Rd

CRANLEY

Park Ave S.

ETHELDENE

Muswell Hill Rd

Park Rd

Wood Vale

Highgate
Wood

Queen's
Wood

MOSELLE

PRIORY BROOK

Great North Rd

Shepherd's Hill

Highgate

Archway Rd

Avenue Rd

CHOLMELEY BROOK

N

W   E

S

visible bodies of water

lost river

start   finish

● • • • • • • ■

walk route

Practicalities

Distance – 7¾ miles
Start – Queen's Wood, Highgate
Getting there – Highgate
Station, then a 5 minute walk to
Queen's Wood
End – Markfield Park, South
Tottenham

Getting back – Seven Sisters
Station, a 15 minute walk from
Markfield Park
Note – this walk should be
completed during daylight
hours, as parks along the route
close at dusk.

Introduction

The Moselle, up against stiff competition, is possibly the best named of London's many rivers. Partly lost and partly missing in action it has been corralled into culverts and tunnels and exploited by dodgy plumbers for illegal outfalls. While its better known cousin is one of the glories of Northern Europe, the version of the Moselle that runs from Highgate to Tottenham is under-appreciated to the extent that people from outside the area seem to doubt its very existence.

Yet residents of Muswell Hill, Hornsey, Wood Green and Tottenham know well that the valley of the Moselle shapes the Borough of Haringey, linking the apparently separate neighbourhoods of Highgate and Tottenham. A local saying claims that "Hornsey's rain, brings Tottenham Pain. When Tottenham Wood is all afire, Tottenham Street is all but mire."[1] This summarises the unequal relationship between Hornsey and Tottenham which, at first glance, do not seem directly connected. In fact, they are interdependent because Tottenham receives all the water that flows down from Muswell Hill on its way to the River Lea, much of which carried by the Moselle.

Contained entirely within the rectangular-shaped borough, the river flows down from the Highgate ridge past Crouch End, through the centre of Wood Green, and into the River Lea via a sweeping Tottenham

---

1 Pinching, Albert & Dell, David, *Haringey's Hidden Streams Revealed*. Hornsey Historical Society, 2005, p63

meander. Its broad watershed is fed by multiple streams and has been subjected to flood prevention work since the Middle Ages, making its course a maze of tributaries and diversions. The river drains into the Lea via its parallel feeder stream, Pymmes Brook, at four separate points south of Tottenham Hale.

The Moselle – variously referred to as the River Moselle, Moselle Brook, Mose, Mosewell, Mosa, Mosella, Muswell, Muzzle or, apparently, Muscle[2] – is one of three main streams that run down from the Muswell Hill watershed. The Muswell Stream flows north, meeting Pymmes Brook near Palmers Green (which connects it eventually back to the Moselle, which runs into Pymmes Brook at Tottenham). The Mutton Brook flows west, through East Finchley and Bounds Green. The Moselle flows east. The name 'Moselle' seems to have the same source as 'Muswell', both variations on the 'mossy well' that formed the source of the Muswell Stream. Remarkably, this well was in use until 1861 when, amid local controversy, it was buried under new housing, specifically No.40 Muswell Road.

Tracking the route of the Moselle unfolds an anatomy of the changing city. Lost rivers often run through edge areas, land between places that were developed late due to their propensity for flooding. A consistent theme of the early 21st century Moselle is the remodelling, rebuilding and intensification of housing at several locations along its route, often highly contentious. Passing through parts of the city that are little visited, the walker can assess the state of the ordinary, and perhaps observe how the apparently unexceptional is the site of conflict and change. Amid the turmoil, the Moselle remains constant, still flowing under the streets of N10, N22 and N17, in that order.

---

2 ibid, p30

Route

• Starting point: from Muswell Hill Road enter Queen's Wood by the path signposted 'Café'.

On the approach to Queen's Wood from Highgate tube station, Muswell Hill Road dips sharply into a substantial valley. In fact, the road is the watershed for the area, the flank of the Hampstead and Highgate ridge that drops sharply down towards Crouch End and Hornsey. On the left-hand side of the road, water flows west in the form of the Mutton Brook, with its sources in Highgate Wood, and eventually ends up in the River Brent. On the right-hand side, the landscape from Highgate to Muswell Hill falls away into valleys like the fingers of a spread hand, with streams flowing east to feed the Moselle and, eventually, the River Lea.

In Queen's Wood, the river's main source is seasonal and often mostly dry, but its channel is clearly visible above ground. This section of the Moselle's headwaters has been labelled 'Queen's Wood Stream' by local authors Pinching and Dell, a name invented to distinguish it from the four other streams in the vicinity that also feed the Moselle. To the north, three small streams are named after the side streets they pass through, once the gardens of large houses where they formed ponds: the Cranley and the Etheldene, which meet at the foot of Muswell Hill, and the St James's Brook or Muswell Hill Brook. To the south are two further streams. The Priory Brook has its source behind Highgate Underground Station and flows along the backs of houses on Priory Gardens. The Cholmeley Brook is formed by three headwaters that meet on Cholmeley Crescent, where clear gaps between the houses mark their courses. It then runs under Archway Road – the A1, which it caused to collapse in 1929 – and curves round towards Crouch End, gathering another couple of feeder streams on the way. This entire matrix of waterways all converges into a single river, the Moselle, a mile away at Hornsey High Street.

Queen's Wood itself is a slice of ancient woodland, the remains of Tottenham Wood. This is said to have been part of the Great Forest of Middlesex which covered most of the county, stretching 20 miles from the gates of the City of London until deforestation in the early 1200s. However, this was probably more of a 'wood-pasture' than a traditional forest, with a combination of trees and open heath used for grazing. The trees in the wood today include oaks, hornbeams and the wild service tree, all markers of its ancient origins.

The wood was bought for public use in 1898 by the Borough of Hornsey, after public protest at plans by the Ecclesiastical Commissioners to develop it for housing. Its name was updated from Churchyard Bottom Wood to Queen's Wood in honour of Victoria's Diamond Jubilee, providing instant status, while Gravelpit Wood across the road was similarly renamed Highgate Wood.

Tottenham Wood was said to determine the weather in Tottenham village, three miles to the east. Early Tottenham historian and local vicar, Rev. Wilhelm Bedwell, wrote in 1631 that "It is obseued that whensouer a foggy thicke mist doth arise out of this wood, and hange ouer it, or houer aboute it in manner of a smoake, that it's generally a sign of raine and foule weather."[3] Foul weather on the hill would also have sent floodwaters flowing down the Moselle valley towards Tottenham, a perennial problem yet to be entirely solved.

• *Fork right after the cafe, following the Capital Ring sign.*

The Queen's Wood Stream runs in a channel to the right of the path, before crossing to the other side in a pipe. It flows under the path beside the remains of the Ancient Bank Enclosure, a combined ditch and earth bank once topped with a fence or a hedge. It dates from the reign of Henry VIII when legislation required the enclosure of woodland across England for the protection of young trees, to build up the nation's timber stocks.

---

3 quoted in Roe, W.J., *Ancient Tottenham*. The Percy Press, 1950, p112

• *Fork left to follow the sign to Frog Pool.*

What is now known as Frog Pool, on the line of the stream, is a recent creation on the site of a concrete-lined paddling pool known locally as 'The Dogs' Pool'. This itself had been installed in 1935, replacing a natural pond, so the current landscape has returned the stream to something more like its natural state.

After the pool, the stream leaves the park under a boundary wall which has an overflow vent to allow water through, as well as a grille covering the main channel running underneath. The wall appears to play a role in holding back the waters of the Moselle during heavy rain, which would explain the alarming crack running from top to bottom, as the river seems to be in the process of slowly sweeping it away. On the opposite side of the wall, a tall green pipe vents the culvert below.

• *Carry straight on to cross the wood, exiting on the Greenways path. Cross Wood Vale and follow the Greenways path as it continues on the other side between fences. Shortly afterwards, turn right towards the cricket pavilion and follow the tarmacked path to the left.*

Water can be heard flowing under the road at the start of the Greenway. While the Greenway is the main route, the walk diverts to the right along a path that follows the precise line of the underground stream, which ran above ground through the playing fields until the 1920s. These fields, known as Crouch End Open Spaces or Shepherd's Cot after the farm that was here in the 19th century, sit in the river valley, overlooked by Alexandra Palace perched on the heights away to the north. The 'Beware Cricket Balls' sign should be probably be taken seriously: there are six cricket fields in the immediate vicinity.

• *Where the path meets Park Road cross, and continue straight ahead along Park Avenue South.*

The Moselle passes through houses on the margins of Crouch End, the centre of which is further to the right along Park Avenue South. The

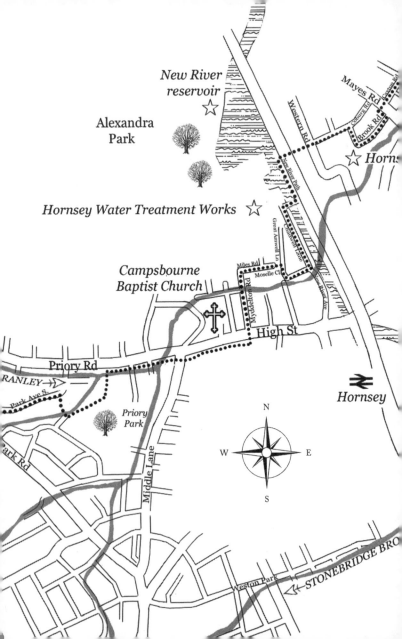

Borough of Hornsey, when first constituted in the early 1900s, was sold as 'Healthy Hornsey' – a retreat from the London smoke. George Gissing described the encroachment of the suburbs on farmland at the end of the 19th century in his 1889 novel *The Nether World*: "for the present Crouch End is still able to remind one that it was in the country a very short time ago. The streets have a smell of newness, of dampness; the bricks retain their complexion, the stucco has not rotted more than one expects in a year or two; poverty tries to hide itself with venetian blinds, until the advance guard of houses shall justify the existence of the slum."[4]

The poverty noted by Gissing is no longer a dominant characteristic of desirable Crouch End, but is still in evidence a short distance away in Hornsey. In the 1945 novel *London Belongs to Me*, Norman Collins' character Mrs Josser remembered exploring the "lovely country all about Crouch End" when she was looking for a cottage with her husband, in her younger days. When she arrived with her daughter, however, the illusion of countryside was gone: "They took one look at the rows of houses and the buses and decided to go on still further into the unknown."[5]

• *Turn right next to No. 82 Park Avenue South, along a path marked with two bollards. At the end of the path turn left into Priory Park.*

The path passes through a pair of metal barriers, tops smoothed by years of hands brushing past. On Abbeville Road, by the entrance to the park, a distinct dip indicates the path of the river while on the right the round drain cover marked 'Borough of Hornsey' conceals the river and shows that it was culverted before 1965, when Hornsey became part of Haringey.

• *Walk straight ahead to cross Priory Park.*

Priory Park opened in the 1890s, as the suburb of Hornsey developed. It was part of the grounds of a Regency Gothic mansion called The Priory. A section of its gardens are now occupied by housing, including the part once

4 Gissing, George, *The Nether World*. The World's Classics, Oxford University Press, 1889 [1992], p364
5 Collins, Norman, *London Belongs to Me*. Penguin Books, 1945 [2008], p264

dominated by a large pond, which is why no trace of the Moselle is visible above ground in the park. The lost pond was the point at which the various headwaters finally combined to form the Moselle, with the Cholmeley flowing around the east side of the park, the Queen's Wood Stream along the west side and the Muswell Hill Brook along Priory Road.

• *Turn left at a T-junction by the paddling pool.*

The path to the left follows the route of the Queen's Wood Stream, but the path to the right leads towards the line of the Cholmeley Brook, flowing under the eastern park boundary. In this direction there is also a hefty granite fountain originally located in St Paul's Churchyard, gratefully passed on by the Cathedral in the 1890s.

• *Exit and turn right along Priory Road.*

The first turning on the left after the school, Rectory Gardens, is worth a quick detour. In the road between No.41 and No.43, where the road turns to the left, is a manhole cover under which the Moselle can be heard flowing. As its name implies, the road is built on the gardens of the former rectory, and the river marked the garden boundary. It ran through the grounds of The Rectory until the 1960s, when the building was demolished for the current primary school, and the river culverted.

The Edwardian houses on the right were built over the large pond in the gardens of The Priory, taking a wedge out of Priory Park and obliterating the spot where the multiple Moselle streams meet that might otherwise be the heart of Hornsey. The river is sometimes known as 'Hornsey's river' and this fate seems appropriate for Hornsey, which is one of the more obscured parts of inner London. Since the abolition of its borough, it has been eclipsed by the rising profiles of neighbouring Crouch End and Muswell Hill, and many Londoners would be hard pressed to locate it.

Hornsey High Street may be a low profile place but the landscaping on the opposite side is unusual, a 'rain park' designed to slow the transition of rainwater to the underground river. Until the 1850s there was even more water around as The New River, the early canal built to channel drinking water to London from Hertfordshire, originally passed through the centre of Hornsey. The construction of the New River was expensive, difficult and opposed by landowners along its route. Rev. Bedwell wrote that "The New riuer, brought with an ill will from Ware to London, runneth with many crookes and windings through the west end of this parish."[6] These meanders took the New River across the Moselle at the junction of Priory Road and Nightingale Lane, but the 'Hornsey Loop' was straightened out and the river now runs instead past the eastern edge of Hornsey.

In 1867 Joseph Bazalgette, analysing the drainage problems of London as he planned his city-wide sewer system, noted that Hornsey had no drainage at all and its effluent flowed into cesspools and watercourses. The Tottenham Local Board of Health had just taken out an injunction against the Parish of Hornsey in an attempt to prevent its sewage draining into the Moselle and the Lea. Shortly afterwards, Hornsey commissioned the Hornsey Outfall Sewer, running south through Harringay to Bazalgette's main Northern Outfall Sewer, which released some of the pressure on the Moselle and Tottenham (although less so in Harringay, where part of the sewer collapsed in 2007 taking two houses on Cavendish Road with it).

At No.32 a plaque marks the site of the first David Greig store, a national grocery chain that vanished in 1972, absorbed by Key Markets (itself now a long-lost brand). The shops are still remembered because their tiled interiors and thistle motif survive across London and beyond. Greig himself was a local boy and benefactor, and the Greig City Academy opposite is part-funded by his charitable trust.

The street called Campsbourne, on the left beside Campsbourne Baptist Church, is named after Campsbourne House, a name that seems to mean 'fields by a stream'. However, this section of the river is also said to have been known as The Campsbourne "in earlier times."[7]

---

6 Bedwell, Rev. Wilhelm quoted in Roe, W.J., *A Briefe Description of the Towne of Tottenham Highcrosse*. The Percy Press, 1950, p108

7 Pinching, Albert & Dell, David, *Haringey's Hidden Streams Revealed*. Hornsey Historical Society, 2005, p41

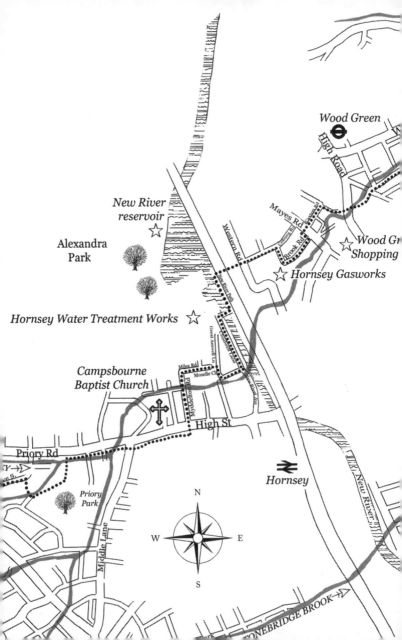

In *The Beauties of Middlesex* published in 1850, gardener William Kean appreciated the lake formed by the river in the grounds of Campsbourne House, and its "cut-leaved alder, fifty-feet in height and ten-feet eleven inches girth... a noble specimen, probably the finest in the country."[8]

• *Take the fourth left along Myddleton Road. Turn right on Miles Road. Continue straight ahead as the road becomes Moselle Close. Follow an alley between buildings next to No. 12.*

Myddleton Road is named after Hugh Myddleton, who funded the construction of the New River in the early 1600s, indicating that we are approaching its current course.

In his 1848 novel *Vanity Fair*, William Makepeace Thackeray used Hornsey as an example, alongside Hampstead and Dulwich, of the supposedly "beautiful suburbs of London". The wealthy Miss Crawley is whisked away into a semi-rural exile there by one set of relatives to keep her and her money out of the clutches of another, but the strategy is not a success and "After a brief space, she rebelled against Highgate and Hornsey utterly."[9]

The Victorian houses in this part of Hornsey were built in the 1860s but within twenty years were in bad repair, suffering from flooding because of their location over the Moselle. By the 1920s Campsbourne was the poorest area in the Borough of Hornsey and known as Campsbourne Slum. There was severe overcrowding, with 26 people discovered living in a single house. It took until the 1960s for the houses to be cleared by the council, and replaced with the current estate. However, after only another twenty years the blocks were in poor repair, with serious social problems including drug dealing. In 2008 the local MP described it as "a forgotten backwater".[10] Since then, improvements have been made, but the area still suffers, whether directly or indirectly, from its situation above the buried river.

8 Keane, William, *The Beauties of Middlesex*. T Wilsher, 1850, p254
9 Thackeray, William Makepeace, *Vanity Fair*. Penguin English Library, 1848 [1968], p236
10 Featherstone, Lynne quoted in Hinshelwood, John, *The Campsbourne Estate: a History of its Development and Re-development*. Hornsey Historical Society, 2011, p2

• At the T-junction, turn right along Great Amwell Lane and then first left along New River Avenue.

Great Amwell Lane is named after the Hertfordshire village where Amwell Springs, the original source for the New River, are located. The Victorian house beside the alley, hidden behind fences, is Moselle Cottage. This is the former New River Company Surveyor's house, built during construction of the waterworks. It is an isolated remnant of the late Victorian buildings on the edge of Hornsey, an area sometimes known as Moselle Park or the Campsbourne Estate.

The Moselle passes under Cross Lane and around the new blocks ahead, and then alongside the New River, crosses under both it and the railway in a brick-lined tunnel. It was diverted along this course during the construction of Hornsey Waterworks, now occupied by the sandy brick and glassy grey blocks of the New River Estate, built on former filter beds during the 2000s. The housing project required the diversion of the Moselle into a new culvert, which skirts around the edge of the housing blocks, and the existing brick-lined tunnel under the river was exposed during excavations.

The walk now detours to the left to cross the New River, before picking up the Moselle again on the other side.

• Turn left to walk alongside the New River. Where it meets a tarmacked path at a T-junction, turn right. Follow the bridge across the New River, turning left on the other side. Follow the path as it turns right under the railway and into Coburg Road.

The New River, completed in 1613, is an artificial channel, but in Haringey it is much more visible than the natural rivers of the area, which gives a misleading impression of the area's topography. The natural watercourses in the area flow from west to east and drain into the River Lea, but the north-south course of the New River gives the false impression that it is heading for the Thames. In fact it always stopped short in Islington, and backfilling means it now disappears below ground in Canonbury.

To the left, beyond the surviving filter beds, is the New River Reservoir. The river flows under what was the site of Hornsey Gasworks, to the right. It has been cleared, awaiting major redevelopment of much of the area between here and Wood Green High Road, but the footprints of a single vast gasholder and two smaller sister structures remain clearly visible in aerial photographs. The tallest, Hornsey Gasholder No.1 which was demolished in 2017, was 140 feet high and a local landmark.

• *Walk along Coburg Road, and take the second right on to Silsoe Road. At the T-junction turn left along Brook Road.*

The 1970s industrial units along Coburg Road were designed by Terry Farrell and house a variety of businesses, not least Turnaround who distributed the first volume of *London's Lost Rivers*. The Chocolate Factory building on the left is the former factory for Barratt's, who moved here in the 1880s and, by the early 20th century, had become the largest confectionery firm in the world. The building was known then as the Biscuit Factory, but sweets were made here too. In 1975 Barratt's (Blackjacks, Fruit Salad, Refreshers, Sherbet Dib Dabs) became part of the very similar-sounding Bassett's (Jelly Babies, Liquorice Allsorts, Murray Mints) and moved out although, through various corporate convulsions, the two companies are now separate again. A chocolate firm called Caxton's moved into what then became known as the Chocolate Factory, but it closed for good in 1984 and is now used as work space.

Major redevelopment was planned for much of Wood Green, including this estate and the town centre, as well as much of Haringey's council housing stock. However, local opposition to the Haringey Development Vehicle, an agreement with developers Lendlease that included handing over council property to the private sector, aroused significant local opposition. The Labour council leader was ousted in a party coup in 2018, and the council taken over by a Momentum-led coalition. The deal was then cancelled, leaving the future of the town centre development and various housing estates uncertain.

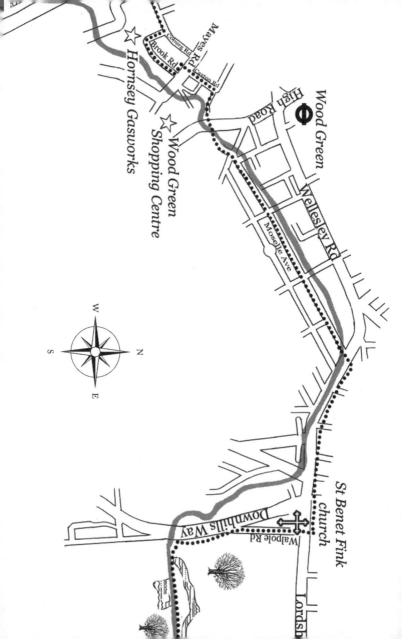

• *Cross Mayes Road, turn left, and then right along Caxton Road.*

The red-brick behemoth ahead, equipped with concrete access ramps, is Wood Green Shopping City which opened in 1981 and dominates the town centre, while drifting unstoppably towards obsolescence. The river passes behind the shopping centre site and then turns right to cross Wood Green High Street.

The shopping centre includes flats at its upper levels, known as 'Sky City', which became closely associated with urban isolation following the discovery in 2006 of the skeleton of Joyce Vincent. She had died three years earlier, and sat undiscovered on the sofa in her bedsit on the upper level of Shopping City, the television on all the while and a pile of unopened Christmas presents on the floor. She was only 38 when she died and her case became widely discussed and the subject of a film. There was no clear explanation for her dramatic isolation in the middle of a densely populated city, but it seemed to have come about partly because she was hiding from an abusive partner. Her fate was also linked to the design of the development which, it is claimed, enables such extreme disconnection between people living in close proximity.

• *At the T-junction, turn right along an alley with a wooden fence along the right side.*

Before the Wood Green Shopping Centre was built, the Moselle ran above ground beside the now vanished Blenheim Road, to the right. It passed the lost Noel Park and Wood Green Station, which was located on the east side of the High Street and closed in 1964. The station was on the Palace Gates line from Liverpool Street to Alexandra Palace, which eventually lost out to competing routes from King's Cross. However, the route of the proposed Crossrail 2 line would replicate part of the line, with an option for a route reconnecting Wood Green to Alexandra Palace.

• At the junction with the High Road cross and continue along the alley on the opposite side of the road beside the red brick Wood Green shopping centre.

Before Wood Green was remodelled as the town centre for the new Borough of Haringey, it was a lower-profile suburb, more middle-class than working class Tottenham. It had developed around the Great Northern Railway station that opened here in 1859 out on its own beyond the villages of Hornsey and Crouch End, which themselves were far from built-up London. It was "almost an independent colony"[11] according to an account of the 1880s, until the suburbs eventually washed up around it.

• When the alley reaches Gladstone Mews turn right, then left on to Pelham Road.

The river runs through the Noel Park Estate, a planned working class estate built by the Artisans, Labourers and General Dwelling Company from the 1880s. The company had previously been responsible for tenement-style estates in Battersea and Queen's Park, but the low-rent houses built here took a more suburban, low-rise approach. It is named after bewhiskered Victorian MP Ernest Noel who was chairman of the company (not be confused with a well-known 20th century Australian MP who was, confusingly, called Ernest Noel Park).

The estate was saved from 1960s plans for Wood Green town centre which involved diverting the High Street through it to make more space for pedestrian shopping, although some houses on the edge of the area were demolished for Shopping City.

• At the T-junction with Gladstone Avenue turn right, then turn left along Moselle Avenue.

The wide, flat valley of the Moselle can be sensed in Noel Park despite the houses. The presence of the river is perhaps also evident in the subsidence

---

11 Clarke, W.S. quoted in Cherry, Bridget & Pevsner, Nikolaus, *London 4: North. Buildings of England*. Yale University Press, 2002, p593

that seems to have claimed a number of front walls and porches along the route. The river flows underground behind the houses on the right-hand side of the street. It forms the back boundary of their gardens, easily distinguished from the air by its gently wobbling line.

Take a very short detour along the first street on the left, Vincent Road. At the back of the houses on the left a small section of garden wall incorporates brick arches, the remains of a bridge over the river. The Moselle was above ground at the bottom of these gardens when the houses were first built, but was buried in the 1920s.

• *At the T-junction with Lordship Lane, turn right.*

The Moselle also turned south-east at this point, flowing along the right-hand side of Lordship Lane where the pavement remains much wider than on the opposite side of the road, over the river's course.

• *After 1/3 mile turn right after a wide crossroads with shops (Downhills Way), along Walpole Road.*

Here, the river makes a sharp turn to the south, taking it around the rising ground ahead on Lordship Lane.

The first street on the right, Pennistone Close, leads to a long, winding alley that precisely mirrors the route of the river which flows underneath. It runs all the way along the backs of houses and through an industrial estate to Lordship Recreation Ground, but it is gated and frustratingly inaccessible. Pennistone Close itself is also a very long dead end, so the walk follows Downhills Way instead before rejoining the river where it enters the park.

Behind a fence to the left, the red brick church is St Benet Fink (Robert Finke [sic] was a benefactor), built to replace a church of the same name in the City of London, on Threadneedle Street. It had been destroyed in the Great Fire and rebuilt, but was demolished by the Corporation of London in 1846 and the proceeds from the sale of its site and furnishings put towards the new church in Tottenham, where the population was growing quickly.

• *Where the road reaches Lordship Recreation Ground, turn left to enter the park. Turn right inside the park.*

Lordship Recreation Ground was opened as a park in the 1930s, having previously been a field beyond the grounds of Downhill House, to the south, also now a park. The Moselle, still above ground, formed the boundary of what were once the gardens.

Thanks to a major restoration project, the Moselle now appears to cross the park in a natural course. The river previously ran in a concrete culvert, which was dismantled in the 2000s. The water here, though, still has a reputation for pollution caused by the number of grey water and sewage pipes which, either illegally or incompetently, discharge directly into the river upstream. This situation, reminiscent of the pre-sewage system era, is finally being addressed by Haringey Council which is repairing the misconnected outlets. The quality of the water has improved noticeably.

On the right by the river, the Moselle Gate marks the spot where the river enters the park, having passed under the long, unnamed back alley from Lordship Lane to beneath the Frankum and Kaye site and Downhills Way.

The Recreation Ground includes a 'Model Traffic Area', a scaled-down road network complete with road markings and, originally, traffic lights and signs built in the 1930s by the Ministry of Transport. It was intended to educate children about road safety by allowing them to ride bicycles and toy cars in supposedly realistic conditions, and included natural hazards for them to deal with. Bicycles and cars could be hired and it proved very popular before the Second World War, before falling into disrepair. The street furniture is gone, but the road markings have been restored.

• *Turn left to cross the park on a path with a pond to the right. Ignore bridges to the right, and walk past a building behind a green fence. Leave the park and walk straight ahead along Adams Road.*

At the far side of the park, the river disappears through a big grille and dives under the Broadwater Farm Estate, named after the Moselle. The estate is a system-built development, completed in 1971 which, before the end of the decade, had gained a reputation as the epitome of urban decay. It was constructed on Broadwaters (sic) Farm, land that had never been developed which is unsurprising as the estate is located directly above the Moselle. Due to the flood risk inherent in its location the blocks are raised on stilts, leaving little apart from garages and cut-throughs at ground level. This has an exceptionally alienating effect and it is described, accurately, by the *Buildings of England* as "a coarsely detailed concrete megastructure".[12]

Despite various improvements to the estate, including the removal of some of the high-level walkways, it remains a difficult place to love. This is all the more unfortunate as a generation has passed since the estate's moment of infamy during the 1985 riots, when the murder of PC Keith Blakelock, hacked to death by a mob on the estate, came to symbolise the problems of Britain's inner cities. It was a low point both for race relations, and for modernist urban reconstruction. The riots, which followed the death of Cynthia Jarrett during a police raid in Tottenham, were exceptionally violent: 250 police officers were injured, including police and journalists hit by shotgun pellets ricocheting off riot shields. Blakelock's murder was the first death of a British policeman in a riot for 150 years.

The Metropolitan Police counted 'The Farm' as a symbolic target, one of London's black-dominated 'no-go areas' alongside All Saints Road in Notting Hill, Railton Road in Brixton, and the Stonebridge Estate in Harlesden, all territory to be retaken. In this racially charged atmosphere, three men were wrongly convicted of PC Blakelock's murder, spending four years in prison before they were released. Two police officers were then acquitted of fabricating evidence. In 2013, 38 years after the riots, another man was tried and acquitted of the murder, and it remains a dark and unresolved episode.

• *Take a combined pedestrian and cycle path to the left, after the school and Moira Close.*

The Moselle crosses Adams Road near the junction with Moira Close, taking a turn to the north. It flows behind the Brookside Flats block to the right.

---

12 Cherry, Bridget & Pevsner, Nikolaus, *London 4: North. Buildings of England*. Yale University Press, 2002, p589

• *At Lordship Lane cross, turn left along the opposite side, then turn right into Bennington Road.*

Not far to the left along Lordship Lane was the original Broadwaters Farm, which not only had the Moselle crossing its land, but also a tributary stream flowing up from Adams Road to the back garden of the farm house, where it formed a pond. This had disappeared by the 1930s and the farm was surrounded by the standard London interwar bay-windowed terraces that still line the south side of the road. The farm itself was replaced by the glories of the much lamented Tottenham Lido, which closed in 1985. Lido Close now occupies the site. On the north side of Lordship Lane, the houses of the Tower Gardens Estate are distinctive and appealing. This purpose-designed working class housing was inspired by the garden town movement, and built by the London County Council on farmland beside the Moselle. Building, which began in 1903, continued into the 1920s culverting the river in the process. The *Buildings of England* appreciates the estate's "picturesque... variety... of slate-hung and tile-hung gables, hipped roofs and bay windows."[13] The river flows underground behind the houses on the right, parallel to Bennington Road. A drain cover in the right-hand pavement marks the place where the river turns to cross Bennington Road, just before the junction with Roundway.

• *Turn right along Roundway. Continue straight ahead along All Hallows Road. At a T-junction, turn left along Church Lane.*

At this point, the Moselle makes an extravagant about turn, swinging left and then right in a lazy curve around the back of Tottenham Cemetery, which lies ahead. It then heads back the way it came, south towards central Tottenham and then Tottenham Hale and the Lea. Rev. Bedwell described it neatly as "running through the middest of the town in a Meander fashion or after the manner of the Greek capital Omega."[14]

13 Cherry, Bridget & Pevsner, Nicklaus, *London 4: North. Buildings of England.* Yale University Press, 2002, p588
14 Bedwell, Rev. Wilhelm quoted in Roe, W.J., *Ancient Tottenham.* The Percy Press, 1950, p104

With no through route on the line of the river, we detour to the right to find the cemetery entrance and pick the river up on the other side.

Bruce Castle Park, ahead, is the grounds of a remarkably old house – a 16th century mansion – which stands a little to the right. Next to the house a stumpy red brick Tudor tower standing on its own is even older, dated by some to the early 1500s. It had been around long enough that, by 1700, its purpose had been forgotten. The house stands on the site of an earlier castle. The name refers to the Bruce family, and the early medieval ownership of the manor of Tottenham by the Scottish Royal Family. In 1254 the estate was divided among heirs and Bruce Castle, possibly the site of an earlier castle, belonged to Robert Bruce, Earl of Annandale and grandfather of the Robert Bruce everyone knows. He owned one third of the manor of Tottenham while John Balliol, his rival for the throne of Scotland, owned another third. Balliol became a notably unsuccessful king in 1292, deposed after fewer than four years on the throne by Edward I of England. However, when his grandson Robert the Bruce revolted against the English, he triumphed, becoming King of Scotland in 1306. His English properties were then seized by Edward II, ending Tottenham's Scottish link.

The building behind a brick wall and iron gate to the left is The Priory, now the vicarage of All Hallows Church, ahead. It was built in 1620 for Joseph Fenton, a barber-surgeon, and gives the impression of persisting in a parallel era.

• *After a zebra crossing, take a pedestrian path to the left through the churchyard.*

All Hallows Church is said to have been founded by David I, mid-12th century King of Scotland, another element of the peculiar Scottish-Tottenham connection. The church was described by Rev. Bedwell as "inunironed [environed] on the West, North and East with the riueret Mose."[15] More specifically, he describes the river as running between the church and the original parsonage, which was on a hill to the north of All Hallows. This is now the site of Tottenham Cemetery.

---

15 Bedwell, Rev. Wilhelm quoted in Roe, W.J., *Ancient Tottenham*. The Percy Press, 1950, p108

• *Follow the path past the church (Church Path) and between fences through the cemetery to White Hart Lane.*

The cemetery contains the self-designed family tomb of Victorian architect William Butterfield, the prolific Gothic revival architect known for his polychrome brickwork and church restorations, who controversially remodelled All Hallows Church in the 1870s. It is also home to the grave of Ted Willis, writer of *Dixon of Dock Green* and, later, Labour peer.

Church Path drops distinctly downhill as it approaches the Moselle and crosses the river on a footbridge. After the bridge, detour to the left through the cemetery to see the point where the Moselle emerges from its culvert to flow above ground again in what Pinching and Dell describe as "a small ravine."[16]

Another stream joins at this point from the north, a tributary called the Lesser Moselle. This arrives from the west where, in the late 19th century, it flowed along both sides of White Hart Lane, rising in the vicinity of what is now helpfully called Rivulet Road, half a mile away back towards Wood Green. Just out of site there is also a large pond, fed by a spring, which flows into the Lesser Moselle. The pond and spring are in the former grounds of the Parsonage, a large Tudor mansion with, in the 1660s, a moat and 13 hearths. In the 1860s it was occupied by Colonel William Gillum, who commissioned Arts and Crafts architect Philip Webb to build him a cottage in the grounds, a replica of one in which he had taken refuge when wounded in the Crimean War. House and cottage were pulled down just before the First World War.

Rev. Bedwell mentions the "Byshops Well", the location of which has been lost. He describes it as "a spring issuing out of the side of an hill in a field opposite unto the vicarage, and falleth into the Mose" where, he claims, "Many ancient people do yet tell of many strang cures done vnto the diseased and impotent by the meanes of these waters."[17]

---

16 Pinching, Albert and Dell, David, *Haringey's Hidden Streams Revealed.* Hornsey Historical Society, 2005, p51

17 Bedwell, Rev. Wilhelm quoted in Roe, W.J., *Ancient Tottenham.* The Percy Press, 1950, pp113-114

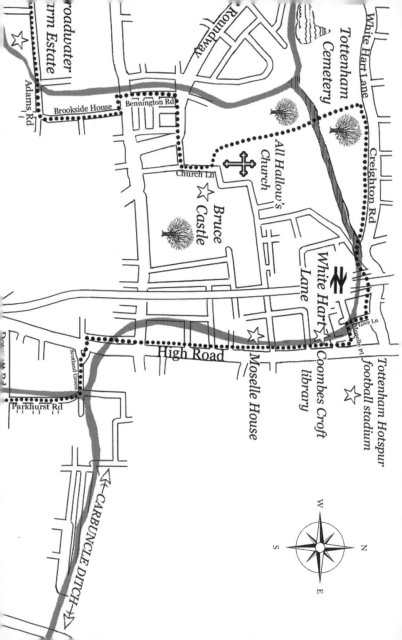

• *Turn right along White Hart Lane, continuing straight ahead across a mini-roundabout as it becomes Creighton Road.*

After it leaves the cemetery, the river turns right and then back on itself around the centre of Tottenham, the remainder of Rev. Bedwell's 'Omega'.

From White Hart Lane downstream through Tottenham, there have been persistent problems with flooding caused by the Moselle. Roe, writing in 1950, remembers flooding closing the railway line at White Hart Lane, and a curate from All Hallows rescuing a child from drowning in floodwaters on the road outside.

Tottenham is strongly linked with flooding, as recorded in a folk song called 'The Tottenham Toad', recorded in the Southern Appalachians in 1921 by collector Cecil Sharp where, like many traditional English songs, it had washed up with early settlers. It begins, "The Tottenham Toad came trotting up the road / With his feet all swimming in the sea." The Toad courts a "pretty little Squirrel" from Enfield, but their romance is interrupted by their constant need to cross the Moselle to see one another.

The Somerset Gardens Estate on the left was built on the site of the imposing mock Tudor Tottenham Grammar School, founded at a date before 1631 and closed in 1988. It was the alma mater of, amongst others, Thatcherite economic guru Lord Harris of High Cross and Mike Winters, of Mike and Bernie Winters comedy duo fame (Mike won a scholarship, Bernie did not).

Wedge House, the former offices of Percy Wedge & Co. at the roundabout, is pleasingly wedge-shaped. The Moselle crosses under White Hart Lane at this point, going straight on under the railway line while the road bears left.

• *After the railway bridge, turn right along Love Lane. Take the first left along Moselle Street, which becomes Moselle Place before reaching the High Road.*

At the junction with Love Lane new paving includes a swale, to absorb rainfall and reduce flooding, and a vent for the Moselle beneath.

The river crosses Love Lane after White Hart Lane Station, and flows to the left of Moselle Street behind Moselle House, the housing block on the left. Its course could be seen in the curving property boundaries north of Moselle Place until redevelopment in the 1960s. It then turns right under Moselle Place, before the junction with the High Road ahead, to flow under the west side of the main road.

The area between White Hart Lane Station and the High Road is the subject of a major redevelopment proposal, which would involve demolishing the housing blocks of the Love Lane Estate and rebuilding, with public space linking the station to the football ground. The football club seems determined to disassociate itself from White Hart Lane, and plans to have the station renamed 'Tottenham Hotspur'.

• *At the T-junction with the High Road, turn right.*

The part of the Moselle at the junction with White Hart Lane was culverted in 1836, earlier than many other parts of the river. The houses at this end of Tottenham date back to the early-18th century, built as out-of-town residences for well-off merchants when Tottenham was a village some way north, beyond the City of London.

It is impossible to miss the rebuilt Tottenham Hotspur football stadium, which was set back from the High Road before its lengthy reconstruction, but now looms over it. The scale of the stadium lays bare the difference between the neighbourhood club that occupied the previous stadium, and the global financial concern that it has become. It is argued that keeping the club in its traditional home is a price worth paying, but Spurs seem unconvinced that the neighbourhood is worthy of their investment, and have suggested the High Road should be upgraded to provide more appropriate surroundings. They echo the reported attitude of Roman Abramovich who, looking for a London club to buy, is said to have discounted Spurs after driving down Tottenham High Road and declaring it to be "worse than Omsk".

Opposite the stadium the precise course of the river, running parallel to the High Road in a culvert, can be determined in Coombes Croft Library. The library extension includes a glass panel in the floor to the right of the reception desk, which provides a view of the river running far below. This depends on whether the light installed in the shaft is working, which is not always the case, and whether you are willing to crawl on your hands and knees under the table the library has unhelpfully placed above it.

After the junction with Church Road, the 18th century Moselle House is set back from the main road. The open space in between, running alongside Tottenham High Road, was once occupied by the buried river.

Further along, the building on the left with a Whitbread clock tower is a remnant of the Bell Brewery, bought by Whitbread in 1896. The Victorian shops and flats opposite the brewery, on the other side of the High Road, are called Criterion Parade and were built over the Moselle in the 1880s. Where they end, a tiny stretch of the Moselle ran above ground in a gap between blocks at the end of the 19th century.

• *Continue along the road for half a mile. After the Lansdowne Road crossroads, take the next left into Scotland Green.*

The building on the corner of the High Road and Lansdowne Road, home at the time of writing to Sports Direct, became the symbol of the riots that broke out across London and then much of Britain in 2011. They began in Tottenham after a man called Mark Duggan was shot dead during a police stop at Tottenham Hale. On 6 August 2011 a protest marched from Broadwater Farm to Tottenham Police Station. A group of 300 people gathered and the situation was soon out of control. Police cars and a double-decker bus were set alight, and looting began on the High Road, in Tottenham Hale and Wood Green, continuing all night. The next night looting took place across London, and the following night all over the country. By the time the riots petered out on 10 August five people had died and more than 3,000 had been arrested, in Britain's worst recorded civil unrest. The corner building, then an Allied Carpets store, was shown repeatedly in flames on news footage. It was entirely destroyed, but was rebuilt after the riots and a close inspection is needed to see that this is now a replica of the original 1930 building.

On the other side of the crossroads, No.7 Bruce Grove has the only blue plaque in Tottenham, which commemorates the former home of

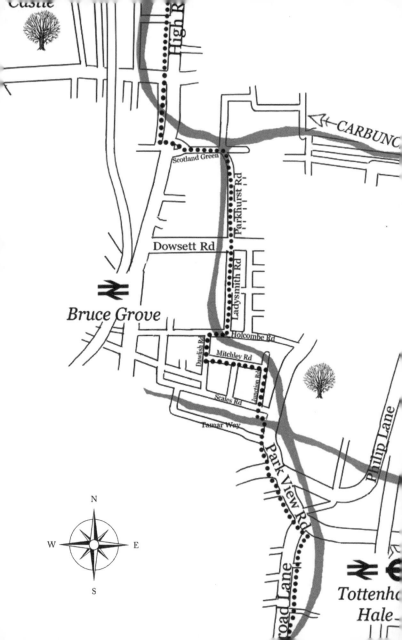

Castle

High Rd

← CARBUNC

Scotland Green

Parkhurst Rd

Dowsett Rd

Ladysmith Rd

Bruce Grove

Holcombe Rd

Dawlish Rd

Mitchley Rd

Scales Rd

Lancelin Rd

Tamar Way

Park View Rd

Philip Lane

Road Lane

Tottenho
Hale-

N
W   E
S

Luke Howard, 'namer of clouds'. Howard ran a pharmaceutical company in Stratford during the 19th century, but was an amateur meteorologist. He recorded the London weather in detail, and devised the system still in use for describing different cloud formations, which he based on natural history classification systems.

Scotland Green is another reference to the ever-present Bruce family. The point where the High Road meets Scotland Green there was a bridge over the Moselle. In the words of Rev. Bedwell this was "a great stone Bridge, where it suddenly maketh a right angle".[18] This was known as Lordship Bridge.

• *Turn first right along Parkhurst Road.*

Hartington Park was created in the 1970s, during the final throes of the slum clearance programme, by demolishing the late 19th century terraced housing on the site.

Where we turn right to follow the main course of the Moselle, Scotland Green continues ahead as Carbuncle Passage. This follows the course of the Carbuncle Ditch, a diversion of the Moselle running in a straight line from here into Pymmes Brook and the River Lea, three-quarters of a mile away. The Ditch is a 15th century flood relief channel, built to relieve the flooding upstream towards White Hart Lane. It was first recorded in the Middle Ages as Garbells Ditch, but its condition may have encouraged corruption of the name.

The river was controlled by sluice gates at Scotland Green until the 1830s, when they were removed. However, the river remained uncovered alongside Scotland Green until 1906 when it was arched over by, judging from a photograph of the works, a team of men with very large moustaches. Perhaps the decision to bury it was influenced by an event seven years earlier, when a bridge over the Ditch collapsed under the weight of several hundred people, who had gathered to watch a brewer's horse being rescued from the water. No-one was hurt, as the river was very shallow, but it was evidently getting in the way. According to Fred

---

18 Bedwell, Rev. Wilhelm quoted in Roe, W.J., *Ancient Tottenham*. The Percy Press, 1950, p104

Fisk, writing not long afterwards, "The Moselle, which ran at the side of the road, had been a great source of trouble and annoyance since time immemorial, not only to the residents, but to traffic in general."[19]

Carbuncle Ditch flows due east beneath Carbuncle Passage, an alleyway between the backs of houses. It then passes under the railway lines south of the Northumberland Park Victoria Line depot, before crossing Tottenham Marshes to Pymmes Brook. The latter is a tributary of the River Lea now channelled alongside the Lea Navigation. The Carbuncle Ditch still flowed above ground along its entire course at the end of the 19th century but is now almost all underground, except for a short stretch just before the railway at Northumberland Park. However, the outfall into Pymmes Brook can still be seen by peering through railings on the far side of the marshes.

• *Cross Dowsett Road and continue straight ahead along Ladysmith Road.*

To the right No.62 Dowsett Road, unlike the other houses on the street, has an archway where its front room should be, marking the point where the Moselle passes underneath.

The river continues under Ladybur Estate on the right (its name is a mash-up of Burbridge Way and Ladysmith Road), which is built on the site of the former Caoutchouc Company India Rubber Works. Pinching and Dell suggest the water of the Moselle may have been used by the factory, which had a landmark chimney 160 feet high, demolished in 1903. The river flowed above ground beside Ladysmith Road until the Second World War, when the housing estate replaced the factory.

• *At the T-junction turn right along Holcombe Road, then left along Dawlish Road.*

The space between the backs of houses on the left – those fronting on to Holcombe Road and those on to Mitchley Road – is unusually wide. This

---

19 Fisk, Fred, *The History of Tottenham*. Fred Fisk, 1913, p101

is because the Moselle turns sharp left at this point, running between the backs of the gardens.

• *Turn first left along Mitchley Road. At the end of the road, turn right along Junction Road.*

To the left, Junction Road extends to a gate which closes off a green lane between the back gardens of the houses. This is the route of the covered Moselle, placed underground along this section during the 1920s.

• *At the T-junction, turn left along Scales Road, and then right along Park View Road.*

On the right, a narrow alley between houses, Tamar Way, marks the point where a short tributary joins the Moselle from the vicinity of Tottenham Police Station on the High Road. The alley, which ran between the backs of 19th century terraces, follows the same route through the Chestnut Estate. The stream ran above ground beside the path, and the path still shadows its route. A culvert, the most recent of the many diversions that have been added to the Moselle, runs due west from the end of Tamar way to Pymmes Brook and the River Lea. This was built in 1968 as a further flood relief measure.

• *Turn left along Monument Way, then cross Hale Road and Ferry Lane via the lights to the right. Walk ahead along The Hale.*

Tottenham Hale was known as The Hale before it became connected to Tottenham by 19th century development. The hale was a hoist located at the point where goods were transferred to and from barges on the River Lea.

The novelist Stella Gibbons wrote of the immediate post-war period that "on the outskirts of the city, out towards Edmonton and Tottenham in the north... there was a strange feeling in the air, heavy and sombre and thrilling, as if History were working visibly before

one's eyes."[20] A new network of roads was powering north, and the age of the car had arrived but these same characteristics now weigh the area down. Road widening has eroded the centre, creating a series of semi-accessible islands, with an out-of-town shopping centre as if to prove this is no longer the city. This approach is now being rethought, and major redevelopment is coming to Tottenham Hale with high-rise residential blocks replacing the low-rise sheds. The busy gyratory remains, though, and it is not yet clear what sort of place the new Hale will be.

• *Cross Station Lane, then cross Ferry Lane at a three stage pelican crossing. Walk straight ahead along Broad Lane.*

The shooting of Mark Duggan, the event that sparked the 2011 riots, took place beyond Tottenham Hale Station on Ferry Lane, the road that leads to the River Lea crossing.

Beyond The Hale we enter South Tottenham, which retains something of the reputation for ordinariness that it clearly had in 1893, when George Gissing described it as a good place to find "a suitable house, very small and of a very low rental."[21]

• *Where Broad Lane turns to the right, turn left after the pub along Markfield Road. Follow Markfield Road under two railway bridges into Markfield Park.*

The Moselle flows to the left of Markfield Road under the industrial estate. The stretch through Tottenham Hale was placed underground in the early 1900s, but this section remained visible for longer. It was gradually covered over as factories expanded between the wars to occupy the space above it.

---

20 Gibbons, Stella, *Westwood*. Longmans, Green, 1946, p1
21 Gissing, George, *The Odd Women*. Penguin Classics, 1893 [1993], p138

• *Bear right, then left to cross Markfield Park and reach the River Lea.*

Markfield Park is partly a reclaimed sewage works, which accounts for the ghostly remnant cement structures that create an unusual atmosphere. This is the site of Tottenham Sewage Works, which operated for just over a century, closing in the early 1960s. The playing fields to the south opened in 1938 – one of the King George's Fields, a national project in memory of George V – but the area to the north, occupied by the sewage works, was derelict until it was incorporated into the park in the mid-2000s. Not only was the area filled with filter and precipitating beds to treat sewage, but it also incorporated a smallpox hospital, now completely demolished, on the car park beside the cafe.

The Markfield Park Beam Engine is less well known than the famed Crossness Pumping Station, on the other side of the Thames, but is an equally impressive piece of Victorian engineering with much decorative, painted ironwork. Powered by steam, it still operates on open days and dates from 1888 when the sewage works, a pioneering facility when it opened in 1852, was upgraded to prevent raw sewage entering the River Lea. Nowadays, sewage is pumped all the way to Beckton for treatment instead.

Unusually, at the very last minute just as the river reaches its end, another lost tributary comes on the scene. The Stonebridge Brook also flows into the Lea at Markfield Park, having come all the way from Crouch End, where it has its source behind Hornsey Town Hall. The Stonebridge, which is joined near the Seven Sisters Road by its own tributary, the Hermitage Brook, is the most obvious outlet in the park. It now flows under the centre of the park, and its outfall is at the exit to the Lea towpath.

The Moselle is more hidden but flows above ground beside the railway, around the northern edge of the park. Its outfall can be seen to the left along the towpath, beside the railway bridge. Before the sewage works were built, the Stonebridge Brook joined the Moselle just before it met the Lea, but the two were separated and the Brook diverted to the south. Writing in 1915, George Grocott claimed that the river "not long prior to 1856, could have claimed to be called 'The Sparkling Moselle', as even at the date I am describing it, it had a plentiful supply of fresh water, with abundance of fish in its upper parts. The River Lea, by this outlet, was a favourite spot for anglers as the tit-bits conveyed into the river through this stream, caused swarms of fish to congregate there."[22]

This is not so fanciful, given that Izaak Walton fished the waters of the Lea at Tottenham. His work *The Compleat Angler* begins with a scene in Tottenham, a meeting at the Tottenham High Cross between Pescator (a fisherman), Venator (a hunter) and Auceps (a falconer). After a day on the Lea during which Pescator wins Venator over to the art of fishing they return to the High Cross, which still survives on the High Road. Here they rest in "a sweet, shady arbour" where Venator thanks Pescator and "requites a part of your courtesies with a bottle of sack, milk, oranges, and sugar, which, all put together, make a drink like nectar".[23] Markfield Park can feel like a world apart, and in the right light the ghost of Walton and his companions lingers over the Moselle and the heavy 19th century engineering that shaped the industrial Lea Valley.

The Mannions Prince Arthur pub, back along the walk route at the corner of Markfield Lane, is a solid choice to toast the Moselle.

22 Grocott, George, *Hackney Fifty Years Ago*. Potter Bros, 1915, p53
23 Walton, Izaak, *The Compleat Angler*. Harrap, 1676 [1984], p218-219

Stamford Brook East

'*A complex network of streams spreads across Acton, Chiswick and Hammersmith, entering the Thames like a trident, at three different places.*'

Stamford Brook East

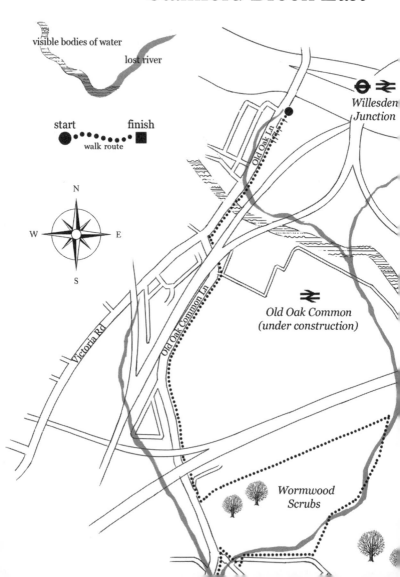

visible bodies of water

lost river

start ●•••••• finish ■

walk route

N
W — E
S

Old Oak Ln

Willesden
Junction

Victoria Rd

Old Oak Common Ln

Old Oak Common
(under construction)

Wormwood
Scrubs

Practicalities

Distance – 4 miles (Hammersmith Creek Route), 6½ miles (Parr Ditch Route)
Start – Webb Place, off Old Oak Common Lane
Getting there – Willesden Junction Station
End – Furnivall Gardens, Hammersmith (Hammersmith Creek Route); Thames Path at Chancellor's Road, Hammersmith (Parr Ditch Route)
Getting back – Ravenscourt Park Station (Hammersmith Creek Route) or Hammersmith Station (Parr Ditch Route)

Introduction

The eastern arm of Stamford Brook is part of the complex network of streams that spread across Acton, Chiswick and Hammersmith. This walk tracks the branch that rises close to Willesden Junction Station and flows south through East Acton into Stamford Brook, the neighbourhood named after the river. It then splits into two outfalls – Hammersmith Creek, formerly Hammersmith's miniature docklands, and the Parr Ditch which forms the edge of Hammersmith, its course in the shape of a reversed 'c'. The Stamford Brook East and West routes overlap, with a short, shared section in the Starch Green/Wendell Park area of Chiswick, before the river splits to enter the Thames like a trident, at three different places.

The eastern arm of the Stamford Brook is as significant in defining its part of London as the western arm. From the Grand Union Canal, close to its source, all the way to the Thames, the Parr Ditch route forms the western boundary of the modern Borough of Hammersmith and Fulham. The route of the Brook, from source to Thames, is also the boundary between the Boroughs of Ealing, to the west, and Hammersmith to the east. The Brook was the historic boundary between Acton and Hammersmith, although this has now been straightened out around Wormwood Scrubs. It previously followed the precise line of the buried river, cutting across the Willesden Junction railway yards and over Wormwood Scrubs.

The easternmost segment of the Brook is a sweeping watercourse called the Parr Ditch, which flows around Hammersmith. It is generally referred to as Parr's Ditch, but some sources call it the Parr Ditch. Either way, the identity of Parr is lost, but the name suggests that the stream may have been co-opted by a landowner for drainage or, more specifically, as the local sewer. It may even have been an entirely man-made channel, although its role in defining the area suggests it is of long standing.

Route

• *Starting point: Webb Place, off Old Oak Lane.*

At the corner of Webb Place, between No.7 and the railway wall, is a drain cover, and the sound of rushing water can be heard coming from below. The drain, and the street, occupy the site of a stream marked on maps from the 1870s running beside Old Oak Common Lane. It originates somewhere just to the north of Webb Place, on a site now obscured by railway lines. This is the main source for the buried eastern arm of the Stamford Brook. Little ponds and springs were scattered around the junction, but the largest was squeezed between the road and the railway embankment, just to the south of Webb Place.

At the time, the surrounding area featured virtually nothing beyond a spaghetti junction knot of tracks at Willesden Junction, surrounded by fields. The nearest houses were at the villages of Harlesden Green to the north and East Acton to the south, beyond the edges of London which only reached as far as Kensal Green to the west. Willesden Junction was, and to some extent still is, a place of magnificent isolation.

Willesden Junction is an infamously baffling station. Originally called Holsden (an earlier version of Harlesden) its current name is unhelpful, with Willesden a mile from the station and Harlesden located in between. It opened in 1866, and the combination of five low-level platforms and two separate sets of high-level ones, led to its becoming known as 'Bewildering Junction'. William Morris wrote to his daughter May, advising "*put yourselves in a cab*" [Morris's italics] rather than attempt to navigate Willesden Junction, "as it is a mere trap for the unwary, everything is arranged so that you shall miss your trains there; there are scarcely any men about, & what there are refuse to answer questions."[1] In 1912 more low-level platforms were added creating another station, Willesden Junction New, that was both part of and separate from Willesden Junction.

---

1 Henderson, Philip, *William Morris: His Life, Work and Friends.* HarperCollins, 1986, p131

The station was also surrounded by an increasing acreage of carriage sheds and sidings. The area became dominated by the railway and it still is, but the station has lost some of its presence if none of its complexity. The original main line platforms and the entrance buildings on Old Oak Common Lane disappeared in the 1960s when the West Coast Main Line was electrified, leaving a strange gap.

Nevertheless, the bridge at Willesden Junction is a potent London location. The view of the railway marshalling yards, described by Iain Sinclair as a "flood pool of railway tracks",[2] was painted in the 1960s and 1970s by London painter Leon Kossoff. His works are "triumphs of inhibited spontaneity, elemental forces choked back by the broken ribs of cancelled strokes, weighed down under a curtain of solid smoke".[3]

• *Turn left out of Webb Place along Old Oak Lane. Cross Old Oak Lane at the pedestrian island and walk ahead along an unmarked alley between houses. Turn left along Goodhall Street.*

The Victorian houses here, and on Old Oak Common Lane, are known as the Island Triangle, with railways on three sides and the Grand Union Canal on the fourth. They were built for London and North Western Railway workers, while the managers lived on a different island at Wells House Road. Some of the houses were squatted in the 1980s, but the terraces of Goodhall Street and Stephenson Street, beyond, have become a favourite location for filmmakers looking for archetypally English housing within easy reach of central London. No.45 Stephenson Street is 'Our House' in the video for the single by Madness, while the exterior of No.68 Goodhall Street appears in Pulp's 1995 'Common People' video. The Triangle has also supplied post-industrial dereliction and appears in several films, from *The Ipcress File* (1965) to David Cronenberg's *Spider* (2003), in which the camera pans from the houses on one side to the railway yards on the other.

2 Sinclair, Iain, *London Overground*. Hamish Hamilton, 2015, p178
3 ibid, p189

• *At the T-junction, turn left along Channel Gate Road, then right into Old Oak Lane.*

The stream flowed beside Old Oak Common Lane to the canal, at which point it turned sharp left. Further to the east, right in the middle of the railway sheds and sidings, another pond was the source for a tributary stream. It flowed south to meet the main branch of the Brook near Hythe Road, just before the Brook plunges under the Grand Union Canal. As there is no public access through the railway depots on the south side of the canal, the walking route continues along Old Oak Lane, picking the route of the stream up again on Wormwood Scrubs.

A small cluster of ponds beside the canal, shown on 1870s maps, were in fact lagoons belonging to a naphtha works. Naphtha was a fuel oil used in lamps and stoves, made by processing coal gas with india rubber and gutta-percha. It was a particularly noxious process, which is why the factory was remarkably isolated with nothing closer than Willesden Junction Station, and the nearest house half a mile away.

The British Railways Hotel was demolished for the construction of Channel Gate Road which, as its name suggests, was built to access the North Pole depot used by Eurostar trains serving the Channel Tunnel when they departed from Waterloo. When the route switched to St Pancras Eurostar moved out, and it is now a work site for the High Speed 2 railway (HS2).

• *Cross the Grand Union Canal.*

The Collective, which occupies a large grey box beside the canal, is a product of London's housing crisis, renting student-sized rooms to people who are not necessarily students.

Old Oak Common was originally called Old Holt Wood but, by 1590, the trees had been cleared and the land was scrub, although oaks are said to have remained along field boundaries until the early 19th century. The original wood was the northern part of a wide area of oaks which extended across Acton during the Middle Ages. Despite local resistance it was eventually enclosed in 1862, when a landowner argued

successfully that he was entitled to fence it because common use of the land had arisen through 'a blunder'.

Although still described as Old Oak Common, the area is almost entirely occupied by railway yards and the former Rolls Royce factory at Hythe Road which is now, along with most of the immediate neighbourhood, owned by the second-hand car dealer Car Giant. It is planned that this will become the centre of a new town next to Old Oak Common Station. A small patch of woodland does exist on the south side of the canal beside the railway site, although the trees are post-Second World War. The boundary of the wood is shaped by the underground course of the Brook which flows along its edge.

• *At the mini-roundabout bear left to continue along Old Oak Common Lane.*

After the railway bridge, the land ahead drops away into what is already become the valley of the river. Housing, under construction at the time of writing, is filling a pocket of land between railway lines that was previously the site of the enormous British Railways Hostel which, at least in photographs, resembled a prison.

Further along to the left, Old Oak Common Station is due to open in 2026. As the only meeting point between HS2 and the Elizabeth Line, it is expected to become one of the busiest stations in Britain. A less likely location would be hard to find, as the future station site is surrounded by an area where remarkably few people live for central London. This will change on a spectacular scale, if plans to build a new town to go with the station are fulfilled. High rise housing is beginning to appear, and much more is proposed, possibly served by new Overground Stations on Old Oak Common Lane and Hythe Road. Until then, Old Oak Common Lane feels very much on the wrong side of the tracks.

To the right, in front of what will soon be the main station entrance, is Wells House Road, with a hand-made oak symbol on the corner house. The road, which is raised above the main road because of the slope down into the valley of the Brook, was built for railway managers. Its houses are larger than those of the Island Triangle, and the road is even more of an island, surrounded by railways on all sides with two access points. A station called Old Oak Halt, on a site between Wells House Road and the first railway bridge to the south, closed in 1947 but was for railway staff use only.

It was built on the site of Wells House, a remnant of the Acton Wells spa. A tributary stream flowed south-east from the site of the Wells to meet the main Stamford Brook a little further along.

Also called Old Oak Wells, it is first mentioned in the early 1600s. The water which came from three wells was said to be sweet, unlike Epsom water, which was salty, but still packed powerful purgative properties. As spas became popular during the 1700s Acton Wells gained customers, who bought its water which was sold across London, and attended its assembly room. For a time the spa even boasted a racecourse. Spas lost their appeal in the 19th century and generally disappeared. By the 1870s the site was marked on maps in the Gothic script used for lost antiquities. The assembly rooms were demolished in 1902, having been used as a farmhouse and as a school.

• *Just before the railway bridge marked 'Low Bridge' cross to the right-hand side of the road at the island, as there is no pavement on the left. After the bridge cross back again at pedestrian lights and continue along Old Oak Common Lane. Turn left into Wormwood Scrubs at the first gap in the fence, to follow a tarmacked path.*

Wormwood Scrubs provides a sense of how Old Oak Common once looked. It was also originally oak woodland: Worm Holt Wood. Until the 1980s, the section of the Scrubs closest to the Lane was described as Old Oak Common, and the larger part to the east was labelled Wormwood Scrubs, but this distinction seems to have disappeared. The Stamford Brook flowed above ground over the Scrubs until the 1920s, when it was culverted. Its course is now very difficult to discern on the ground, but this walk crosses the Scrubs to the point where the Brook emerges from under the railway. The walk then follows the Brook south-west across the common, using paths that run close to the line of the Brook.

• *Where the path turns left, continue ahead across the grass, bearing left. Keep left to walk alongside the railway embankment.*

Wormwood Scrubs remains undeveloped because it was reserved for military exercises, first used by the 36th Middlesex (Paddington) Rifle Volunteer Corps from 1860. Rifle ranges were built on what is now the Linford Christie Stadium and, later, an early aircraft hangar as the common became a landing ground. For some time after the First World War it was used as Wormwood Scrubs Naval Air Station.

• *Continue, passing a model aircraft warning sign, to the point where the path curves right around a thicket of thorns. Turn right immediately after the thicket along a grass track. Where it meets the main path turn left. Shortly after, double back to the right along another path that joins the main path at an acute angle.*

The turrets of HM Prison Wormwood Scrubs are visible on the far side of the common. The prison is likely to close in the next few years, conditions having been repeatedly condemned by Her Majesty's Inspectorate of Prisons. The first prison, a corrugated iron structure which opened in 1874, was replaced by a permanent brick building constructed by selected prisoners. It has housed a number of celebrated prisoners including composer Ivor Novello, who was made an example of during the Second World War, sentenced to four weeks for misusing petrol coupons. During the war the prison also housed MI8c, the Radio Security Service, which tracked enemy agents, and MI8d, which was the Chief Cable Censorship Department.

Russian spy George Blake was sprung in 1966 after four years inside, using the straightforward method of climbing through a window and over the perimeter wall, using a rope ladder thrown over by three ex-inmates. They then smuggled him across the Channel in a camper van. Former Labour MP and Postmaster General John Stonehouse served his sentence in the Scrubs, having been extradited from Australia where he had fled after faking his own death to escape a fraud investigation. On his release he joined the Social Democratic Party.

• *At the edge of the Scrubs, turn right, then left at the next gap in the trees to exit on to Braybrook Street.*

There seems to be no link between Braybrook Street's name and Stamford Brook. However, a tributary stream joins the Brook at this point, flowing from Acton Wells. It meets the Stamford Brook at the point where the railway bridge now crosses. In the late 19th century there was a small basin on the right-hand side of Old Oak Common Lane, and a short stretch close to the road appears to have been used by industries along its banks. This section of stream vanished when the Central Line was built in the 1910s.

Braybrook Street, which is clearly in East Acton, is known for the so-called Shepherd's Bush Murders that took place here in 1966. Three policemen were shot dead when they stopped a van that had parked suspiciously close to the prison. The three men inside were not, in fact, organising an escape but they were armed criminals who seem to have panicked at being caught carrying guns. The killings caused outrage but the leader, Harry Roberts, also became the darkest of folk heroes. He was released on licence in 2014 after 48 years in jail, by then the only survivor of the Braybrook Street shootings. A granite police memorial commemorates the murdered policemen.

• *Turn right along Braybrook Street. At the T-junction turn right on to Wulfstan Street. Shortly afterwards, turn left along Old Oak Lane.*

'At the junction of Wulfstan Street and Old Oak Common Lane, the author saw water gushing from an inspection cover in late 2018, suggesting the confluence of the Brook and its tributary is barely contained beneath the pavement. The joint stream flows under the main road towards the Westway, ahead.

The Old Oak Estate is an early London County Council Estate, built partly just before the First World War, with a second section built in the 1920s. Heavily influenced by the urban cottages of Hampstead Garden Suburb, it was initially known as the Acton Wells Estate. It surrounds East Acton tube station which opened in 1920. On the opposite side of Old Oak Common Lane, 'Homes for Heroes' houses were built by the Ministry of Health in 1920 to demonstrate new construction techniques. They include concrete 'Selfridge' houses, named after Selfridge's Oxford Street store which was the first reinforced concrete building in London.

Like Braybrook Street, Norbroke Street on the left does not seem to be connected to the lost river, although it sounds as though it should be. It probably relates to the Northbrokes, which were the northern areas of the manors of Palingswick and Gunnersbury, to the south.

• *Follow Old Oak Lane until it reaches the junction with the Westway. Cross both carriageways at the lights and continue straight ahead along Old Oak Road (not to be confused with Old Oak Common Lane, to the right).*

Before the First World War, the Brook ran above ground beside Old Oak Common Lane, through what is now the centre of the enormous crossroads with the Westway, diving under the island of terraced houses on the other side.

On the far side of the Westway, to both left and right, new buildings are filling what was, for nearly 20 years, a derelict strip. In the 1990s 150 houses and offices on this side of the road were demolished amid great controversy, in preparation for widening the A40. In 1997 the incoming Labour government cancelled the Conservatives' road building programme, leaving the Westway in limbo.

The first street to the right, East Acton Lane, was the only street in East Acton until after the First World War. London rapidly filled the spaces around what was a small, isolated village with a few large houses, fewer small ones and the East Acton Stud Farm, which dominated the village centre. Building of the tube station north of the Westway shifted the centre of East Acton, and the lane has lost any sense that it was a high street. The Brook flows across open ground to the right after this turning, then follows the line of Old Oak Road.

Streets to the left are named after plants, some of which are surprisingly dangerous (Hemlock Road, Yew Tree Road, Sundew Avenue). This area is the Wormholt Estate, also a garden city-inspired design, built from 1919 to relieve the crowded slums of Hammersmith.

Look along Armstrong Road to the right, beside the redundant 1930s church, for a glimpse at the very end of the "ultra-austere"[4] former Ministry of Pensions building, which looks suspiciously like the model for the Ministry of Truth.

• *Follow Old Oak Road for ½ mile until it reaches a crossroads with Uxbridge Road/ The Vale. Cross and turn right along The Vale.*

Stamford Brook seems to have flowed briefly along The Vale to the right, before turning south, which is the course of the borough boundary. However, the picture is clouded by the presence of a channel, which can be seen on maps from the 1860s, running along the north side of The Vale (then Uxbridge Road) from the Old Oak Common Lane junction to the railway bridge, three quarters of a mile away. Pumps were located at various points along its route, and it is possible that this was a diversion of the Stamford Brook providing Acton with drinking water. This would explain why its course across Uxbridge Road is not apparent, but the river does appear again a little further on.

To the right on the Vale is the former Newman Hire Company building. The firm, now based in Hayes, hires props for 'Film, Television, Theatre, Exhibition and Photography'. They boast cheerfully that "Michael Gambon's dead body in Gosford Park was lit by our table lamps".[5]

• *Take the first left along St Elmo Road.*

The Stamford Brook now enters Starch Green, an area that has retained the name of the village that was once at its centre, although it is now indistinguishable from the surrounding Hammersmith streets. Although there were laundries in the area, the name goes back to the 17th century, and may have referred to a green used for drying washing, although this is not clear.

---

4 Cherry, Bridget & Pevsner, Nikolaus, *London 3: North West. Buildings of England*. Penguin Books, 1991, p158
5 http://www.newmanprophire.co.uk/AboutNewmanPropHire.aspx

The river flowed along the right-hand side of the road and then, at the junction with Jeddo Road ahead, made a sharp turn to the right passing around the boundaries of a large nursery which occupied the site until the late 19th century.

• *Turn second right along Jeddo Road.*

The borough boundary follows the line of the stream to the right, behind the buildings on Jeddo Road. A gated alleyway between the backs of the houses runs along the Brook's precise route but is, unfortunately, inaccessible to the public.

Titian Studio on the right is a specialised restorer of historic furniture, the people to call if you have a Chippendale, a Sheraton or a Hepplewhite in need of attention. The converted building next to it is the Old Laundry, the last evidence of the laundry district. In the 1880s the large Peal's boot factory was on the street which, the Booth Survey commented, produced "boots made by machinery to look like handsewn".[6]

• *Continue to follow Jeddo Road as it turns left and becomes Lefroy Road.*

The Brook continues straight ahead, but the walk turns left with the streets, picking up the river again at Emlyn Road.

The streets between here and Askew Road, to the east, were the Starch Green small laundry district in the late 19th century, as recorded by the Booth Survey. Its notes summed up the area, where four rooms were home to two entire families, as "small employers giving work to 9 or 10 women & 4 or 5 men, who are drivers, dollymen, labourers; washerwomen very independent; careless of their children; drink much beer; noisy; relations loose but not for hire."[7]

6 Booth/B/361 p3
7 Booth/B/361 p3

• *Turn right along Cobbold Road.*

The Brook crosses Larden Road to the right and then flows behind houses and under the new development to meet Stamford Brook West at Warple Way. The two streams then flow together for a relatively short distance to Stamford Brook Road, where they split. The next section follows the combined route, also included in Chapter 9: Stamford Brook West, and then stays with Stamford Brook East as the streams diverge.

Combined Route: Stamford Brook East and West

• *Turn first left along Emlyn Road.*

The Stamford Brook continues along Warple Way a little further before turning east to cross Emlyn Road, after the junction with Wendell Road. A stink pipe can be seen next to an alleyway between Nos.64 and 66, marking the point where the Brook crosses. There is no through route, so the walk continues along Emlyn Road.

The borough boundary between Hounslow and Hammersmith and Fulham used to follow the route of the Brook precisely from Canham Road to the Thames, so precisely that No.65 Emlyn Road was divided in half. The boundary was rationalised in 1994 and is now less exacting, running to the west of Emlyn Road, but it still follows the Brook for much of its course.

• *Turn second right along Palgrave Road, then right at the T-junction along Hartswood Road.*

The Brook runs behind houses on Hartswood Road, before crossing under the street a little way to the left and passing under the back gardens of the houses on the other side to reach Stamford Brook Road. No.19 Hartswood Road, which has a pond and fountain in its front garden, is

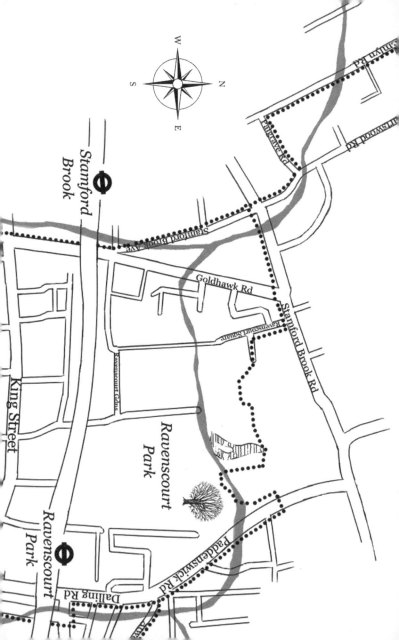

on the route of the stream. A valley is visible where Hartswood Road meets Stamford Brook Road.

• *Cross Stamford Brook Road via the zebra crossing, and continue straight ahead along Stamford Brook Avenue.*

The green space to the right, Stamford Brook Common, is the first appearance of the lost river's preferred name. The river crosses the main road at Stamford Bridge, and the bridge was located to the left of the junction with Hartswood Road. The two newer houses at Nos. 18 and 20 fill what was once a gap, marking the route of the river.

The Common, now separate, was part of a continuous band of open land that connected to the west via Turnham Green and Acton Common. It was later surrounded by houses in one of which – an 18th century villa called The Brook to the left – the Camden Town group painter Lucien Pissarro lived from 1901 until his death in 1944. The son of the impressionist Camille Pissarro, he had his studios in the building which is marked with a blue plaque.

Stamford Bridge is also the name for the point where the neighbouring lost river to the east, Counter's Creek (Chapter 4), crosses Fulham Road, and for the neighbouring Chelsea FC ground. The two rivers and the bridges are unconnected, but close enough to cause regular mix-ups.

The Brook passes between the houses of Stamford Brook Avenue and those on Goldhawk Road, to the left. From Stamford Brook Common to the River Thames, the line of the buried Brook forms the boundary between Chiswick and Hammersmith, with the boroughs of Hounslow to the west and Hammersmith and Fulham to the east.

The two branches of the Stamford Brook also part company again behind the Stamford Brook Avenue houses, where a branch of the stream turns sharply to the east. It crosses Goldhawk Road between Nos. 354 and 352, heading towards Ravenscourt Park. The Hammersmith Creek Route, below, picks up this branch of the stream, while the Chiswick Route follows the main Stamford Brook West branch to the Thames.

• *Cross Goldhawk Road at the roundabout and turn next right into Ravenscourt Square. Turn first left along Ravenscourt Square to enter Ravenscourt Park.*

Stamford Brook flows behind the houses on the right-hand side of Goldhawk Road where the borough boundary also runs. A branch then departs from Stamford Brook West, crossing Goldhawk Road and running along the route of Invermead Close. As this is a dead end, the walk takes the next turning to the right to meet the river again.

The Brook crosses Ravenscourt Square further ahead, past the left turn into Ravenscourt Park, where it can be spotted under a drain cover. In the 1860s it ran above ground along the park boundary, confidently labelled 'Stamford Brook (west branch)' on Ordnance Survey maps. It is not clear what the eastern branch was thought to be, as it is not labelled anywhere.

The river was culverted in the 1880s when the park opened to the public. It had been the grounds of a lost medieval manor house, Paddenswick House, which was surrounded by a moat. The park lake is said to be the remains of this moat and would have been fed by the Stamford Brook, until it was incorporated into the sewer system.

Paddenswick Manor, then Palingswick, was the house of Alice Perrers, mistress of Edward III. The daughter of an Essex tiler, she entered the service of Philippa, Edward's Queen, when she was 18. By the time the Queen died in 1469 she was the King's mistress. She rose quickly to a position of great wealth and power, becoming the richest woman in the country, and making many jealous. Stories circulated that she used her influence over the King for her own profit and bribed judges. According to the *Chronicon Angliae* she was accused in Parliament of employing a magician: "Yt was tolde in the parlement, that the sayed Ales had a long tyme kepte with her a certayne freir of the order of St. Dominike [prechers] whoe in outwarde show professed physicke, and practised the sayme arte, but he was a magician, geven to wycked enchauntementes, by whose experiments Ales allued the Kynge to her unlawfull love, or els, as I may trulyer say, into madness."[8] The magician in question was

---

8 Translated in Bird, James & Norman, Philip, eds., *Survey of London: Volume 6, Hammersmith*. London County Council, 1915, p98-113

later arrested at Palingswick by two noblemen who arrived in disguise, bearing urine samples, and entrapped him into to taking money to "cure infirmities". Just before Edward's death in 1477, he was persuaded to pass a law against women who exercised undue influence over 'the king's court'. Alice then had her property, including Palingswick, seized by the Sheriff of London and was briefly exiled. However, she returned to see the King on his deathbed where, according to the *Chronicon Angliae*, she stripped the rings from his fingers.

Ravenscourt Park is named after a Regency manor, Ravenscourt House, which belonged to Thomas Corbett whose coat of arms included a raven as a pun on his name (corbeau being French for raven). Built in 1812 its landscaped gardens, now the park, were designed by Humphry Repton who was famed for gardens from Woburn Abbey to Russell Square. It was being used as a library when it burned to the ground during the Blitz.

Nicholas Royle reports that, in the late 1990s, west London magus J.G. Ballard could occasionally be sighted in the park, some distance from his Shepperton home territory. [9]

• *Bear right and then turn left on tarmacked paths to cross a playing area and then past the lake, on the right. Loop around the lake to the right. Turn left at the two cedar trees, left again, and then right to exit the park on to Paddenswick Road.*

The ex-moat, now lake, disappears under the path and leaves the park, passing under the walled garden beside the path. It then turns right with Paddenswick Road.

• *Turn right along Paddenswick Road.*

In the 1860s, the triangle of land between Paddenswick Road and Dalling Road was Paddenswick Green, the village green of a small settlement in the process of becoming surrounded by new housing. The District Line to the south brought new access and development that linked up hamlets

9 Royle, Nicholas, Do You Remember Derek Marlowe?, in: *Time Out London Walks Volume One*. Time Out Guides Ltd, 1998, p262

beyond Hammersmith. At the junction with Dorville Crescent a house stood on its own on the course of the Brook, with a well and a small pond. Closer to the junction with Dalling Road there was also a Pump House.

To the right, behind a red pillarbox on the corner with Ravenscourt Road, is a tall, elegant, grey stink pipe indicating the river beneath.

Further along, the Thatched House pub and the junction with Dalling Road mark the point where the Brook splits again. The Parr Ditch route, below, follows the course of the river as it loops to the left. The Hammersmith Creek route follows the branch that continues straight ahead to the Thames.

Route: Hammersmith Creek

• *Continue to follow Paddenswick Road. Just before the railway viaduct, turn left along Glenthorne Road. Turn first right on to Studland Street.*

After the Parr Ditch separated to the left, the river flowed along the left-hand side of Paddenswick Road and then to the left on Studland Street. The back fences of the buildings still follow the line of the Brook. It then crossed under King Street ahead.

• *Follow Studland Street to the junction with King Street. Cross King Street on the zebra crossing to the right and continue ahead along Nigel Playfair Avenue.*

On the right, the 'Welcome to Chiswick' sign marks the boundary between the boroughs of Hammersmith and Fulham and Brentford which follows this branch of the Brook.

The place where the Brook crosses King Street, the main road through Hammersmith, was the 'Stamford', probably a stony or sandy ford, from which an entire system of watercourses takes its name. On the opposite side of King Street, to the right, is the Hampshire Hog pub. The alley beside it – Hampshire Hog Lane – used to be called the Warple Way. It was a 'warple' or alleyway, running beside the Brook. However, this end of the river does not seem to have been known as the Warple. Instead, the final stretch leading to the Thames was called Hammersmith Creek.

Until the 1930s, Hammersmith Creek was navigable from King Street to the Thames, a short distance ahead, and was used by Thames sailing barges. It was an industrial area known as Little Wapping, with a small but concentrated selection of riverside activities. The Creek was filled in 1936, the wharves having already closed, and the new Hammersmith Town Hall was built astride the river, which was channelled into an enormous pipe.

The town hall complex now combines the 1930s building at the back with a brutalist extension at the front, built on the original gardens in the 1970s, joined by a maze of multiple walkways. Two vast heads of Old Father Thames, one of which features on the cover of this book, are carved into the steps at the river end of the Town Hall, giving it the appearance of a water gate opening on to the ever-flowing Great West Road.

Nigel Playfair Avenue is named after the actor-manager, who ran the Lyric Theatre, Hammersmith. He had died in 1934, shortly before work began on the Town Hall. On the right-hand side the cinema built at the same time at the Town Hall, originally the Regal, later the ABC, was demolished in 2017. This site and the car park beyond were occupied by industrial waterside buildings before the Creek was filled, including malt houses belonging to the Town Brewery, and boat builders.

• *Take the subway to cross under the Great West Road. On the other side, walk straight ahead across Furnivall Gardens to the River Thames.*

Furnivall Gardens is named after Dr Frederick Furnivall, who was a philologist and co-founder of the Oxford English Dictionary, but also a rowing enthusiast. He campaigned for gender equality in rowing, founding the Hammersmith Sculling Club for Girls. He rowed from Hammersmith to Richmond and back every Sunday until his death in 1910, at the age of 81.

The open space was created by the demolition of Little Wapping after the Second World War. The Town Hall was untouched, but V1 bombs landed on either side, including one that destroyed the remaining riverside buildings. The small neighbourhood had been an island of older buildings, with picturesque 17th century cottages and wharves around the mouth of the Creek, as well as uncompromising industry in the form of the Phoenix Lead Mills. The path to the right continued, crossing the Creek mouth on a wooden bridge called the High Bridge. Its location is marked by the circular flower bed.

Dove Pier, which is now used by a small houseboat community, was built for the Festival of Britain in 1951. It provided a passenger steamer service to the Festival sites at Battersea Park and on the South Bank. This only lasted as long as the Festival and afterwards the pier was bought by the owner of the Dove pub, next door. It now belongs to the boat dwellers.

Further to the right past the gardens is Kelmscott House, home of writer and artist William Morris and the house he advised his daughter to reach by cab. His private printing house, Kelmscott Press, was based a few doors along the road. Another Arts and Crafts printer was based at No.1 Hammersmith Terrace, a street away, from the 1890s. Dove's Press was owned by two artists – T.J. Cobden-Sanderson (a friend of Morris) and Emery Walker – who produced classics of the printer's art, including the Dove Bible printed using their Doves Type lettering. However, the partners fell out and Cobden-Sanderson destroyed the typeface to prevent Walker from inheriting it. From 1916 he made what he claimed were 170 night-time trips to Hammersmith Bridge, where he secretly dropped the heavy metal blocks into the Thames. Astonishingly, these were recovered from the river bed by divers in 2015 and the typeface has now been reassembled.

The outfall, to the left of the pier directly ahead, is marked with a concrete pillbox stacked on the river wall. Peering over the wall and around the corner, a Thames Water sign can be seen warning of a storm outlet. Below, the culverted Creek still cuts a path through the mud to the Thames.

Hammersmith Creek is right next to the Dove, one of the most famous riverside pubs in London. Turn right to find it in an alley beside Furnivall Gardens.

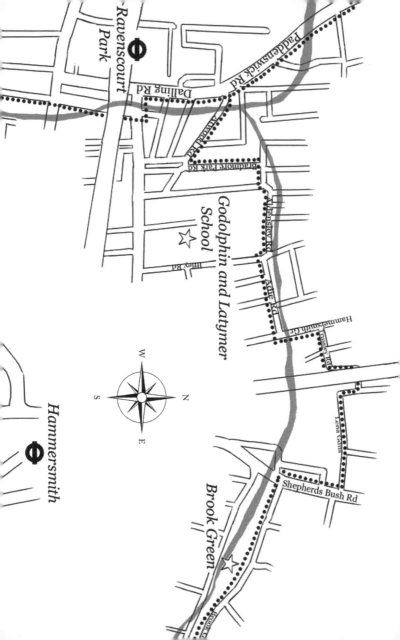

Route: The Parr Ditch

• *After the Thatched House pub, turn left to cross Dalling Road on the zebra crossing. Turn right on the other side, and then first left along Atwood Road.*

The turning is marked by a landmark green stink pipe where another branch of the Stamford Brook, the Parr Ditch, flows to the east. It is not clear how much of this stream is a man-made drainage channel, but the upper reaches appear natural on late 19th century maps. The Ditch flows across Dalling Road and south of Furber Street, but there is no through route on foot, so the walk diverts along Atwood Road.

• *Take the second left along Bradmore Park Road.*

The walk route returns to the course of the Ditch at the top of Bradmore Park Road, which is named after Bradmore Farm. The stream ran through its fields until covered over for housing in the 1880s.

• *At the junction with Brackenbury Road, turn right along Aldensley Road.*

At the junction of Aldensley Road and Carthew Road there is a tall grey stink pipe. This is roughly where the buildings of Bradmore Farm were located while the next turning on the right, Banim Street, is the route of the farm drive which bridged the river at the junction with Aldensley Road. The rear boundaries of the gardens to the right follow the line of the river. Tabor Road, to the left, has recently has a sewer upgrade from Thames Water to prevent the stream flooding basement flats.

Godolphin and Latymer Girls' School is also behind the houses, an independent school that used to be a boys' state school. Next door on Banim Street, the controversial West London Free School, fronted by Toby Young, was the first of an experimental approach to school funding introduced by David Cameron's Coalition government.

• *At the T-junction, turn right on Iffley Road and immediately left along Adie Road.*

A tall grey stink pipe is at the junction of Adie Road and Iffley Road, and another at the junction of Overstone Road.

The neighbourhood is a classic example of property industry branding, often referred to by estate agents as Brackenbury Village.

• *At the T-junction turn left on to Hammersmith Grove. Turn first right along Trussley Road.*

The Ditch continues straight ahead under houses and then the railway, while the walk diverts to the left to pass under the tracks.

• *Follow Trussley Road as it turns left and then right to pass under the railway viaduct. Turn right into Sulgrave Road and continue to follow it as it turns left and becomes Lena Gardens.*

The river flows under the Tesco supermarket to the right, which was the home of the Brook Green Works belonging to the Osram Lamp Factory. In operation for a century until demolition in 1988, the company broke the Edison hold on incandescent bulbs with a new patent system. The factory's dome with Osram Lamps signs remains.

• *At the T-junction turn right along Shepherd's Bush Road. Cross at the pelican crossing, turn right on the other side and then left along Brook Green.*

The long, thin Brook Green, was landscaped as a park in the 1880s, and reflects the course of the river running below. It curls to the south east, the start of the Parr Ditch's unusual course which takes it back round on itself to reach the Thames. The parish boundary and, before it was reformed, the boundary between the Hammersmith North and Hammersmith South constituencies, ran along the middle of Brook Green, and followed the curving line of the Parr Ditch all the way to the Thames.

In the 1930s, before the new Hammersmith Town Hall was built over Hammersmith Creek, plans to build it on Brook Green were strongly opposed by residents.

St Paul's School on the left has a plaque commemorating Gustav Holst, who was director of music in the early 20th century and wrote his *Brook Green Suite* while teaching at the school. The school was built on the grounds of The Grange, the house of champion Victorian actor Henry Irving.

A small tributary joined the Ditch from the left, flowing between Caithness Road and Aynhoe Road. It flowed down from Blythe Road, a little way to the north, which was also known as Blinde Lane and was said, in the 1830s, to be almost impassable in winter conditions.

• *Continue to follow the north side of Brook Green all the way to Hammersmith Road.*

At the far end of the Green, a large, round, elaborate drain cover covers the river which runs beneath.

At this point another lost river, Counter's Creek (Chapter 4) runs only ⅓ mile to the west, on the far side of the Olympia Exhibition Centre.

• *Cross at the lights, turn right on the other side, then left along Edith Road.*

The Parr Ditch was also known as the Black Bull Ditch, after the inn that it ran beside on the south side of Talgarth Road. It was replaced by the red brick Gothic buildings on the right, designed by Alfred Waterhouse. They were built for St Paul's School, which had relocated from the Cathedral and are now a hotel. While the girls' school remains at Brook Green, the boys' is now across the Thames in Barnes.

• *Follow Edith Road as it becomes Gliddon Road.*

The Ditch runs to the right of Edith Road, under the huge 1970s Hammersmith College complex. On the far side of the College is

Great Church Lane, which was another of the warples to be found in Hammersmith.

• *Cross Talgarth Road at the lights and continue along Gliddon Road.*

At the junction a green stink pipe marks the point where the Ditch crosses. Talgarth Road was built in the 1960s, an expressway carrying the A4 over the Hammersmith Flyover before it becomes the Great West Road, with the demolition of most of the houses between the road and the District Line, ahead. However, St Paul's Studios on the far side of Talgarth Road survived. The houses, with double-height north-facing windows, were designed by Frederick Wheeler as purpose-built artists' studios in a setting that was then much more rural. Later, Margot Fonteyn lived at No.149, with the Sadler's Wells Ballet School in the adjacent building.

To the right, the space created by road widening was eventually occupied by the Ark, the office block designed by Ralph Erskine and completed in 1992, which floats in the distance.

In Terry Taylor's 1961 novel *Baron's Court, All Change,* the station is the gateway to London. The Piccadilly line dives underground, marking the transition point from the endless Middlesex suburbs with their stifling family hierachies and mind-numbing shop assistant jobs, to the London of "foreign accents", jazz clubs, and mind-opening substances (mostly "Indian hemp" or "charge"). The scene changes "from black and white into technicolour".[10]

• *Turn first right along Margravine Gardens. Turn left into Margravine Cemetery.*

The Ditch flows along the boundary of the cemetery, behind the houses on Margravine Gardens, and then turns north to run parallel with the railway line, along a route with no pedestrian access. The walk continues through the cemetery to pick the river up again on Fulham Palace Road.

---

10 Taylor, Terry, *Baron's Court, All Change.* Four Square, 1961, p44

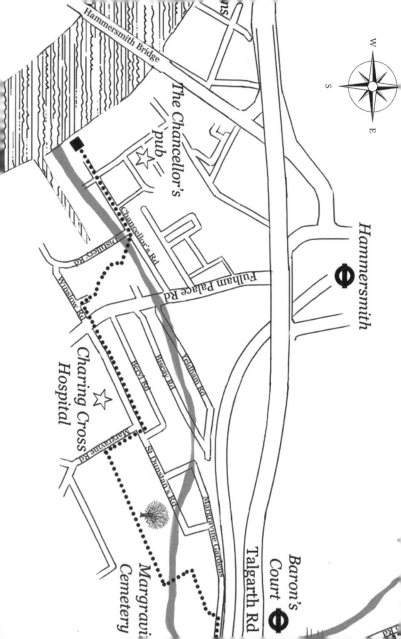

Margravine Cemetery was opened in 1869 by the Hammersmith Burial Grounds Committee, to relieve overcrowded graveyards in the parish. It has a non-conformist chapel and used to have an Anglican chapel, which was demolished in the 1930s.

• *Cross the cemetery turning left, and then right to follow the main path to exit on to Margravine Road. Turn right along Margravine Road, and first left along St Dunstan's Road.*

Charing Cross Hospital to the left transferred from its previous site just off The Strand. It was rebuilt in 1973 on the site of Fulham Hospital (on the south side of the Ditch and therefore in Fulham rather than Hammersmith). The hospital, known at first as Charing Cross Hospital, Fulham, consists of slab blocks in the shape of a cross.

• *Cross Fulham Palace Road at the lights and walk ahead into Winslow Road.*

Fulham Palace Road dips a little towards the junction with Yeldham Road, where the river passes underneath. The road crossed the Parr Ditch on a bridge, known as Parr Bridge, which was at the far end of Great Church Lane which crossed common land in between.

• *Turn first right, enter Frank Banfield Park and follow a path across to the far corner.*

Frank Banfield Park, named after a former mayor, was created when Elmdale and Playfair Streets were demolished in 1974. A private asylum called Brandenburg House had been demolished to build the streets in the late 19th century. It was named after an earlier Brandenburg House on the Thames, at the mouth of the Parr Ditch which was the home of the Margravine of Brandenburg, who has left her name attached to the area. She lent it to Caroline of Brunswick, wife of the Prince Regent, who died here in 1821. Caroline was brought over from Germany in 1795 for what turned out to be an infamously disastrous marriage. Like the Prince she lived an uninhibited life, but he did not appreciate her freedom. She was the subject of 'the Delicate Investigation' in 1806. She and the Prince had separated but he wanted to divorce her, and appointed a commission to investigate accusations of adultery. She had adopted a boy and convinced many people that he was her child, even pretending to be pregnant, apparently as a joke that went too far. The commission discovered that the child was not hers. Jane Austen wrote, "Poor woman, I shall support her as long as I can, because she is a woman and because I hate her husband." Afterwards she went into exile but returned in 1820 when the House of Lords threatened to pass a bill dissolving her marriage. She turned up uninvited at the Prince Regent's coronation as George IV in 1821. She was turned away, and was never crowned Queen, dying a few months later.

The house later became the site of the Hammersmith Distillery and the Manbré & Garton Saccharine Works (see also Chapter 5: Falcon Brook), and is now occupied by the gargantuan Distillery Wharf development.

• *Leave the park in the far corner to exit on to Chancellor's Road. Turn left to follow Chancellor's Road to the River Thames.*

Thames Water has works on either side of Chancellor's Road, the Hammersmith Depot and the Hammersmith Sewage Pumping Station, which makes it clear that the street is a significant water management spot. The Ditch ran behind buildings to the right of the street where a stretch was still above ground in the early 20th century. Water is now audible under a solid drain cover in the pavement on the left-hand side of the road.

Hammersmith Bridge is a particularly beautiful, much-loved symbol of the river. Compton Mackenzie, in this 1913 novel *Sinister Street*, described it as "ethereal in the creeping river-mist and faintly motionable like a ship at anchor".[11] It was designed by the multi-talented Joseph Bazalgette, taking a break from culverting London's rivers. It opened in 1888, replacing a previous suspension bridge which was the first on the Thames.

---

11 Mackenzie, Compton, *Sinister Street*. Penguin Books, 1969 [1913], p320

Hammersmith Bridge has, surprisingly, been targeted by the IRA three times. During the 1939 IRA bombing campaign, virtually forgotten in the light of events later that year, a passer-by found a suitcase on the pavement emitting sparks and smoke. He picked it up and threw it in the Thames where it exploded, throwing up a water spout 60 feet high, followed by another bomb on the other side of the bridge which survived, with damage to its girders. The bridge became a symbolic target as a result and had narrow escapes in 1996, when the Provisional IRA planted two bombs at the south end which failed to explode, one of which was the largest anyone had attempted to use in Britain. Then, in 2000, the Real IRA exploded a bomb under the south side, which closed the bridge for two years.

The Pathé news report of the 1939 attack announced, in tones of disbelief, that the "bomb outrage" had taken place "...almost on the eve of the Boat Race. What kind of thoughts do these maniacs entertain?".[12] This stretch of the river is at the centre of the Championship Course, which runs from Mortlake to Putney, over which the University Boat Race and many other less well-known races are rowed. The former Harrods Furniture Depository on the opposite bank is a course landmark.

The new development along the riverfront includes a statue of Lancelot 'Capability' Brown, who lived on Hammersmith Mall for many years before his appointment as Royal Gardener, which came with an apartment at Hampton Court Palace. The outfall of the Ditch, in the embankment to the right of the statue, is almost undetectable from the shore. In fact, there is a grille in the river wall that can only really be seen from a boat. However, an indent in the mud is visible at low tide showing where the outfall is located, giving a sense that something of the river is still present.

Trace your steps back along Chancellor's Road and turn left into Crisp Road to find The Chancellor, a better pub than anything in the new riverside development.

---

12 British Pathé, 30 March 1939

Stamford Brook West

‘ *Stamford Brook West slides between places, its elusive course passing through edge locations and several different versions of West London.* ’

Stamford Brook West

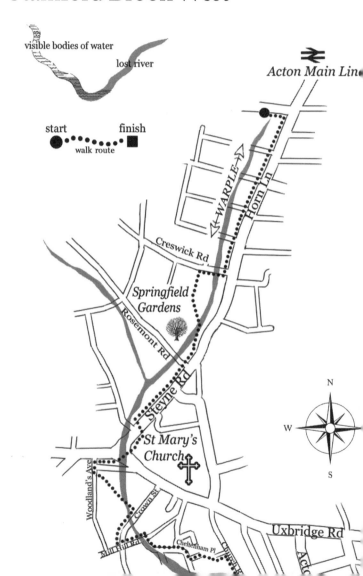

Practicalities

Distance – 3¾ miles (Stamford Brook route) or 4 miles (Hammersmith Creek Route)
Start – Corner of Lynton Gardens and Horn Lane, Acton
Getting there – Acton Main Line Station, followed by a short walk along Horn Lane

End – Either Chiswick Mall, Hammersmith or Furnivall Gardens, Hammersmith
Getting back – Stamford Brook Station (Stamford Brook Route) or Ravenscourt Park Station (Hammersmith Creek Route)

Introduction

The Stamford Brook, with an entire Chiswick neighbourhood named after it, not to mention a tube station, seems at first glance a straightforward lost river. However, it proves surprisingly elusive, each piece of new knowledge making its course more uncertain. There are actually two Stamford Brooks – the eastern branch (covered in Chapter 8: Stamford Brook East) and the western branch – which require two separate walks to follow their complete routes. The two Brooks combine only briefly into a single river before splitting again into three separate streams, which all flow into the Thames at different points between Chiswick and Hammersmith.

The Stamford Brook West tributaries also present complications. A short stream, sometimes called the Warple, joins the main Brook close to the centre of Acton, but this name is also applied to the whole river. The stream then flows past the Mill Hill Park Estate, where it is sometimes called the Mill Hill Stream. Although this is no more than an alternative name for this section of the Stamford Brook, it is wrongly described by some sources as a separate tributary. There is further confusion, with some sources believing that Bollo Brook, which also flows through Acton to the west, is another branch of Stamford Brook. The streams run close to one another and may have met across Acton Common in times of flood, but Chapter 2 traces an independent course for the Bollo Brook with no link to Stamford Brook.

Stamford Brook West flows through the centre of Acton and meets Stamford Brook East in the backlands of Acton Vale. The two branches flow together for the short distance to Stamford Brook Green, where they split again. One route continues due south, past Stamford Brook Underground Station to meet the Thames at Chiswick Mall. The other turns east, splitting into two further branches – Hammersmith Creek and the Parr Ditch. The middle section of the route where the two Stamford Brooks briefly meet is included both in this walk and in Chapter 8: Stamford Brook East.

The route of Stamford Brook West slides between places, through edge locations that prove to have been more significant than they might seem, hosting at different times both aristocratic mansions and dense housing and industry. Several lost versions of West London are revealed at once by unpeeling the vast change that has buried the Brook leaving us to piece together its now elusive course.

Route

• *Starting point: Lynton Road, just off Horn Lane.*

The source of the Stamford Brook is now beneath Lynton Court, the block of dark brick 1930s flats on the corner of Horn Lane and Lynton Road. The block opposite is called Springfield Court, providing a clue to the fields on which these houses were built. The streets were already traced out in the 1880s and mostly completed a decade later. However, the Lynton Court site was not filled until the 1930s, and a stream can be seen clearly flowing above ground, a short stretch of the Stamford Brook running beside Horn Lane.

The majestic chestnut tree on the corner of Lynton Road is another clue to the pre-development landscape. At the end of the 19th century London came to an end at Acton Station, as it was then known, and the Great Western Main Line. Beyond were farms, open fields and Springfield Brickworks to the west and, when Lucien Pissarro painted the railway bridge to the east of Acton Station (now Western Avenue) in 1907, it still looked like a rural railway. Twenty years later houses had crossed the railway and extended as far as North Acton.

• *With Lynton Road on your right, walk down Horn Lane.*

Horn Lane runs along a valley, with side roads climbing to both the east and west, and the land slopes downhill from here through the centre of Acton.

Acton is famous for its many stations, matching its many districts. There is one for every point of the compass – North Acton, South Acton, East Acton, West Acton – and a few more – Acton Town, Acton Central, and Acton Main Line. There used to be another, when Chiswick Park Station was called Acton Green. In the 1990s there was an informal competition for the fastest journey visiting all the Acton stations, a serious challenge as they are mostly on different lines without interchanges. The station situation reflects the succession of districts, enabled by new rail connections, that popped up around the edges of Acton in the first half of the 20th century. Before then, Acton had been a village on the main road from London to Oxford, known as Church Acton to distinguish it from East Acton, a separate hamlet a mile to the north-east.

Acton Main Line is one of the least useful of the Acton stations, but this is about to change, although its unimaginative name will stay the same. When the Elizabeth Line opens this end of Horn Lane will, at least on paper, become a transport hub. Until then its surroundings continue to feel neglected, as they have for several decades. The main station buildings were derelict as far back as 1964, when they appeared in The Beatles' film *A Hard Day's Night*, and were pulled down later the same decade.

On the left the blue sign for Nemoure Road was put up by the 'Council of Acton', when Acton was an urban district council. It became a borough in 1921, with its own coat of arms of an oak tree, crowned with an oak sprig. The landscape of the Stamford Brook was not always open fields. Acton was wooded in the Middle Ages, the name thought to mean 'oak town', with trees spreading all the way to Old Oak Common, next to Wormwood Scrubs. Acton was incorporated into the Borough of Ealing in 1965, which took the Acton oak as its own coat of arms.

• *At a fenced park, turn right along Creswick Road and then left through the fence to enter Springfield Gardens. Bear left to follow the path across the park.*

The housing on the corner of Creswick Road is on the site of the Territorial Army Centre, demolished in the 2000s. Like many West London buildings within easy reach of BBC studios it was used as a *Doctor Who* location, in this case the operations base for Group Captain Gilmore as he tracked strange vibrations in the 1988 Sylvester McCoy story Remembrance of the Daleks.

In the corner of the park by the junction with Creswick Road is a large, fat black stink pipe, a green junction box and a set of concrete platforms with access hatches. This serious infrastructure has been built to contain and manage the underground flow of water, showing that the Brook is more than just a trickle. Springfield Gardens is not, as is sometimes claimed, the source of the Stamford Brook, but the stream flowed above ground across open land here until before the Second World War. The land was then bought by Acton Council to dump soil from constructing sewers, which also buried the stream, before a park was laid out in the 1930s. It no longer has the tennis courts, putting and bowling greens and open-air theatre originally provided.

• *Leave by the corner at the junction of Horn Lane and Rosemont Road.*

To the right, the tributary known as the Warple joins the Stamford Brook. A valley can be spotted on Rosemont Road, passing under Rosemont Court, where the stream crosses to meet the main Brook. It is a short tributary, running under houses beside Rosemont Road for a quarter of a mile. Ordnance Survey maps for the area show a very short stretch of the river still above ground in the back gardens of the houses at the junction with Buxton Road, but this no longer seems to be the case.

Where Horn Lane turns to the left, a valley extends to the right under the estate. This low point can be seen to pass under the Steyne Estate beside Moreton Tower, and a damp drain in the middle of the hard-surfaced parking appears to sit directly above the course of the Brook.

• *Turn right to walk along Horn Lane as it becomes Steyne Road.*

The lower end of Horn Lane, to the junction with Uxbridge Road, is known as The Steyne, a name likely to be derived from an Old English word for a stony place. There were indeed pits at one time alongside the Brook, where in 1622 tenants were ordered to stop digging for gravel. There was also a parish well – Trafford's Well – which by 1832, had unfortunately been "rendered unusable by a nearby privy."[1]

Factories of various types occupied this site over several centuries, making use of the Brook's water, probably beginning with a watermill. By the 1720s Steyne Mills was a tanning yard, and by the 1800s a rug mill. The Steyne Mills Laundry burned down spectacularly in 1867, prompting Acton to set up its own fire brigade. In the 1880s there was a

---

1 Bolton, Diane, Croot, Patricia and Hicks, M.A. *A History of the County of Middlesex: Volume 7, Acton, Chiswick, Ealing and Brentford, West Twyford, Willesden.* Victoria County History, 1982, p32

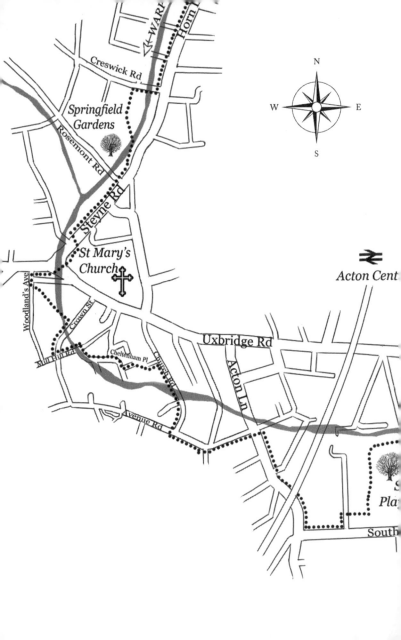

scouring and dyeing works, and by the 1950s a large preserve factory. The Steyne Estate was built on the site.

• Just before the junction with the High Street cross Steyne Road at the pedestrian lights and turn right.

To the left, the wide-open spaces of the Morrisons car park dominate Acton's key road junction. The supermarket is on the site of a much smaller grocery store called Waite, Rose and Taylor, which opened in 1904, the first in what became a national chain. When Taylor left in 1908, the business was renamed Waitrose and began expanding in Acton and then to the west of London, joining the John Lewis Partnership in 1937.

The dip in the road where Steyne Road meets Uxbridge Road was called Acton Bottom, a name that has dropped out of use. Uxbridge Road was, until the construction of the new route for the A40 in the 1920s, the main road from London to Oxford. Its condition was therefore a constant concern, both for travellers and for the inhabitants of Acton who were tasked with keeping it in good repair, cutting back hedges to prevent robbers concealing themselves. The river crossing was a difficult point on the road, at the foot of Acton Hill which rises to the west. The crossing was a 'water splash' or ford here, with a steep drop down from the hill. By the 18th century there was a bridge, rebuilt in 1769, but the hill continued to create an obstacle for wagons throughout the 19th century and the RSPCA provided free use of an extra horse (a trace horse) to help haul loads up it. The bridge disappeared when the Brook was culverted in the mid-19th century.

Because of its location on the western road out of London, Acton plays a supporting role in the Civil War. The forces of the Earl of Essex and the Earl of Warwick rendezvous-ed at Acton, before marching to defeat by the Royalists at the Battle of Brentford. Oliver Cromwell, returning victorious from the last battle of the Civil War, the Battle of Worcester in 1651, was met at Acton by a grand welcoming committee including peers, MPs, the Council of State and the Lord Mayor of London.

The Aeronaut pub, to the right, is named after Acton's pioneering pilot George Lee Temple, the first man to fly a plane upside down. He died young, in a plane crash. The pub, which survived a spectacular fire on New Year's Eve 2017, was previously The Redback, a pub which in its 1990s heyday attracted busloads of Antipodean revellers from across London.

Further to the left is St Mary's Church. The church is raised above the level of the high street on the sloping sides of the Stamford Brook valley. A row of cottages between the church and the road, now demolished, needed a raised footpath in front of them because of the valley gradient. The Acton town pump, which supplied drinking water on the High Street until 1919, has been relocated beside the church door. A plaque explains "It replaced the Thorney Conduit Water Troughs of 1610 that were fed from the ancient well." These had been set up by Thomas Thorney in the grounds of the Bell pub, where the Town Hall is now, to provide a public water supply.

• *Cross the High Street at the island after the roundabout and turn left into Woodlands Avenue. Turn left into The Woodlands park. Follow the path across the green space.*

The Woodlands are the former gardens of a Victorian house, demolished in 1903 and bought by the council. They contain an ice house and a pretty pond next to the buried Brook, fed by its springs. It was originally a round concrete municipal pond, but was remodelled in the 2010s in a more natural fashion.

On the right at the end of the park the Library for Iranian Studies, the largest Persian language repository outside Iran, opened on this site in 1994. Further to the right, an information board records the presence of the Stamford Brook, "Acton's underground stream."

• *Exit on to Crown Street and turn right. At the next junction turn left along Mill Hill Road. Turn right by the Talbot pub along Cheltenham Place.*

The Brook continues straight ahead in an obvious valley, passing under Crown Street and Sidney Miller Court, crossing Mill Hill Road and disappearing behind The Talbot pub. Mill Hill Road, with the buried Bollo Brook at the other end, is perhaps the only street in London with two separate lost rivers. The Stamford Brook formed the eastern boundary of Mill Hill Fields, named after a windmill that sat on a mound in the vicinity of Avenue Road. These became the grounds of Acton Hill House in the early 19th century and were then developed in the 1870s as the Mill Hill Park Estate, a proposed garden suburb that never quite lived up to its ambitions.

• *Follow Cheltenham Place as it turns to the left, then to the right. After a block of flats called Harleyford Manor turn left into an unnamed road. Bear left to follow an alley up steps to Church Road.*

The South Acton Estate is partly built on the grounds of the demolished Berrymead House, also called Berrymead Priory. Stamford Brook ran through the grounds of the house, which extended north from here all the way to Uxbridge Road.

The derelict Priory, by then used as the Constitutional Club, was demolished in 1984 and replaced by the Town Hall car park. The house was not in fact a priory, but a piece of creeper-draped Gothic architecture built in the very early 1800s. There had been a house on the site since the time of Henry VIII which had, variously, belonged to the Marquesses of Halifax and Dukes of Kingston, important politicians of the Stuart and the Hanoverian eras. The novelist Edward Bulwer-Lytton lived in the house briefly in 1835-6, and in the 1840s a young cavalry officer called George Trafford Heald, who had recently come into an inheritance, bought the property. He moved in with his new wife Eliza Gilbert, who was better known by her stage name of Lola Montez.

An infamous stage performer and lover of the famous, she had already eloped once, had affairs with Franz Liszt and Alexandre Dumas, and been the mistress of King Ludwig I of Bavaria. There she had been the power behind the throne and was made Countess of Landsfeld, but was obliged to flee Bavaria when revolutionaries forced Ludwig from the throne. Her move to Acton sounds like much-needed relaxation, but she and Heald could not stay long. They were in fact both already married, and fled the country when they were accused of bigamy. Heald apparently later drowned, and Montez moved to the United States to start again. Her house in Grass Valley, California, is now a US National Monument.

• *Turn right along Church Road. At a T-junction turn left along Avenue Road.*

The Brook continues straight ahead, crossing Church Road from the right after the Michael Flanders Centre, heading under houses. The walk takes a short diversion to catch up with its route a little way ahead at Acton Lane.

The Michael Flanders Centre is a day care centre for disabled people, named after the actor, writer and singer. Flanders, one half of the comedy musical duo Flanders and Swann, was obliged to use a wheelchair after contracting polio while serving in the Navy during the Second World War.

The South Acton Estate is undergoing a large-scale rebuilding programme as Acton Gardens. Building in South Acton began in the 1860s, and a dense district of terraces sprang up very quickly. Equally rapidly, it became known for its overcrowding, with a family of 18 recorded as living in single, small house in the 1890s. It was also the laundry district of London, known as 'Soapsuds Island', with 180 laundries at its peak, some of which had relocated from Kensington and Notting Hill. The softer water in the area, from springs that fed the Bollo Brook and the Stamford Brook, were said to be one of its advantages. In 1901, 2,448 women and 568 men worked in the laundries, and South Acton remained a laundry centre until the 1950s. Soon after, the terraces were replaced wholesale with modernist estate blocks, now themselves being replaced.

• *At a crossroads, cross and turn right along Acton Lane.*

The Brook passes diagonally under the crossroads to flow under houses and then the railway line. The latter blocks the pedestrian through route, so the walk continues along Acton Lane to catch up with the Brook further ahead, at Southfields Recreation Ground.

In contrast to its neighbour, Ealing, the newly expanded Acton, despite being very well connected to central London, gained a reputation during the 20th century as a dead-end. This seems to have been partly due to the negative stereotypes that were a reaction against London's new suburbia. In Anthony Berkeley's 1936 crime classic *The Poisoned Chocolate Case* it is described airily as "a bleak spot somewhere beyond the bounds of civilisation".[2] Later, post-War poverty and torpor descended. The painter Patrick Caulfield, born in Acton in a place that "doesn't exist anymore"[3], worked in factories and was grateful to escape in 1960, to the Royal College of Art. Pete Townshend of The Who, also from Acton, wrote the song 'Stardom in Acton' about getting out, and getting a tan in California.

• *Follow Acton Lane under the railway bridge and, at a mini-roundabout, turn left along Southfield Road.*

Despite the industry and employment available during the first half of the 20th century, behaviours more associated with remote rural areas were recorded here. Folklore collector Edward Lovett carried out research in Acton in 1914, where the medical inspector of schools told him that children wore necklaces of glass beads to protect against bronchitis. The beads, which were sometimes dark blue, white or yellow but "the colour is almost always sky blue", were a charm, and could never be taken off. Lovett then found the same beads for sale in shops "of the lower class"[4] across London. Bronchitis was a serious problem in the damp, overcrowded housing in areas such as South Acton. Hidden rivers, despite being below ground, often brought damp conditions with them that called for protection from folk magic.

2 Berkeley, Anthony, *The Poisoned Chocolates Case*. Penguin Books, 1936, p165
3 Caulfield, Patrick, *National Life Stories: Artists' Lives*. The British Library Board, 1996-98
4 Lovett, Edward, *Magic in Modern London*. Occult Art Company, 1925 [2014], p59-60

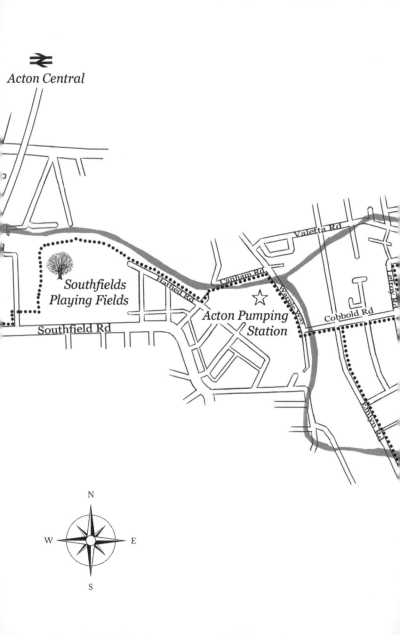

• Turn second left along Wilkinson Way, then right into Southfield Recreation Ground. Turn left after the low, white building and follow the path around the far perimeter of the park to the Hatfield Road exit (the second exit you pass).

The river runs under the northern boundary of Southfields Recreation Ground, originally the South Field. Wilkinson Way commemorates the Wilkinson Sword factory, which was sited on the north west section of the park from 1904. It made swords as well as razors, but also specialised in bayonets, producing two million during the First World War, as well as tractors, cars, bicycles and motorbikes. The firm moved to Park Royal in 1972.

The area between here and Acton Vale, to the north, was entirely occupied by large engineering works, and was a centre for the motor industry well into the 1970s. In the early 1900s firms included D. Napier & Son, who developed the first six-cylinder engine in 1903, and a series of forgotten names all based in the Vale including W. & G. du Cros and French firms Panhard & Levassor and Darracq-Clement-Talbot, where the famed Sunbeam Talbot Ten saloon was manufactured. The Evershed & Vignoles factory, on Acton Lane until 1986, was an electrical defence manufacturer making targeting equipment for the Navy during the First World War and aircraft instruments in the Second World War. By the 1930s engineering employed four-fifths of the workers in the area, and most of the others worked for chemical firms and other Acton Vale manufacturers.

As well as the Stamford Brook, a lost railway ran along the northern edge of Southfields Park. This was the Hammersmith Branch of the North and South West Junction Railway, connecting Acton Central to Hammersmith. It was opened in 1857 but was gradually undermined by better services on the District Line and closed to passengers in 1917. The track was kept to serve the Acton Coal Depot and, when this closed in 1965, the railway went too.

• *Leave the park to walk along Hatfield Road. Take the first turning on the left into an unmarked street (Rugby Road), and continue as the street becomes a path. At the end of the path turn right along Canham Road.*

To the right, an abandoned suburban Victorian villa, complete with hanging tiles and dated 1887, is stranded on the Thames Water site. This is the location of the Acton Storm Tanks, a pumping station built to deal with the water that passed through the area when the Stamford Brook reached full capacity during heavy rain. It was built in 1905, with six open tanks to hold extra water for discharge into the Thames. A new tunnel is now being built from here to the river at Fulham, where it meets the Thames Tideway sewer, preventing sewage from discharging into the Thames.

The tanks are located at this point because the Stamford Brook West stream meets Stamford Brook East at the junction of Canham Road and Warple Way, flowing in from The Vale, to the east. The flow of water is therefore doubled, requiring the extra capacity to prevent flooding. For around three-quarters of a mile, Stamford Brooks East and West follow the same route.

• *At the T-junction, turn right along Warple Way and then first left on to Cobbold Road.*

Warple Way is the first and last appearance in the streetscape of the alternative name for Stamford Brook West. 'Warple' is an antiquated word for a footpath or a bridleway, which is found elsewhere in London and the South East. It probably refers to a path that ran alongside the Brook, or to this particular warple which leads all the way to The Vale.

The electricity-themed housing – Ampere House, Tesla Court, Edison Court, Watt Court – refers to the CAV (later Lucas CAV) which moved to Acton in 1904. Charles A. Vandervell's company made early dynamo-charged car batteries and the first electric lighting for buses. Later it specialised in electronics and fuel-injection systems. New facilities were built in the 1960s, including a sleek, modern factory shed and a research building. The firm eventually moved from Acton in 2005, although only as far as Greenford.

Combined Route: Stamford Brook East and West

• *Turn first right along Emlyn Road.*

The Stamford Brook continues along Warple Way a little further before turning east to cross Emlyn Road, after the junction with Wendell Road. A stink pipe can be seen next to an alleyway between Nos.64 and 66, marking the point where the Brook crosses. There is no through route, so the walk continues along Emlyn Road.

The borough boundary between Hounslow and Hammersmith and Fulham used to follow the route of the Brook precisely from Canham Road to the Thames, so precisely that No.65 Emlyn Road was divided in half. The boundary was rationalised in 1994 and is now less exacting, running to the west of Emlyn Road, but it still follows the Brook for much of its course.

• *Turn second right along Palgrave Road, then right at the T-junction along Hartswood Road.*

The Brook runs behind houses on Hartswood Road, before crossing under the street a little way to the left and passing under the back gardens of the houses on the other side to reach Stamford Brook Road. No.19 Hartswood Road, which has a pond and fountain in its front garden, is on the route of the stream. A valley is visible where Hartswood Road meets Stamford Brook Road.

• *Cross Stamford Brook Road via the zebra crossing, and continue straight ahead along Stamford Brook Avenue.*

The green space to the right, Stamford Brook Common, is the first appearance of the lost river's preferred name. The river crosses the main road at Stamford Bridge, and the bridge was located to the left of the junction with Hartswood Road. The two newer houses at Nos.18 and 20 fill what was once a gap, marking the route of the river.

The Common, now separate, was part of a continuous band of open land that connected to the west via Turnham Green and Acton Common. It was later surrounded by houses in one of which – an 18th century villa called The Brook to the left – painter of railway bridges and other London scenes, Lucien Pissarro, lived from 1901 until his death in 1944. He was the son of the impressionist Camille Pissarro and the building, where he also worked, is marked with a blue plaque.

Stamford Bridge is also the name for the point where the neighbouring lost river to the east, Counter's Creek (Chapter 4), crosses Fulham Road, and for the neighbouring Chelsea FC ground. The two rivers and the bridges are unconnected, but close enough to cause regular mix-ups.

The Brook passes between the houses of Stamford Brook Avenue and those on Goldhawk Road, to the left. From Stamford Brook Common to the River Thames, the line of the buried Brook forms the boundary between Chiswick and Hammersmith, with the boroughs of Hounslow to the west and Hammersmith and Fulham to the east.

The two branches of the Stamford Brook part company again behind the Stamford Brook Avenue houses, where a branch of the stream turns sharply to the east. It crosses Goldhawk Road between Nos.354 and 352, heading towards Ravenscourt Park. Chapter 8: Stamford Brook East follows this branch of the stream on its two different routes to the Thames, while this chapter continues along the main Stamford Brook West branch.

To follow Stamford Brook West, continue along the route below. To follow the Hammersmith Creek route, switch to Chapter 8: Stamford Brook East.

• *Continue straight ahead along Goldhawk Road.*

At the junction the Brook meets Goldhawk Road and runs straight down the middle of the street to King Street ahead.

Cult London writer Derek Marlowe, author of *A Dandy in Aspic* among other works, lived in the red brick mansion blocks behind houses to the left during the second half of the 1980s, at No.80 Hamlet Gardens, before moving to Blue Jay Way in Los Angeles, where he died in 1996.

• *Walk under the railway bridge and past Stamford Brook Station. Cross Chiswick High Road at the pedestrian lights and continue straight ahead along British Grove.*

Stamford Brook Station, the only tube station named directly after a lost river was also, in 1964, the first to have automated ticket barriers. It is one of three Chiswick stations that are not served by the Piccadilly Line, which passes through at high speed on the way to Hammersmith or Acton. The station does not have enough platforms, so eastbound trains have nowhere to stop even if they wanted to.

The place where the Brook crosses the main road is also where King Street (Hammersmith) becomes Chiswick High Road. This was becoming the edge of London when London County Council was established in 1888, grabbing chunks of surrounding counties. This included Middlesex, which had Westminster as its county town. Chiswick was outside London until the next expansion, in 1965, brought it into Hounslow. The lost station to the right on Chiswick High Road, the terminus of the North and South Western Junction Railway demolished in the 1970s, was originally called Hammersmith, to suggest a greater proximity to central London than was the case in reality.

The atmospheric British Grove follows the line of the Brook, which is channelled under the road. The H. Crowther Studio has been making lead garden ornaments on this site since 1908, and restores the lead statuary favoured by 18th century sculptors such as John van Nost and John Cheere, and found in gardens such as those at Longleat House.

Further along on the left is British Grove Studios, a recording complex owned by Mark Knopfler of Dire Straits, which opened in the former Royal Chiswick Laundry building in 2002. It contains the analogue consoles from EMI's Milan Studio, used to record La Scala performances of Maria Callas, and those from EMI's Lagos Studios which, more prosaically, were used for Wings' *Band on the Run*. The studios are part of a record label cluster in this part of Chiswick. Island Records' former offices on St Peter's Square back on to the British Grove site, and their Fallout Shelter studio is in the basement. Musicians signed to Island recorded here in the 1970s, including Sandy Denny, Nick Drake,

Bob Marley and Traffic. Close by, Metropolis Studios on Chiswick High Road is known for 2000s work with the likes of Pete Doherty and Amy Winehouse, while Richard Branson's Townhouse Studios on Goldhawk Road, responsible for both Phil Collins' 'In the Air Tonight' and Elton John's 'Candle in the Wind 1997', is now housing.

• *At the Great West Road turn right and walk along to the underpass.*

The underpass, the only route past the behemoth Great West Road, takes us away from the line of Stamford Brook. It flowed straight ahead along British Grove, which was cut in half when the Great West Road was extended through Chiswick in the early 1960s. The Brentford section, known as the Golden Mile because of its Art Deco factories, was built much earlier in 1925 but it channelled traffic through the centre of Chiswick and Hammersmith. The Great West Road is effectively a bypass, but it forms a barely penetrable barrier between the town and the river. Berestede Road, to the left off British Grove survived but a matching street, Hughenden Road, disappeared under the dual carriageway.

• *Turn left on the other side to Netheravon Road South. Turn right, and immediately left along the unlabelled British Grove Passage.*

To the left the stub street, British Grove South, picks up the route of the Brook again as it emerges from under the Great West Road.

• *At the red and white striped vehicle barrier turn right into Miller's Court, which leads to Chiswick Mall.*

The Miller's Court estate is on the site of Miller's Bakery, which moved flour and bread from its wharf on the Thames. The Brook passes straight ahead along what was the boundary of the bakery, while the route through the estate takes a path to its left.

• *Turn left along Chiswick Mall.*

Chiswick Mall was renamed in the early 19th century after Pall Mall, perhaps to seem more appealingly urban. Until the early 20th century there was a combination of fine houses, recalling the wealth of earlier inhabitants, and serious industry. Not far along the riverfront to the west is the Fuller's Griffin Brewery, still in operation, and until 1909 the shipbuilder Thornycroft & Co. was based nearby.

There is no sign of an outfall from the street as this section of the riverfront is, unusually, private gardens. However, the Stamford Brook passes the rounded end of Cedar House to the right, which was once the home of the Miller's Bakery manager. In earlier times this stretch of the Thames had a number of maltings, including one on this site that was used by the brewery. It probably used a Stamford Brook inlet as a river wharf.

A small parish boundary stone by its front door marks the spot where the Brook crosses Chiswick Mall. It passes under gardens straight ahead, running along the fence between gardens before reaching the Thames. The borough boundary also follows this line and, when it marked the edge of the County of London, it extended across the narrow island beyond, Chiswick Eyot, meaning that its eastern tip was once in London and the rest in Chiswick. Since then the island's tips seems to have eroded away, and the whole island is now in Hounslow.

However, further to the right an enormous green stink pipe on the corner of Eyot Gardens, is an indication of the presence of underground water.

Turn left and walk along the Thames for the best collection of riverside pubs in London, grouped around Upper Mall, including the Old Ship, the Black Lion and, further along, the Dove.

Bibliography

A

Aaronovitch, Ben, 2012. *Rivers of London*. Gollancz.

Ackroyd, Peter, 2019. *Peter Ackroyd's Historical Tour of Covent Garden*. https://www.coventgarden.london/content/peter-ackroyds-historical-tour-covent-garden-1 (accessed 22.7.19).

B

Balchin, Nigel, 1942. *Darkness Falls From the Air*. Collins.

Baron, Alexander, 2001. *The Lowlife*. The Harvill Press.

Barton, Nicholas & Myers, Stephen, 2016. *The Lost Rivers of London*. Historical Publications.

Beckett, Samuel, 1970. *Murphy*. Calder and Boyars.

Bedwell, Rev. Wilhelm, 1631. *A Briefe Description of the Towne of Tottenham Highcrosse*. The Percy Press.

Berkeley, Anthony, 1936. *The Poisoned Chocolates Case*. Penguin Books.

Billington, Michael, 1997. *The Life and Work of Harold Pinter*. Faber and Faber.

Bird, James & Norman, Philip (eds.), 1915. *Survey of London: Volume 6, Hammersmith*. London County Council.

Bolton, Diane K., Croot, Patricia E.C. & Hicks M.A., 1982. *A History of the County of Middlesex: Volume 7, Acton, Chiswick, Ealing and Brentford, West Twyford, Willesden.* Victoria County History.

Booth, Charles, 1902-03. *Life and Labour of the People in London. 1st Series, Poverty.* The Macmillan Co.

Borrow, George, 1851. *Lavengro.* John Murray.

Braddon, Mary E., 1862 [1985]. *Lady Audley's Secret.* Virago Modern Classics.

British Pathé, 30 March 1939. *Hammersmith Bridge Bombed.* Pathé Archive.

C

Caulfield, Patrick, 1996. *National Life Stories: Artists' Lives.* The British Library Board.

Cherry, Bridget & Pevsner, Nikolaus, 1991. *London 3: North West. Buildings of England.* Penguin Books.

Cherry, Bridget & Pevsner, Nikolaus, 2001. *London 2: South. Buildings of England.* Penguin Books.

Cherry, Bridget & Pevsner, Nikolaus, 2002. *London 4: North. Buildings of England.* Yale University Press.

Cherry, Bridget, O'Brien, Charles, Pevsner, Nicklaus, 2005. *London 5: East. Buildings of England.* Yale University Press.

Christie, Agatha, 1929 [1962]. *The Seven Dials Mystery.* Pan Books.

Collins, Norman, 2008. *London Belongs to Me.* Penguin Books.

'C.R.T.', 13 May 1857. Letter to the Editor. *The Times.*

D

Davies, Caitlin, 2015. *Downstream: A History and Celebration of Swimming the River Thames.* Aurum Press.

Dickens, Charles, 1843. *The Life and Adventures of Martin Chuzzlewit.* Chapman and Hall.

Dickens, Charles, 1868. *The Old Curiosity Shop.* Chapman and Hall.

Doyle, Arthur Conan. 2006. *Sherlock Holmes: The Complete Stories.* Wordsworth Editions.

E

Elks, Laurie, 2017. *Hackney: Portrait of a Community 1967-2017*. Hackney Society.

F

Faulkner, Thomas, 1820. *History and Antiquities of Kensington*. T. Egerton, Payne & Foss and Nichols & Son.

Feret, Charles James, 1900. *Fulham Old and New*. The Leadenhall Press Ltd.

Fisher, Allen, 2005. *Place*. Reality Street.

Fisk, Fred. 1913. *The History of Tottenham*. Fred Fisk.

Fitzgerald, Penelope, 1979. *Offshore*. 4th Estate.

Fowler, Christopher, 2006. *The Water Room*. Bantam Books, London.

'F.R.C.S.', 1893. *Glimpses of Ancient Hackney and Stoke Newington*. A.T. Roberts & Co.

G

Gay, John, 1730. *Trivia or the Art of Walking the Streets of London*. Bernard Lintot.

'GES262', 2014. *High Level Sewer, London*. http://www.guerrillaexploring. com/gesite/public_html/index.php?option=com_content&view=arti cle&id=394:ges262-high-storm-relief-sewer&catid=53:draining&It emid=68 (accessed 3.18.19).

Gibbons, Stella, 1946. *Westwood*. Longmans, Green.

Gilbert, Bob, 2018. *Ghost Trees: nature and people in a London parish*. Saraband.

Gissing, George, 1889 [1992]. *The Nether World*. The World's Classics, Oxford University Press.

Gissing, George, 1893 [1993]. *The Odd Women*. Penguin Classics.

Glinert, Ed, 2004. *The London Compendium: A Street-by-street Exploration of the Hidden Metropolis*. Penguin Books.

Goodwin, Tom, 1 September 2011. Reggae record shop Dub Vendor to close after 35 years due to riot damage. *New Musical Express*.

Grocott, George, 1915. *Hackney Fifty Years Ago*. Potter Bros.

Grossmith, George & Grossmith, Weedon, 1892 [1965]. *The Diary of a Nobody*. Penguin Books.

H

Hackney Citizen, 29 November 2008. *At Home with Iain Sinclair. Hackney Citizen*. https://www.hackneycitizen.co.uk/2008/11/29/at-home-with-iain-sinclair/ (accessed 3.18.19).

Hare, Augustus J.C., 1901. *Walks in London Vol.II*. George Allen.

Henderson, Philip, 1986. *William Morris: His Life, Work and Friends*. HarperCollins.

Hinshelwood, John, 2011. *The Campsbourne Estate: a History of its Development and Re-development.* Hornsey Historical Society.

Hobhouse, Hermione (ed.), 1994. *Survey of London Volumes 43 and 44, Poplar, Blackwall and Isle of Dogs*. London County Council.

Hough Clinch, C., 1890. *Bloomsbury and St. Giles's Past and Present*. Truslove and Shirley.

Hughson, David & Reid, William Hamilton, 1817. *Walks Through London*. Sherwood, Neely, and Jones; Murray; Clarke; Lindsell; Chapple; Colnaghi; Walker; Taylor and Hessey; J.M. Richardson; Cowie and Company; Blackwood; Brash and Reid; M. Keene and J. Cumming.

I

Inglis, Lucy, 2014. *Georgian London*. Penguin Books.

'J.F.B.' 24 November 1883. The Old Falcon Inn, Battersea. *Notes and Queries. 6th Series Vol. VIII*. John C. Francis.

J

Johnson, B.S., 1964 [2004]. *Albert Angelo*. Picador.

K

Keane, William, 1850. *The Beauties of Middlesex*. T. Wilsher.

L

Le Carré, John, 1961 [2016]. *Call for the Dead*. Penguin Books.

Lovett, Edward, 1925 [2014]. *Magic in Modern London*. Occult Art Company.

M

Machen, Arthur, 1936 [2010]. *N*. Published for the Stoke Newington Literary Festival by the Friends of Arthur Machen and Tartarus Press.

MacInnes, Colin, 1959. *Absolute Beginners*. New English Library.

Mackenzie, Compton, 1969. *Sinister Street*. Penguin Books.

Marriott, John, 2011. *Beyond the Tower: A History of East London*. Yale University Press.

McCullin, Don, 2002. *Unreasonable Behaviour: an autobiography*. Vintage, London.

Mills, A.D., 2001. *A Dictionary of London Place Names*. Oxford University Press.

Moore, Alan & Campbell, Eddie, 2000. *From Hell*. Knockabout.

Moore, Alan & Perkins, Tim, 2000. *Highbury Working, A Beat Seance*. RE:.

Morgan, Frances, 2002. The Village of Visionaries, in: *Time Out Book of London Walks. Volume 2*. Time Out Guides Ltd.

N

Nairn, Ian, 1966. *Nairn's London*. Penguin.

O

Oldham, Mark, 29 August 2008. White Riot: The week Notting Hill exploded. *Independent*.

On the Record, undated. *A Hackney Autobiography* https://www.ahackneyautobiography.org.uk.

P

Parton, John, 1822. *Some Account of the Hospital and Parish of St. Giles in the Fields, Middlesex*. Luke Hansard and Sons.

Parton, John, 1826. St. Giles in the Fields, in: *The Gentleman's Magazine, Vol.96*, June 1826.

Pepys, Samuel, 1660-1669. *The Diary of Samuel Pepys*. https://www.pepysdiary.com/

Pinching, Albert & Dell, David, 2005. *Haringey's Hidden Streams Revealed*. Hornsey Historical Society.

Priestley, J.B., 1930. *Angel Pavement*. Penguin Books.

R

Reid Banks, Lynne, 1969. *The L-Shaped Room*. Chatto & Windus.

Riley, W. Edward & Gomme, Laurence, 1914. *Survey of London: Volume 5, St. Giles-in-The-Fields*. London County Council.

Roe, W.J., 1950. *Ancient Tottenham*. The Percy Press.

Royle, Nicholas, 1998. Do You Remember Derek Marlowe?, in: *Time Out London Walks Volume One*. Time Out Guides Ltd.

S

Sayers, Dorothy L. & Paton Walsh, Jill, 1998. *Thrones, Dominations*. New English Library.

Sedgemore, Brian, 11 November 1983. *Trowbridge Estate, Hackney Wick*. Hansard.

Shakespeare, William, 1988. *Henry IV Part 2*. The Arden Shakespeare.

Sinclair, Iain, 2015. *London Overground*. Hamish Hamilton.

Sinclair, Iain, 2010. *Hackney, That Rose-Red Empire – A Confidential Report*. Penguin Books.

Sinclair, Iain, 22 June 2009. *London's Lost Rivers: The Hackney Brook and other North West Passages*. Gresham College.

Sinclair, Iain (ed.), 2006. *London City of Disappearances*. Hamish Hamilton.

Sinclair, Iain, McKean, D., 2016. *My Favourite London Devils: a gazetteer of books, lives & brief encounters*. Tangerine Press.

Seymour, Robert & Stow, John, 1735. *A Survey of the Cities of London and Westminster, Borough of Southwark and Parts Adjacent*. J. Read.

Strype, John, 1720. *A Survey of the Cities of London and Westminster*. A. Churchill, J. Knapton, R. Knaplock, J. Walthoe, E. Horne, B. Tooke, D. Midwinter, B. Cowse, R. Robinson, & T. Ward.

Sunderland, Septimus, 1915. *Old London's Spas, Baths and Wells*. John Bale, Sons & Danielsson.

Sutin, Lawrence, 2002. *Do What Thou Wilt: a life of Aleister Crowley*. St. Martin's Griffin.

T

Taylor, Terry, 1961. *Baron's Court, All Change*. Four Square.

Thackeray, William Makepeace, 1848 [1968]. *Vanity Fair*. Penguin English Library.

Thornbury, Walter, 1878. *Old and New London Vol.3*. Cassell, Petter & Galpin

Thrale, Hester Lynch, 1942. *Thraliana. The Diary of Mrs Hester Lynch Thrale 1776-1809. Volume 1 1776-1784*. Oxford University Press.

Trollope, Anthony, 1858 [1984]. *The Three Clerks*. Alan Sutton.

U

Unsworth, Cathi, 2013. *Lynne Reid Banks: "The L-Shaped Room"* - 1960, in: *London Fictions* Ed. Whitehead, Andrew & White, Jerry, World Economic and Social Survey. Five Leaves Publications.

Walford, Edward, 1878. *Old and New London*. Cassell, Petter & Galpin.

Walton, Izaak, 1676 [1984]. *The Compleat Angler*. Harrap.

Webb, W. Arthur, 1907. *Survey of London Monograph 8, Sandford Manor, Fulham*. Guild & School of Handicraft.

Whitehead, Andrew & White, Jerry (eds.), 2013. *London Fictions*. Five Leaves Publications.

Whiteing, Richard, 1899. *No. 5 John Street*. Grant Richards.

Acknowledgements

My thanks to people who have helped greatly by providing kind access to their own research and knowledge: Simon Matthews, who knows more about London than almost anyone; Prof. Ifan Shepherd, who guided me around the recesses of the British Library map room; and Henry Vivian-Neal, the guardian spirit of Kensal Green Cemetery.

Many, many thanks to Mark Pilkington who masterminded operations, SF Said who took the photographs, Lorna Ritchie who designed the maps, Maia Gaffney-Hyde who laid out the text and Richard Bancroft who proofed it.

As always, *London's Lost Rivers Volume 2* is, like *Volume 1*, for my wife Jo Healy who makes all of this possible.

Strange Attractor Press 2019